England's Sea Empire, 1550–1642

EARLY MODERN EUROPE TODAY

Editor: Professor J. H. Shennan

England's Sea Empire, 1550–1642

DAVID B. QUINN

Emeritus Professor of Modern History,
University of Liverpool

and

A. N. RYAN

Reader in History, University of Liverpool

London
GEORGE ALLEN & UNWIN
Boston   Sydney

George Allen & Unwin (Publishers) Ltd.
40 Museum Street, London WC1 1LU, UK

George Allen & Unwin (Publishers) Ltd,
Park Lane, Hemel Hempstead, Herts HP2 4TE, UK

Allen & Unwin, Inc.,
9 Winchester Terrace, Winchester, Mass. 01890, USA

George Allen & Unwin Australia Pty Ltd,
8 Napier Street, North Sydney, NSW 2060, Australia

942.05
Q7e

First published in 1983

British Library Cataloguing in Publication Data

Quinn, David B.
    England's sea empire.—(Early modern Europe series)
1. England—Foreign economic relations
I. Title   II. Ryan, A. N.   III. Series
382.1′0942   HF1532.5.E/
ISBN 0-04-942179-4

Library of Congress Cataloging in Publication Data

Quinn, David B. (David B.)
    England's sea empire, 1550-1642.
(Early modern Europe today)
Bibliography: p.
Includes index.
1. Great Britain—History—Elizabeth, 1558–1603.
2. Great Britain—History—Early Stuarts, 1603–1649.
3. Great Britain—History, Naval—Tudors, 1485–1603.
4. Great Britain—History, Naval—Stuarts, 1603–1714.
5. Great Britain—Colonies—Discovery and exploration.
I. Ryan, A. N.   II. Title.   III. Series.
DA356.Q56   1983   942.05′5   83–11755
ISBN 0-04-942179-4

84-8647

Set in 10 on 11 point Times by Grove Graphics, Tring, Hertfordshire
and printed in Great Britain by Biddles Ltd., Guildford, Surrey.

Contents

Contents

Early Modern Europe Today

In introducing a new historical series it is difficult not to begin by offering some justification for its appearance. Yet if we accept that history is ultimately unknowable in the sense that our perception of the past as distinct from the past itself is forever changing, then no apologia is required. That is certainly the premiss on which this series is posited. In the last several decades the changes have been particularly rapid, reflecting fundamental shifts in social and political attitudes, and informed by the growth of new related disciplines and by new approaches to the subject itself. The volumes contained within this series will seek to provide the present generation of students and readers with up-to-date history; with judgements and interpretations which will no doubt in turn form part of the synthesis of future scholarly revisions. Some of the books will concentrate on previously neglected or unconsidered material to reach conclusions likely to challenge conventional orthodoxies in more established areas of study; others will re-examine some of these conventional orthodoxies to discover whether, in the light of contemporary scholarly opinion, they retain their validity or require more or less drastic reassessment. Each in its own way, therefore, will seek to define and illuminate some of the contours of early modern Europe, a coherent period at once remote from our own world yet crucial to an understanding of it. Each will combine considerable chronological range with thematic precision and each, finally, will be completed by a significant bibliographical chapter. It is hoped that this last, prominent feature, which will make the series especially distinctive, will be of value not only to readers curious to explore the particular topic further but also to those seeking information of a wide range of themes associated with it.

List of Maps

(Maps drawn by Alan Hodgkiss of the University of Liverpool)

Cover illustration shows John White's map of Virginia, *ca* 1585. White was an artist and later governor of the 1587 colony, whose duties included surveying and draughting this map. The Royal Arms and those of Ralegh who promoted the colony are also depicted.

An Introduction

In May 1553 three English ships commanded by Sir Hugh Willoughby and piloted by Richard Chancellor sailed from the Thames to the Arctic seas in search of a passage to Asia around the north cape of Norway and the northern coast of Russia. In the same year Thomas Wyndham, also in command of three ships, including two men-of-war, sailed from Portsmouth to the Guinea coast of Africa in quest of gold, ivory and pepper. The expeditions, both of which were financed by commercial magnates of the City of London, members of the court and government and officials of the navy, seem in retrospect to have released maritime energies which were to drive England to world empire founded upon dominion of the seas.

The projectors possessed neither a blueprint of empire nor a recipe for naval mastery. They were concerned in gloomy and dangerous times in saving themselves from possible ruin through risky, though potentially profitable, speculation and in saving the Tudor state and society from the ills afflicting it in mid-century. The obvious crisis was that exports of finished and unfinished cloth to the Continent of Europe through the port of Antwerp were unmistakably in decline. The shrinkage of the cloth market, apart from its adverse impact upon important agricultural interests, was a threat to England's greatest industry, bringing with it the prospect of widespread distress which might, especially as England had yet to find a religious consensus, endanger such social stability as existed, and indeed the regime itself. There is evidence of the existence in the City of London of a recognition that it was desirable to vary the traditional, and hitherto rewarding, patterns of the export trade in cloth. This was a theme to which the commercial propagandists of the Tudor age returned again and again throughout the century.

But we should not let them convince us that a search for new cloth markets was the sole, or the most potent, driving force behind the maritime reconnaissances of 1553. They were directed towards Asia and Africa, areas of the world which, the available evidence suggested, were sources of untold wealth in spices and other expensive commodities and, more attractive again, in bullion. The acquisition of bullion was a bait to adventurers in both public and private life. They belonged to a generation which had seen speculators enrich themselves in land deals following Henry VIII's ecclesiastical revolution. Now at a time of financial and political uncertainty with the coinage unstable and the social fabric under strain, they tended to veer away from investment in land and conventional commerce and to risk capital in novel ventures.

The quest for trade with the extra-European parts of the world, particularly the quest for trade with Asia, was in itself hardly new. It had flitted in and out of English history since the last decade of the fifteenth century and the Cabot voyages from Bristol. The elderly Sebastian Cabot, son of John who had crossed the Atlantic from Bristol in 1497, was now again resident in England after years in the Spanish maritime service. He was a living link with the great age of the Bristol voyages and an advocate of the view that there existed in northern waters a navigable passage to Asia. We should not, however, exaggerate the importance and influence of Sebastian Cabot. There was a native tradition of propaganda, also emanating from Bristol, in favour of the establishment of trade with Asia by a passage through the Arctic seas. It's literary relics are the *Declaration of the Indies* by Robert Thorne (1527) and the 'Brief Summe of Geography' by Roger Barlow (1541). Although there were spasmodic Atlantic enterprises under Henry VIII, the ideas of Thorne and Barlow were largely neglected in both official and unofficial circles. Nor was there any widespread support for practical efforts, such as those of the Hawkins family of Plymouth, to extend Anglo-Spanish trade into African and American waters. The lack of speculative investment tended to restrain the maritime activities of the English and to contain them within traditional limits.

The enterprises launched in 1553 should not be viewed as peaceful commercial ventures. It is significant that their moving spirit in government was John Dudley, Duke of Northumberland, the most powerful member of the regency acting on behalf of Edward VI, and that Northumberland, a former lord admiral, had in 1551–2 been involved in discussions about a possible raid on Peru, site of the Spanish silver mines. Though not such flagrant acts of aggression, the 1553 enterprises were directed towards areas over which the Iberian states, Spain and Portugal, asserted monopolistic claims based on rights of prior discovery and occupation. In other words, the intruders might meet with armed resistance and had to be prepared in their turn to meet it with force of arms. Behind this English readiness to fight their way into a trade and to respect no occupation other than effective occupation was the spirit later to manifest itself in the widespread, and often indiscriminate, privateering of Elizabethan times. Already during the 1540s, in the last of Henry VIII's French wars, there had been a ready response, especially in the west country, to the offer of licences to private citizens to prey upon enemy shipping. The response was not confined to seamen, shipowners and merchant adventurers, but embraced also landed gentry, who saw here a way of enhancing their fortunes, and officials of the Tudor navy. The lawlessness of the privateersmen of the 1540s was a feature of the movement, as was the emergence among them of anti-Spanish sentiments, though England was officially at war with France. The first illegal seizure of a Spanish treasure ship by an Englishman occurred in 1545. The maritime nation-in-arms which was to make the sea a focal area of investment in the hope of profitable returns through both seizures and illicit trade was awaiting its opportunity.

The public manifestation of the sea power of England in the 1550s was the line of great warships built and purchased by Henry VIII, which was moored in the River Medway below Rochester bridge. Ships, for the most part, of majesty and force, they constituted a fleet which had been seen by its founder as a bulwark against hostile designs of the French. They were floating fortresses designed to fight in the English Channel and ill-equipped to operate in distant waters. The aggressive, offensive arm of English sea power was largely in private hands. The age which dawned in 1553 was to be dominated by private adventurers afloat and ashore who, frequently in alliance with members of both court and government, risked their lives or their capital − in many cases both − in a hazardous game of fortune seeking: a game in which an increasing number saw themselves as defenders of Protestantism in a conflict to the death with Catholic Spain. In the quest for plunder and trade, an alliance − sometimes an uneasy alliance − was forged between the regular element of the Crown and the forces of the private adventurers. The history of their trials and experiences is the history of the English discovery of sea power and dawning consciousness of what it meant.

Bibliographical Essay

(Unless otherwise stated, the place of publication is London)

General

The standard bibliographies of British history in the sixteenth and seventeenth centuries are Conyers Read, *Bibliography of British History: Tudor Period, 1485–1603*, second edition (Oxford, 1959) and Godfrey Davies and Mary Frear Keeler, *Bibliography of British History: Stuart Period, 1603–1714*, second edition (Oxford, 1970). M. Levine, *Tudor England, 1485–1603* (Cambridge, 1968) is a useful supplement to Read, *Bibliography of British History*, though on a less comprehensive scale. J. S. Morrill, *Seventeenth-Century Britain, 1603–1714* (1980) is the second volume in the series *Critical Bibliographies in Modern History*. John Roach (ed.), *A Bibliography of Modern History* (Cambridge, 1968), is a bibliographical companion to the *New Cambridge Modern History* and a helpful guide to writings in many languages on European and extra-European history. The wide-ranging bibliographical sections in Pierre Chaunu, *Conquête et exploitation des nouveaux mondes (xvi siècle)* (Paris, 1969), and Fredéric Mauro, *L'Expansion européenne (1600–1870)*, second edition (Paris, 1967), are valuable. The relevant sections of the Historical Association's *Annual Bulletin of Historical Literature* (1912–) should be consulted, particularly for recent publications. Other annual compilations to be noted include *Indice Histórico Español* (Barcelona, 1953–) and *Bibliographie annuelle de l'histoire de France* (Paris, 1956–).

For the oceans in European history, a good start can be made with J. H. Parry, *The Age of Reconnaissance* (1963), and the same author's *The Discovery of the Sea* (New York, 1974), both of which, apart from other merits, are strong on technical aspects. C. M. Cipolla, *European Culture and Overseas Expansion* (Harmondsworth, 1970), and Charles Verlinden, *Les Origines de la civilisation atlantique: De la Renaissance à l'Âge des Lumières* (Neuchatel, 1966), explore the economic and social dynamics of expansion. J. H. Elliott, *The Old World and the New, 1492–1650* (Cambridge, 1972), is a perceptive discussion of the process of assimilation by Europeans of the discoveries. K. M. Pannikar, *Asia and Western Dominance* (1953), is an Asian interpretation of the consequences of the rise of European oceanic power.

The study of early modern maritime and imperial rivalry must, if it is to make sense, be rooted in its European context. The *Fontana History of Europe* is a serviceable introduction: G. R. Elton, *Reformation Europe, 1517-1559* (1963); J. H. Elliott, *Europe Divided, 1559-1598* (1968); Geoffrey Parker, *Europe in Crisis, 1598-1648* (1979). Charles Wilson, *The Transformation of Europe, 1558-1648* (1974), is an admirable general survey. E. E. Rich and Charles Wilson (eds), *Cambridge Economic History of Europe*, Vol.IV: *The Economy of Expanding Europe in the Sixteenth and Seventeenth Centuries* (Cambridge, 1967), contains a wealth of information on population, prices and trade. For those who wish to explore modern interpretations of this economic activity, Fernand Braudel, *Capitalism and Material Life* (1973) and I. Wallerstein, *The Modern World System*, Vol.I: *Capitalist Agriculture and the Origins of the European World Economy in the Sixteenth Century* (New York, 1974); Vol.II: *Mercantilism and the Consolidation of the European World Economy, 1600-1750* (New York, 1980), may be recommended. J. H. Shennan, *The Origins of the Modern European State, 1450-1725* (1974) is excellent for developments throughout Europe. International relations in the sixteenth and seventeenth centuries are surveyed by Gaston Zeller, *Histoire des relations internationales*, Vol.II: *Les Temps modernes: de Christophe Colomb à Cromwell* (Paris, 1953), and Henri Lapeyre, *Les Monarchies européenes du xvi siècle: les relations internationales* (Paris, 1967). Garrett Mattingly, *Renaissance Diplomacy* (1955), is a masterly study of power relations and diplomatic procedures in early modern Western Europe with valuable material on Anglo-Spanish affairs.

Spain is well served by J. H. Elliott, *Imperial Spain, 1469-1716* (1963), and John Lynch, *Spain under the Habsburgs*, Vol. I: *Empire and Absolutism, 1516-1598* (Oxford, 1964); Vol.II: *Spain and America, 1598-1700* (Oxford, 1969). R. B. Merriman *The Rise of the Spanish Empire in the Old World and the New*, Vol.IV: *Philip the Prudent* (New York, 1934), though superseded in many respects by recent research, is still useful as a political biography. The latest study in English of Philip II is Geoffrey Parker, *Philip II* (Boston, Mass., 1978). During the first half of his reign, Philip II was preoccupied with Mediterranean problems. For these the great authority is Fernand Braudel's magisterial *La Méditerranée et le monde méditerranéen à l'époque de Philippe II*, second revised edition (Paris, 1966), now translated into English by Siân Reynolds as *The Mediterranean and the Mediterranean World in the Age of Philip II*, 2 vols (1972). A. C. Hess, *The Forgotten Frontier* (1978), is important, as is the same author's 'The Moriscos: an Otto-man Fifth Column in sixteenth-century Spain', *American Historical Review*, vol.lxxiv (1968). Dorothy M. Vaughan, *Europe and the Turk*, second revised edition (Liverpool, 1967), is a thorough account of Ottoman relations with the West. An appropriate way of learning more about the Ottoman Empire when its power was of primary interest to Spain is to consult V. J. Parry, 'The Ottoman Empire, 1520–1566', in G. R. Elton (ed.), *The New Cambridge Modern History*, Vol.II: *The Reformation, 1520–1559* (Cambridge, 1968), and by the same author, 'The Ottoman Empire, 1566–1617', in R. B. Wernham (ed.), *The New Cambridge Modern History*, Vol.III: *The Counter-Reformation and Price Revolution, 1559–1610* (Cambridge, 1968). M. A. Cook (ed.), *A History of the Ottoman Empire to 1730* (Cambridge, 1976), is a useful outline. See also Bernard Lewis, *The Muslim Discovery of Europe* (New York, 1982).

Though aware of Spain's difficulties in the Mediterranean to the extent of being ready to take advantage of them, her European rivals were more conscious of her power than of her problems. An excellent introduction to this theme is H. G. Koenigsberger, 'Western Europe and the power of Spain', in Wernham (ed.), *New Cambridge Modern History*, Vol.III. For the guiding principles of Philip II's policy, see Koenigsberger, 'The statecraft of Philip II', *European Studies Review*, vol.i (1971). Valuable articles by Geoffrey Parker, all dating from the 1970s, have been conveniently assembled in *Spain and the Netherlands, 1559–1659: Ten Studies* (1979). The classic account in English of the Netherlands in the sixteenth century is Pieter Geyl, *The Revolt of the Netherlands, 1555–1609*, first English edition (1932); reprinted (1964). Some of Geyl's conclusions were questioned by G. N. Clark, 'The birth of the Dutch Republic', *Proceedings of the British Academy*, vol.xxxii (1946), now reprinted in Lucy S. Sutherland (ed.), *Studies in History* (1966). The complex history of the Netherlands in the sixteenth and seventeenth centuries has inspired a vast literature, most of it in languages other than English. Some idea of its richness and variety can be gleaned from J. W. Smit, 'The present position of studies regarding the revolt of the Netherlands', J. S. Bromley and E. H. Kossman (eds), *Britain and the Netherlands*, Vol.I (1960). We are highly indebted to Geoffrey Parker for having exploited this literature, and his own archival studies, to give us *The Dutch Revolt*, paperback edition (Harmondsworth, 1979), a fresh interpretation firmly rooted in the international setting. For the later history of the Netherlands, standard works are Pieter Geyl, *The Netherlands in the Seventeenth Century*, 2 vols (1961–4), and K. H. D. Haley, *The Dutch in the Seventeenth Century* (1972). J. I. Israel, 'A conflict of empires: Spain and the Netherlands, 1618–48', *Past and Present*, vol.lxxxvi (1977), should be consulted. Geoffrey Parker, *The Army of Flanders and the Spanish Road: The Logistics of Spanish Victory and Defeat in the Low Countries' Wars* (Cambridge, 1972), is an important study of Spanish military organisation which does much to explain the durability of

Spanish power in the Netherlands; while the debilitating strain upon Spanish resources of the supreme effort to achieve great-power status by both land and sea is a central theme of I. A. A. Thompson's authoritative *War and Government in Habsburg Spain, 1560–1620* (1976).

English involvement in the affairs of the Netherlands continues to prompt debate between distinguished historians. R. B. Wernham, *Before the Armada: The Growth of English Foreign Policy, 1485–1588* (Oxford, 1966), is a lucid exposition of foreign policy as the art of the possible which underlines the significance from the English point of view of French ambitions and power throughout the sixteenth century and generally commends the prudent rationality of Elizabeth I's conduct of foreign affairs. See also Wernham, 'English policy and the revolt of the Netherlands', Bromley and Kossman (eds), *Britain and the Netherlands*, Vol.I; and Wernham, 'Elizabethan war aims and strategy', S. T. Bindoff, J. Hurstfield and C. H. Williams (eds), *Elizabethan Government and Society: Essays Presented to Sir John Neale* (1961). Charles Wilson, *Queen Elizabeth and the Revolt of the Netherlands* (1970), is less impressed by the queen's rationality than by her lack of stomach for a great cause and her dilatoriness in sending aid to the Netherlands. The most detailed studies of Elizabethan policy are Conyers Read, *Mr Secretary Walsingham and the Policy of Queen Elizabeth*, 3 vols (Oxford, 1925); *Mr Secretary Cecil and Queen Elizabeth* (1955); *Lord Burghley and Queen Elizabeth* (1960). For the post-armada phase of the reign, E. P. Cheyney, *History of England from the Defeat of the Armada to the Death of Elizabeth*, 2 vols (New York, 1914–26) is the most sound and complete account, though excessively critical of the queen. H. A. Lloyd, *The Rouen Campaign, 1590–1592: Politics, Warfare and the Early Modern State* (Oxford, 1973), is an illuminating study. French affairs may be followed in outline in J. E. Neale, *The Age of Catherine de Medici* (1943), and in detail in the specialised works of H. G. Koenigsberger, 'The organisation of revolutionary parties in France and the Netherlands', *Journal of Modern History*, vol.xxvii (1955); N. M. Sutherland, *The Massacre of St Bartholomew and the European Conflict, 1559–1572* (1973); De Lamar Jensen, *Diplomacy and Dogmatism: Bernardino de Mendoza and the French Catholic League* (Cambridge, Mass., 1964); Jensen, 'Franco-Spanish diplomacy and the Armada', Charles H. Carter (ed.), *From the Renaissance to the Counter-Reformation: Essays in Honor of Garrett Mattingly* (New York, 1965). See also the interesting use made of art to illuminate the sympathies between the French court and William of Orange by Frances A. Yates, *The Valois Tapestries*, second edition (1975). Articles dealing with critical episodes in Anglo-Spanish relations include Conyers Read, 'Queen Elizabeth's seizure of the Duke of Alva's pay-ships', *Journal of Modern History*, vol.v (1933); J. B. Black, 'Queen Elizabeth, the sea beggars and the capture of Brille', *English Historical Review*, vol.xlvi (1931); J. E. Neale, 'Queen Elizabeth and the Netherlands, 1586–7', *English Historical Review*, vol.xlv (1930). The expedition of 1585 to the Netherlands is partly documented in John Bruce (ed.), *Correspondence of Robert Dudley, Earl of Leycester, during His Government of the Low Countries, in the Years 1585 and 1586,* Camden Society, First Series, Vol.XXVII (1844).

J. R. Jones, *Britain and Europe in the Seventeenth Century* (1966), is an excellent brief introduction with useful pointers on Anglo-Spanish and Anglo-Dutch relations. C. H. Carter, *The Secret Diplomacy of the Habsburgs* (New York, 1964), contains valuable material on Anglo-Spanish relations under James I in the context of the general situation. See also Carter's 'Gondomar, ambassador to James I', *Historical Journal*, vol.6 (1964). S. L. Adams, 'Foreign policy and the parliaments of 1621 and 1624', L. M. Sharpe (ed.), *Faction and Parliament* (Oxford, 1978), adds to our understanding of foreign policy in the closing years of James I. George Edmondson, *Anglo-Dutch Rivalry, 1600–1653* (Oxford, 1911), is a painstaking account now rather outdated and largely superseded by Charles Wilson, *Profit and Power: A Study of England and the Dutch Wars* (1957). For those wishing to study more about Dutch maritime activity, C. R. Boxer, *The Dutch Seaborne Empire, 1600–1800,* paperback edition (1977), is strongly recommended. G. E. Aylmer, *The King's Servants: The Civil Service of Charles I, 1625–1642* (1961), has important things to say about office-holding in the public service, including the naval service. Conrad Russell, 'Parliament and the king's finances', Conrad Russell (ed.), *The Origins of the English Civil War* (1978), brings out the impact of inflationary pressures upon defence expenditure.

Naval and Maritime

The most up-to-date bibliographical aid is R. G. Albion, *Naval and Maritime History: An Annotated Bibliography*, fourth edition, revised and expanded (Newton Abbot, 1975). R. Higham (ed.), *A Guide to the Sources of British Military History* (1972), contains valuable sections on naval affairs with helpful introductory essays. G. E. Manwaring, *A Bibliography of British Naval History: A Bibliographical and Historical Guide to Printed and Manuscript Sources* (1930), is still useful. There is a wealth of learned articles in *The Mariner's Mirror*, published since 1911 by the Society for Nautical Research. Indispensable guides to its contents are R. C. Anderson, *Mariner's Mirror: General Index to Volumes 1–35* (Cambridge, 1955), and Elizabeth Rolfe,

The Mariner's Mirror: Index to Volumes 36–55 (1974). Students of British naval history should familiarise themselves with the publications of the Navy Records Society, established in 1893 for the purpose of printing rare or unpublished works of naval interest. Several of the society's volumes are listed in their appropriate places here. An abundance of contemporary material regarding navigation and voyages is printed by the Hakluyt Society, which distributed its first volume in 1847. Peter Kemp (ed.), *The Oxford Companion to Ships and the Sea* (1976), is a handy work of reference.

There are several general surveys of British naval history, of which the most recent, Paul M. Kennedy, *The Rise and Fall of British Naval Mastery* (1976), is noteworthy for its emphasis upon the economic and financial bases of sea power. Michael A. Lewis, *The Navy of Britain: A Historical Portrait* (1948) is a highly informative and well-illustrated work. See also Lewis's *England's Sea Officers: The Story of the Naval Profession* (1939). Admiral Sir Herbert Richmond, *Statesmen and Sea Power*, second edition (Oxford, 1947), is a powerful analysis of strategic problems faced by British statesmen from the days of Elizabeth I, whom he criticises, not altogether convincingly, for having never understood either the capabilities or uses of sea power. B. Tunstall, *The Realities of Naval History* (1936), C. C. Lloyd, *The Nation and the Navy* (1954), and G. J. Marcus, *A Naval History of England*, Vol.I: *The Formative Centuries to 1783* (1961), all have merits as chronological surveys. Peter Padfield, *Tide of Empires*, Vol.I: *1481–1654* (1979), has more of an international flavour and reflects also the author's interest in the history of artillery at sea. Gerald S. Graham, *Empire of the North Atlantic* (1951), is a thoughtful introduction to maritime strategy. C. C. Lloyd, *The British Seaman, 1200–1860: A Social Survey* (1968), is instructive on lower-deck conditions and the intractability of the manning problem. Romola and R. C. Anderson, *The Sailing Ship: Six Thousand Years of History* (1926; reprinted 1963), still holds an honoured place as a standard work on sail. Björn Landström, *The Ship: A Survey of the History of the Ship from the Primitive Raft to the Nuclear-Powered Submarine with Reconstructions in Words and Pictures* (1961), is a learned and attractive publication. George P. B. Naish, 'Ships and ship-building, *c.*1500–*c.*1750', Charles Singer *et al.* (eds), *A History of Technology* (1957), should not be missed. Developments in weapons are surveyed by F. L. Robertson, *The Evolution of Naval Armament* (1921). J. J. Keevil, *Medicine and the Navy*, Vol.I: *1200–1649* (1957), is a useful and well-documented study. J. B. Hewson, *A History of the Practice of Navigation* (Glasgow, 1951), and E. G. R. Taylor, *The Haven-Finding Art: A History of Navigation from Odysseus to Captain Cook* (1956), are helpful introductory surveys. D. W. Waters, *The Art of Navigation in England in Elizabethan and Early Stuart Times*

(1958), is a major study of the growth of scientific navigation. There are important documentary collections of naval interest. M. Oppenheim (ed.), *Naval Accounts and Inventories of the Reign of Henry VIII*, Navy Records Society [henceforth cited as NRS], Vol.8 (1896) and A. Spont (ed.), *Letters and Papers relating to the War with France, 1512–13*, NRS, Vol.10 (1897), are both useful for the early history of the Tudor navy. J. S. Corbett (ed.), *Fighting Instructions, 1530–1816*, NRS, Vol.29 (1905), sheds light on the beginnings of broadside sailing-ship tactics. Corbett (ed.), *Papers Relating to the Spanish War, 1585–1587*, NRS, Vol.11 (1898), is of value for the pre-armada phase of the war. The official English documents for the armada campaign are printed in J. K. Laughton's indispensable edition of *State Papers Relating to the Defeat of the Spanish Armada, Anno 1588*, 2 vols, NRS, Vols.1 and 2 (1894). For letters of Philip II to Santa Cruz and Medina Sidonia and for Ubaldini's contemporary 'Drake-centred' narrative of events, see George P. B. Naish (ed.), 'Documents illustrating the history of the Spanish Armada', C. C. Lloyd (ed.), *The Naval Miscellany*, Vol.IV, NRS, Vol.92 (1952). M. Oppenheim (ed.), *The Naval Tracts of Sir William Monson*, 5 vols, NRS, Vols.22, 23, 43, 45, 47 (1902–14), contains commentaries on people, campaigns and organisation by an officer who participated in operations during and after the Spanish war. Monson could be both inaccurate and unfair. The problems thus created for the student are taken care of by Oppenheim's scholarly editorial guidance. Maladministration and financial difficulties are the central themes of A. P. McGowan's careful edition of *The Jacobean Commissions of Enquiry: 1608 and 1618*, NRS, Vol.116 (1971). W. G. Perrin (ed.), *The Autobiography of Phineas Pett*, NRS, Vol.51 (1918), covers 1570–1638 and is valuable for shipbuilding and patronage. J. R. Tanner (ed.), *Two Discourses of the Navy, 1638 and 1659, by John Holland; also a Discourse of the Navy 1660 by Sir Robert Slyngsbie*, NRS, Vol.7 (1896), and W. G. Perrin (ed.), *Boteler's Dialogues*, NRS, Vol.65 (1929), are useful for contemporary views of the navy and naval policy, principally under the early Stuarts.

The documentation in print of piracy, privateering and the war of plunder is sparse. R. G. Marsden (ed.), *Documents relating to the Law and Custom of the Sea*, Vol.I: *1205–1648*, NRS, Vol.49 (1915), and Marsden (ed.), *Select Pleas in the Court of Admiralty*, Selden Society, Vols.VI and XI (1892–7), elucidate the legal basis of their study. English and Spanish materials have been exploited effectively by Irene A. Wright (ed.), *Documents Concerning English Voyages to the Spanish Main, 1569–80*, Hakluyt Society, Second Series, Vol.71 (1932); Wright (ed.), *Further English Voyages to Spanish America, 1583–1594*, Hakluyt Society, Second Series, Vol.99 (1951); Kenneth R. Andrews (ed.), *English Privateering Voyages to the West Indies, 1588–1595*, Hakluyt

Society, Second Series, Vol.111 (1959); Andrews (ed.), *The Last Voyage of Drake and Hawkins* Hakluyt Society, Second Series, Vol.142 (1972). The background and progress of a disastrous venture are documented by E. G. R. Taylor (ed.), *The Troublesome Voyage of Captain Edward Fenton, 1582–83*, Hakluyt Society, Second Series, Vol.113 (1959), and Elizabeth Story Donno (ed.), *An Elizabethan in 1582: The Diary of Richard Madox, Fellow of All Souls*, Hakluyt Society, Second Series, Vol.147 (1976). For Cavendish see, principally, David B. Quinn (ed.), *The Last Voyage of Thomas Cavendish, 1591–1592: The Autograph Manuscript of His Own Account of the Voyage with an Introduction, Transcription and Notes* (1975). Richard Hawkins, *Observations of Sir Richard Hawkins, Knight, on His Voyage into the South Sea, AD 1593*, has been edited by J. A. Williamson (1933). Insights into the relationship between piracy and the navy may be gleaned from G. E. Manwaring and W. G. Perrin (eds), *The Life and Works of Sir Henry Mainwaring*, 2 vols, NRS, Vols.54 and 56 (1920–22).

The writings of Michael Oppenheim (1853–1927) remain indispensable as a sustained effort to set the history of the English navy in the totality of English maritime development. Apart from his volumes in the Navy Records Society's series, we should note 'The Royal and Merchant Navy under Elizabeth', *English Historical Review* [henceforth cited as *EHR*], vol.vi (1891); *A History of the Administration of the Royal Navy and of Merchant Shipping in relation to the Navy, 1509–1660* (1896); contributions under 'Maritime history' to the *Victoria County History: Cornwall*, Vol.I (1906); *Suffolk*, Vol.II (1907); *Essex*, Vol.II (1907); *Sussex*, Vol.II (1907); *Dorset*, Vol.II (1908); *Somerset*, Vol.II (1911); *Kent*, Vol.II (1926). His unprinted contribution to the *Victoria County History of Devon* has been edited by W. E. Minchinton as *The Maritime History of Devon* (Exeter, 1968). Three recent contributions to the history of seafaring and ships are David B. Quinn, 'Sailors and the sea', Allardyce Nicoll (ed.), *Shakespeare in His Own Age* (Cambridge, 1964), G. V. Scammell, 'Manning the English merchant service in the sixteenth century', *The Mariner's Mirror* [henceforth cited as *MM*, vol.56 (1970), and K. R. Andrews, 'The Elizabethan seaman', *MM*, vol.68 (1982). Articles dealing with English naval administration include G. E. Aylmer, 'Attempts at administrative reform, 1625–40', *EHR*, vol.lxxii (1957); C. S. L. Davies, 'The administration of the Royal Navy under Henry VIII: the origins of the Navy Board', *EHR*, vol.lxxx (1965); Tom Glasgow, 'Maturing of naval administration, 1556–1564', *MM*, vol.56 (1970); A. W. Johns, 'The principal officers of the Navy', *MM*, vol.14 (1928); Ronald Pollitt, 'Bureaucracy and the Armada: the administrator's battle', *MM*, vol.60 (1974); Lawrence Stone, 'The Armada campaign of 1588', *History*, vol.xxix (1944).

J. S. Corbett, *Drake and the Tudor Navy*, 2 vols (1898), is essential reading for the sixteenth century. But see K. R. Andrews, *Drake's Voyages: A Re-assessment of Their Place in Elizabethan Maritime Expansion* (1967), for searching criticisms of Corbett's interpretation of Drake as a naval strategist. Andrew's fundamental contribution to our understanding of the war of plunder, and hence of sixteenth-century sea warfare in general, may be studied, *inter alia*, in *Elizabethan Privateering: English Privateering during the Spanish War, 1585–1603* (Cambridge, 1964), and *The Caribbean: Trade and Plunder, 1530–1630* (1978). Gordon Connell-Smith, *Forerunners of Drake: A Study of English Trade with Spain in the Early Tudor Period* (1954), is an important study of the growth of animosity towards Spain among English merchants and seamen and the significance of acts of pillage in the 1540s. The British Library's 'Drake Exhibition' in 1977 was accompanied by the publication of *Sir Francis Drake: An Exhibition to Commemorate Francis Drake's Voyage around the World, 1577–1580* (1977), an illustrated introductory survey of Drake's career. Though by no means the last word on the circumnavigation, H. R. Wagner, *Sir Francis Drake's Voyage around the World* (San Francisco, Calif., 1926), is a learned work with much information not otherwise readily accessible. Within a few years of its publication, Wagner's thesis was shown to require modification by E. G. R. Taylor, 'More light on Drake', *MM*, vol.16 (1930), and *Tudor Geography, 1485–1583* (1930). More recently K. R. Andrews has presented a fresh and convincing reinterpretation of the evidence available to Wagner and Taylor in 'The aims of Drake's expedition of 1577–80', *American Historical Review*, vol.lxxiii (1968). Biographies of Drake's illustrious contemporaries include A. L. Rowse, *Sir Richard Grenville of the Revenge: An Elizabethan Hero* (1949); George C. Williamson, *George, Third Earl of Cumberland, 1558–1605* (Cambridge, 1920); J. A. Williamson, *Sir John Hawkins: The Times and the Man* (Oxford, 1927), and *Hawkins of Plymouth* (1949), both of which, though somewhat indulgent towards Hawkins, are authoritative studies of Elizabethan oceanic endeavour and the Elizabethan navy. Rayner Unwin, *The Defeat of John Hawkins* (1960), is a readable account of Hawkins's third voyage to the Caribbean. R. W. Kenny, *Elizabeth's Admiral: The Political Career of Charles Howard, Earl of Nottingham, 1536–1624* (1970), is the most comprehensive study of the lord admiral. There is a short biography of Howard, very thin on his career under James I, by J. K. Laughton, 'Howard', J. K. Laughton (ed.), *From Howard to Nelson: Twelve Sailors* (1899), and one of William Monson by Wilbur C. Abbott, 'A true Elizabethan: Sir William Monson', *Conflicts with Oblivion* (New Haven, Conn., 1924).

Garrett Mattingly, *The Defeat of the Spanish Armada* (1959), is a compelling account of the great campaign firmly located in the context of Anglo-Spanish relations and the general European situation. The technical background of the Armada campaign is currently unsettled. Michael A. Lewis, *The Spanish Armada* (1960) and *Armada Guns* (1961), and D. W. Waters, 'The Elizabethan navy and the Armada campaign', *MM*, vol.35 (1949), also available in the National Maritime Museum's series of *Maritime Monographs and Reports* (Greenwich, 1975), are broadly agreed that the Spaniards were superior to the English in heavy short-range armament and inferior in light-shotted long-range armament. However, the validity of their archivally limited investigations, which made much, though not complete, sense of events in the English Channel, has been called into question by I. A. A. Thompson, 'Spanish Armada guns', *MM*, vol.61 (1975), whose evidence from the Spanish archives suggests that the Spaniards were at a general disadvantage in both weight of shot and range. John Francis Guilmartin, Jr, *Gunpowder and Galleys: Changing Technology and Mediterranean Warfare at Sea in the Sixteenth Century* (Cambridge, 1974), contains useful ideas on the problems of adjustment from Mediterranean to Atlantic naval warfare. Charles J. Ffoulkes, *Gun Founders of England* (Cambridge, 1937), is helpful on the Tudor armaments industry. See also H. R. Schubert, 'The superiority of English cast-iron cannon at the close of the sixteenth century', *Journal of the Iron and Steel Institute*, vol.clxi (1949). The yields of nautical archaeology, while seeming on balance to favour Thompson's conclusions, do not as yet provide clear-cut answers to the problems. The activities and finds of underwater archaeologists are attractively recorded in R. Sténuit, *Treasures of the Armada* (Newton Abbot, 1972), and Colin Martin, *Full Fathom Five: Wrecks of the Spanish Armada* (1975). The starting-point of investigations into wrecks off the Irish coast must be W. Spotswood Green, 'The wrecks of the Spanish Armada on the coast of Ireland', *Geographical Journal*, vol.xxvii (1906), and 'Armada ships on the Kerry coast', *Proceedings of the Royal Irish Academy*, vol.xxvii (1909). Spanish naval documents for the campaign have been published by C. Fernández Duro (ed.), *La Armada Invencible,* 2 vols (Madrid, 1885), and Enrique Herrera Oria, *Felipe II y el Marqués de Santa Cruz en la Empresa de Inglaterra* (Madrid, 1946). Correspondence from the archive of Medina Sidonia has been printed by Gabriel Maura Gamazo, duque de Maura (ed.), *El Designio de Felipe II* (Madrid, 1957). The leadership of the Spanish fleet is discussed by Peter Pierson, 'A commander for the Armada', *MM*, vol.55 (1969), and I. A. A. Thompson, 'The appointment of the Duke of Medina Sidonia to the command of the Spanish Armada', *Historical Journal*, vol.12 (1969). Leon van der Essen, *Alexandre Farnèse: prince de Parme, gouverneur-général des Pays-Bas (1545–1592),* 5 vols

(Brussels, 1933–8), is indispensable for Parma's part in the Spanish designs of 1587–8 and for his campaigns in the Netherlands and France.

Publications of Andrews, Cheyney, Corbett, Oppenheim, Wernham and Williamson already cited deal with many aspects of the English war effort after the campaign of 1588. To them must be added J. S. Corbett, *The Successors of Drake* (1900), which is still the standard comprehensive coverage of naval warfare from 1596 to 1604. R. B. Wernham, 'Queen Elizabeth and the Portugal expedition of 1589', *EHR*, vol.lxvi (1951), is a cautious defence of the queen's policy and a valuable corrective to some of the strictures passed upon her. L. W. Henry, 'The Earl of Essex as strategist and military organiser, 1596–7', *EHR*, vol.lxviii (1953), brings out the contrast between Essex's capacity to formulate strategic ideas and his incapacity to translate them into action. W. B. Devereux, *The Lives and Letters of the Devereux Earls of Essex in the Reigns of Elizabeth, James I and Charles I, 1540–1646*, 2 vols (1853), contains useful letters. For the Irish campaigns, there are Cyril Falls's excellent *Elizabeth's Irish Wars* (1950), and *Mountjoy: Elizabethan General* (1955); Frederick M. Jones, *Mountjoy, 1563–1606: The Last Elizabethan Deputy* (Dublin, 1958). Spanish policy towards Ireland is examined by John J. Silke, *Kinsale: The Spanish Intervention in Ireland at the End of the Elizabethan Wars* (Liverpool, 1970), which is the standard work on this episode. The leadership of the expedition to Ireland has aroused controversy. See the contrasting views of Frederick M. Jones, 'An indictment of Don Juan del Aguila', *Irish Sword*, vol.ii (1955), and Henry Mangan, 'A vindication of Don Juan del Aguila', *Irish Sword*, vol.ii (1956).

For general surveys of the seventeenth century we remain dependent on two older works: J. S. Corbett, *England in the Mediterranean, 1603–1714*, 2 vols (1904), and C. D. Penn, *The Navy under the Early Stuarts and Its Influence on English History* (Leighton Buzzard and Manchester, 1913). Despite their continued usefulness, neither can any longer be regarded as definitive. There is valuable material on the governmental financial crisis and the second commission of inquiry into the navy in Menna Prestwick, *Cranfield: Politics and Profits under the Early Stuarts: The Career of Lionel Cranfield, Earl of Middlesex* (Oxford, 1966). Dorothea Coke, *The Last Elizabethan: Sir John Coke, 1563–1644* (1937), is useful for Coke's service as assistant treasurer of the navy under Fulke Greville, on the second commission of inquiry and as secretary of state under Charles I. Valuable first-hand material concerning the Jacobean and Caroline fleets may with effort be quarried from Coke's papers in Historical Manuscripts Commission, Twelfth Report, Appendix, Parts I and II: *The Manuscripts of the Earl Cowper, KG, Preserved at Melbourne Hall, Derbyshire*, 2 vols (1888–90). Charles Dalton, *The Life and Times of General Sir Edward Cecil, Viscount*

Wimbledon: Colonel of an English Regiment in the Dutch Service, 1605–1631, and One of His Majesty's Most Honourable Privy Council, 1628–1638, 2 vols (1885), is important for the expedition to Cádiz (1625). See also A. B. Grosart (ed.), *The Voyage to Cadiz in 1625: Being a Journal Written by John Glanville, Secretary to the Lord Admiral of the Fleet (Sir E. Cecil)*, Camden Society, New Series, Vol.XXXII (1883). We lack a monograph on naval finance under the early Stuarts, but there are useful articles dealing with ship money: R. J. W. Swales, 'The ship money levy of 1628', *Bulletin of the Institute of Historical Research*, vol.50 (1977); M. D. Gordon, 'The collection of ship money in the reign of Charles I', *Transactions of the Royal Historical Society*, Third Series, vol.iv (1910); L. M. Hill, 'County government in Caroline England, 1625–1640', Conrad Russell (ed.), *The Origins of the English Civil War* (1978). T. G. Barnes, *Somerset, 1625–1640: A County's Government during the Personal Rule* (Oxford, 1961), puts the application of the ship-money writs in Somerset under the microscope with findings which underline the need for further local studies. An impressionistic picture of the Caroline navy in the 1630s and of the social tensions therein may be obtained from David Mathew, *The Age of Charles I* (1951). See also W. R. Chaplin, 'William Rainsborough (1587–1642) and his associates of the Trinity House', *MM*, vol.31 (1945). The significance of the construction of the *Sovereign of the Seas* is discussed in 'The ship and the line', the first chapter of John Ehrman, *The Navy in the War of William III, 1689–1697* (Cambridge, 1953). The influence of sea power in the English Civil War is described by J. R. Powell, *The Navy in the English Civil War* (Hamden, Conn., 1962) and documented by J. R. Powell and E. K. Timings (eds), *Documents relating to the Civil War, 1642–1648*, NRS, Vol.113 (1963). E. H. Jenkins, *A History of the French Navy* (1973), and J. Tramond, *Manuel d'histoire maritime de la France des origines à 1815* (Paris, 1947), are both convenient introductions to the history of the French navy.

Commercial and Colonial

It is not easy, and is probably not desirable, to separate too sharply the materials dealing with English external trade in general from those dealing with the beginnings and development of overseas trade leading to the establishment of commercial bases in the East and to colonies in the west. In the chapters dealing with these topics, they are intermingled as they are here.

J. H. Rose *et al.* (eds), *The Cambridge History of the British Empire*, Vol.I (1929), and for a more limited period, J. A. Williamson, *The Age of Drake* (1938), give a conventional but useful study, as do Williamson, *Sir John Hawkins: The Times and the Man* (Oxford, 1927), and *Hawkins of Plymouth* (1949). A. L. Rowse, *The Expansion of*

Elizabethan England (1955), D. B. Quinn, *Ralegh and the British Empire* (latest edition Harmondsworth, 1973), and K. R. Andrews, *Drake's Voyages: A Re-Assessment of their Place in Elizabethan Maritime Expansion* (1967), all attempt something more than narrative. See also the introductory essay to D. B. Quinn (ed.), *The Voyages and Colonising Enterprises of Sir Humphrey Gilbert*, 2 vols, Hakluyt Society, Second Series, Vols 83–4 (1940).

For the first half of the seventeenth century we still depend on monographs mainly centred on the colonial enterprise and lack a broad synthetic treatment of the whole period, for which what follows can only be an interim report. The more general economic histories of the period, notably E. E. Rich and Charles Wilson (eds), *Cambridge Economic History of Europe*, Vol.IV: *The Economy of Expanding Europe in the Sixteenth and Seventeenth Centuries* (Cambridge, 1967), D. C. Coleman, *The Economy of England, 1450–1750* (1977), and Charles Wilson, *England's Apprenticeship, 1603–1763* (Cambridge, 1965), in their anxiety not to predate the appearance of either a 'commercial' or an 'industrial' revolution, tend to play down the novelties in external trade outside Europe and the growth of capitalist, mercantile and manufacturing groups concerned in it by adopting a strictly quantitative approach. This is not always the most revealing one in a field where novelty in technique and variety in product are often better indications of change. The older general book, G. D. Ramsay, *English Overseas Trade during the Centuries of Emergence* (1957), does not do this; nor does Ralph Davis in his brief *English Overseas Trade, 1500–1700* (1973). B. E. Supple, *Commercial Crisis and Change in England, 1603–1642* (Cambridge, 1959), is the most sophisticated general account of the background so far available for this period. P. H. Ramsey, *Tudor Economic Problems* (1963), his edition of essays, *The Price Revolution in the Sixteenth Century* (1971), and also R. B. Outhwaite, *Inflation in Tudor and Stuart England* (1969), throw light on the background of commercial expansion.

The dispersed papers of F. J. Fisher still remain, if qualified in some respects by later work, the basic introduction to many branches of English external trade. Chronologically they are 'Commercial trends and policy in sixteenth-century England', *Economic History Review* [henceforth cited as *EcHR*], vol.x (1940); 'London export trade in the early seventeenth century', *EcHR*, Second Series, vol.iii (1950); 'The sixteenth and seventeenth centuries: the dark ages of English economic history?', *Economica*, New Series, vol.24 (1957); 'Tawney's century', F. J. Fisher (ed.), *Essays in the Economic and Social History of Tudor and Stuart England in Honour of R. H. Tawney* (Cambridge, 1961). Closely linked in areas with which he was concerned are J. R. Jones, 'Some aspects of London's mercantile history', Norton Downs (ed.),

Essays in Honor of Conyers Read (Chicago, Ill., 1953); Lewis R. Miller, 'New evidence on the shipping and imports of London, 1601–1602', *Quarterly Journal of Economics*, vol.xli (1927); J. D. Gould, 'Cloth exports, 1600–1640', *EcHR*, Second Series, vol.xxiv (1971); Gould, 'The trade depression of the early 1620s', *EcHR*, Second Series, vol.vii (1954–5). N. J. Williams, *Contraband Cargoes* (1959), underlines the caution which must be used in drawing conclusions from official figures since smuggling was so prevalent (as was the corruption of officials).

Focused more directly on new directions in trade and policy are Lawrence Stone, 'Elizabethan overseas trade', *EcHR*, Second Series, vol.ii (1949), and T. K. Rabb, 'The expansion of Europe and the spirit of capitalism', *Historical Journal*, vol.17 (1974), both of which are valuable. But Rabb's book, *Enterprise and Empire, 1575–1630* (Cambridge, Mass., 1967), an early experiment in using computerised technique, must be read with caution. R. Brenner, 'The social basis of English commercial development, 1550–1659', *Journal of Economic History*, vol.xxx (1972), is important if, on some points, controversial. J. C. Riemersa, 'Government influence on company organization in Holland and England, 1550–1650', *Journal of Economic History*, Supplement 10 (1950), has interesting points of comparison to make. It links up on the English side with V. Ponko, 'The Privy Council and the spirit of Elizabethan economic management, 1558–1603', *American Philosophical Society Transactions*, New Series, vol.lvii (1968).

Joan Thirsk, *Economic Policy and Projects: The Development of a Consumer Society in Early Modern England* (Oxford, 1978), puts into clear and original perspective the novelties in Tudor and Stuart productive industries showing that, if their scale was individually small, they created a class of producers and consumers, and new goods for export, which gradually altered traditional patterns of internal production and distribution. This diversity in production cut down imports of certain goods from Europe, but created demands for overseas raw material (cotton for one) and provided a much wider range of articles for sale in overseas markets. Sybil M. Jack, *Trade and Industry in Tudor and Stuart England* (1977), supplies additional information but is weak on interpretation. J. W. Nef, *The Conquest of the Material World* (Chicago, Ill., 1964), modifies his earlier views about the existence of a major industrial revolution in England in the sixteenth and early seventeenth centuries and correctly stresses that a number of capital-intensive industries (however atypical they might be in the general picture) did develop in the period. Several – shipbuilding, the metal industries, sugar-boiling – were to be of special importance in overseas development.

The social background is drawn in Carl Bridenbaugh, *Vexed and Troubled Englishmen*, revised edition (New York, 1974), and is put in a European perspective by Geoffrey Parker, *Europe in Crisis, 1598–1648* (1979). Andrew B. Appleby, *Famine in Tudor and Stuart England* (Liverpool, 1978), and parts of P. J. Bowden, *The Wool Trade in Tudor and Stuart England* (1962), illustrate how epidemics and bad harvests could oppress the poor, enrich rising yeomen and merchants and, especially, encourage emigration as indentured servants. The earlier sixteenth-century background for this is clearly brought out by W. G. Hoskins, *The Age of Plunder* (1976).

When we come to trace specific developments in overseas trade, G. D. Ramsay, *The City of London in International Politics at the Accession of Elizabeth Tudor* (Manchester, 1975), and the text he has edited, *The Politics of a Tudor Merchant Adventurer* (Manchester, 1979), form an excellent foundation for the study of England's conventional external trade in the early years of the period and help to explain why it remained tied to such dependence on the unfinished cloth trade and to such narrow territorial limits. The history of newer chartered companies explain how this network was broken, and we are fortunate to have good histories of most of them. T. S. Willan, *The Muscovy Merchants of 1555* (Manchester, 1953), and *The Early History of the Russia Company, 1553–1603* (Manchester, 1956), are authoritative, while M. S. Anderson, *Britain's Discovery of Russia, 1553–1815* (1958), provides a wider perspective. The Barbary Company is well covered in T. S. Willan, *Studies in Elizabethan Foreign Trade* (Manchester, 1959). Similarly, R. W. K. Hinton, *The Eastland Trade and the Common Weal in the Seventeenth Century* (Cambridge, 1959), and J. K. Fedorwicz, *England's Baltic Trade in the Early Seventeenth Century* (Cambridge, 1979), cover the Eastland Company and other trade with Scandinavia and Poland. For the Levant Company, we have the general history, A. C. Wood, *A History of the Levant Company* (1935), and the more specific treatment in T. S. Willan, 'Some aspects of English trade with the Levant in the seventeenth century', *EHR*, vol.lxx (1955). Alberto Tenenti, *Piracy and the Decline of Venice, 1580–1615* (1967), is somewhat inflated as regards English piratical attacks on Venetian trade. R. Davis, 'England and the Mediterranean, 1570–1670', F. J. Fisher (ed.), *Essays . . . in Honour of R. H. Tawney* (Cambridge, 1961), provides a more balanced picture. For the foundation of the East India Company, Sir William Foster, *England's Quest of Eastern Trade* (1933), is still the most useful introduction. K. N. Chauduri, *The English East India Company* (1965), is the most important monograph. D. K. Bassett, 'Early English trade and settlement in Asia, 1602–1690', J. S. Bromley and E. H. Kossmann (eds), *British and the Netherlands in Europe and Asia* (1968), is a concise and valuable summary. G. N. Clark and W. J. M. Eysinga, *The Colonial Conferences between England and the Netherlands in 1612 and 1615* (Leiden, 1952), underline the problems of Anglo-Dutch competition in Asia, while M. A. P. Meilink-Roelofsz, *Asian Trade and European Influence in the Indonesian Archipelago between 1500 and about 1630* (The Hague, 1962), brings out the context in the Far East. A pamphlet war over the East India Company began in 1615 with pamphlets by Robert Keale, *Trades Increase* (1615) – anti – and Sir Dudley Digges, *The Defence of Trade* (1615) – pro – which are very revealing of contemporary attitudes to oriental and other branches of overseas trade. The controversy continued until long after the middle of the century. English contacts with West Africa have still to be searched for in many places. J. W. Blake, *West Africa: Quest for God and Gold* (1977), covers the period to 1578, while 'The farm of the Guinea trade in 1631', H. A. Cronne, T. W. Moody and D. B. Quinn (eds), *Essays in British and Irish History in Honour of James Eadie Todd* (1949), throws light on a later obscure episode. E. W. Bovill, *The Golden Trade of the Moors,* second edition (1963), is also useful.

Companies for commerce in the remoter parts of the Old World shade into companies for trade and colonisation in the New. For the general context, R. Davis, *The Rise of the Atlantic Economics* (1973), and K. G. Davies, *The North Atlantic World in the Seventeenth Century* (1974), are helpful and stimulating. D. B. Quinn, *England and the Discovery of America, 1481–1620* (New York, 1974), has several studies on their origin, made rather more specific in *North America from Earliest Discovery to First Settlements* (New York, 1977), which goes, however, only to 1612. For the Virginia Company, P. L. Barbour, *The Three Worlds of John Smith* (Boston, Mass., 1964), has something on the beginning of the colony, while E. S. Morgan, *American Freedom – American Slavery* (New York, 1975), gives a graphic account of what he regards as its 'fiasco'. W. F. Craven, *The Southern Colonies in the Seventeenth Century* (Baton Rouge, La, 1949), gives a more consistent account, while *The Dissolution of the Virginia Company* (New York, 1932), remains important. Another work of his was privately printed at Williamsburg, Va, in 1938, *An Introduction to the History of Bermuda*, and has not been superseded, though H. C. Wilkinson, *The Adventurers of Bermuda* second edition (1958), has some value. R. Hamor, *A true discourse of the present state of Virginia* (1615), and Edward Waterhouse, *A declaration of the state of the colony and affaires of Virginia* (1622), give some contemporary light on the first plantation colony. D. B. Quinn (ed.), *Maryland and the Wider World* (Detroit, Mich., 1982), places this colony in its setting and incorporates recent research. Frances Rose-Troup, *The Massachusetts Bay Company and Its Predecessors* (New York, 1930), is still valuable, as is R. Preston, *Gorges of Plymouth Fort* (Toronto, 1953). Gillian T. Cell, *English Enterprise in Newfoundland, 1577–1660* (Toronto, 1969), is now supported by her documentary collection, *Newfoundland Discovered*, Hakluyt Society, 2nd series, vol. 160 (1982), and by G. M. Story (ed.), *Early European Settlement and Exploration in Atlantic Canada* (St John's, Que., 1982). A great deal has been written about early colonial America, but the most relevant material is still to be found for this period in C. M. Andrews, *The Colonial Period of American History*, Vols 1 and 2 (New Haven, Conn., 1934–6).

For the West Indies in perspective, K. R. Andrews, *The Spanish Caribbean, Trade and Plunder, 1530–1630* (New Haven, Conn., 1978), places English activity in perspective. His invaluable *Elizabethan Privateering* (Cambridge, 1964) is mainly concerned with the earliest phase of English activity there. For the early period of settlement, Carl and Roberta Bridenbaugh, *No Peace beyond the Line: The English in the Caribbean, 1624–1690* (New York, 1972), and R. S. Dunn, *Sugar and Slaves: The Rise of the Planter Class in the English West Indies, 1624–1713* (Chapel Hill, NC, 1973), are largely complementary: the latter being more specifically economic in its approach.

For the English in all parts of the Caribbean and North America, the leading periodical is the *William and Mary Quarterly*, published by the Institute for Early American History and Culture, Williamsburg, Virginia. Of the essays in K. R. Andrews, N. P. Canny and P. E. H. Hair (eds), *The Westward Enterprise, 1480–1650* (Liverpool, 1978), those most directly relevant to the present study are Carole Shammas, 'English commercial development and American colonization, 1560–1620', K. R. Andrews, 'The English in the Caribbean, 1560–1620', and Joyce Lorimer, 'The English contraband tobacco trade with Guiana, 1590–1617'. Two fairly general essays by D. B. Quinn may be noticed, 'Renaissance influences in English colonization,' in *Royal Historical Society Transactions*, Fifth Series, vol. xxvi (1976) and 'James I and the beginnings of empire in America', *Journal of Imperial and Commonwealth History*, vol. ii (1974). The latter periodical has been gradually widening its scope so as to take in articles on the earlier colonial developments, notably K. R. Andrews, 'Beyond the Equinoctial: England and South America in the sixteenth century', vol. x (1981).

Some contemporary works of value are [Sir Thomas Smith], *A discourse of the commonweal of this realme of England*, ed. Mary Dewar (Charlotteville, Va, 1969); Richard Eden, *Decades of the East and West India* (1555); *The politics of a Tudor merchant venturer: a letter to the earls of East Friesland*, already mentioned; John Browne, *The marchants avizo, 1589*, ed. P. McGrath (Cambridge, Mass., 1957); John Wheeler, *A treatise of commerce 1601*, ed. G. B. Hotchkiss (New York, 1931); E. G. R. Taylor, *The writings and correspondence of the two Richard Hakluyts*, 2 vols, 1935; Richard Hakluyt, *The principal navigations, 1589*, ed. D. B. Quinn and R. A. Skelton, 2 vols (Cambridge, 1965), *The principal navigations, 1598–1600*, 12 vols (Glasgow, 1903–5), followed by Samuel Purchas, *Hakluytus posthumus, or Purchas his pilgrimes 1625*, 20 vols (Glasgow, 1905–7). To the tracts on Virginia and the East India Company already mentioned, Matthew Sutcliffe, *A ful and round answer to N. D. alias Robert Parsons* (1604), and the invaluable, if not invariably reliable, works of Lewes Roberts, *The merchants increase of commerce* (London, 1636) and *The treasure of traffike* (1641), the latter addressed to the Long Parliament, and both giving an unparalleled conspectus of information and opinions.

CHAPTER 1

Trade and Discovery Overseas, 1550–1585

The first half of the sixteenth century was dominated in the commercial sphere by the continued rise, with few interruptions, of the trade in shortcloths, undyed, unfinished woollen cloth, which was increasingly canalised through the single port of Antwerp. The result was that there was little capital and relatively little interest in other trades on the part of the London merchants and their associates in the larger provincial towns. They were indeed a somewhat closed society, but they commanded most of the sources of capital, leaving little for other enterprises. Consequently, interest in the exploration of new areas of commerce was slight and the means for its achievement were meagre. The western ports, notably Bristol with its strong Iberian and other Atlantic connections, alone had something of a continuing interest in western expansion. But even there it was ill-sustained, and the Newfoundland cod fishery itself, in which Bristol had been the pioneer since at least 1502, if not long before, seems to have shifted to the ports on the south coast, especially in Devon. Had the Tudors found that there were indeed riches to be found to the west by a route to the East, they would have diverted some of their revenue to their exploitation, but instead of a rich Asia an apparently barren North America was all that appeared, while fishing was a lowly trade not worthy of royal interest. And had a North-west Passage around the awkward obstacle of North America been opened up in 1509, Henry VIII might have been diverted from war and sport and lechery to attempt to become another Manoel the Fortunate. The interest and significance of the early Bristol voyages is much more apparent in the twentieth century than it was in the early sixteenth. Moreover, the products of successful Iberian expansion, both in Asia and in the Americas, were fairly readily available, that from the Portuguese trading empire in the East at Antwerp and that from the less productive empire (in its early stages at least) of the Spaniards in the west at Seville. There were individuals like Sebastian Cabot and Robert Thorne who seriously tried to interest both the Crown and the Londoners in plans for English expansion overseas, but they were voices that were scarcely listened to. There was only a little pioneering activity after the outburst of western searches between 1497 and 1509, the most interesting being the Plymouth voyages to Brazil in the 1530s which provide the only serious example in this period of direct intervention for commercial ends in territories enclosed by the papal donation and the treaty of Tordesillas, which had proposed to close the doors to all non-Iberian powers concerned with the new worlds that were being discovered and exploited outside traditional routes.

Not every Englishman was happy about this. Thomas Cromwell was approached and criticised by several projectors who wished to do otherwise. Clement Armstrong in particular wanted to keep English cloth at home and make the foreigner come to England and pay good hard money for cloth there, and this in turn would stimulate home manufacturers and transform the economy. Instead, it was urged English merchants were bringing from Europe exotic products of slight value to the English producer. The consumer was being flattered and provided for, and robbed by high prices in the process, while all except the producers of wool, cloth and their allied products were being neglected and exploited. These proposals met with little or no response, especially since royal customs receipts were growing. Sir Thomas Smith, writing *A discourse of the commonweal of this realme of England* in 1549, could stress the official view:

> What need they beyond sea to travail to 'Perowe' or such far countries or to try out the sands of the rivers of Tagus in Spain, Pactolus in Asia and Ganges in India to get among them after much labour sparks of gold or to dig the deep bowels of the earth for the mine of silver or gold, when they can, in vile clay not far sought for, and of 'pryple' [gem] stones and fern roots make good gold and silver more than a great many of gold and silver mines would make.

This sarcastic and satirical, as well as conservative, view by the secretary of state, indicates the backward state of thinking in England a few years after the discovery of the almost inexhaustable supply of silver from Potosi, the first in a chain of mineral discoveries which was to transform the fortunes of Spain and feed the avarice of the rest of Europe, incidentally contributing, as Smith was to observe, when he revised his treatise in the 1570s, to the rise of prices which provided at the same time a major stimulus to the commerce of the whole of Europe as well as contributing to the hardships of those living on fixed incomes.

The growth of English exploration and commerce for much of the early and middle sixteenth century takes on the character of an arithmetical rather than a geometric progress. There is no outburst of discovery and exploration in a dramatic and romantic form. Trial and error, and the gradual pushing out beyond established boundaries, is characteristic of English expansion until the more spectacular, but not invariably fruitful, forays of the later sixteenth century. At the same time, by mid-century a substantial amount of information about new prospects was becoming available. Henry VIII, even if he had refused all commitments to sponsor voyages within the Iberian sphere, had built up at court a substantial body of information on the world outside Europe, especially sponsoring French cartographers such as Jean Rotz to present cartographically a new and enlarged picture of the world, while French navigational expertise was also made available in several manuscript treatises. The arrival of Sebastian Cabot in England in 1547 brought home a man who had taken part in the early Bristol voyages and then had a long career in charge of the Spanish training school for pilots, as well as leading an expedition himself to the Plate estuary. He knew enough to inform English merchants what might and might not prosper in the way of speculative enterprises overseas. Over the next few years he was to be a seminal influence in many directions, even if his major preoccupation, the discovery of a northern passage, remained still wrapped in mystery when he died a decade later.

The overseas activities of the 1550s did not spring out of nothing, and they are not all, by any means, the consequence of the difficulties the cloth trade encountered during this decade, a hard one for England in many ways. Currency debasement hindered trade; over-production of wool with under-consumption of cloth exports on the Continent made social and religious unrest more serious. At the same time, after 1547, there was certainly mobile capital available such as there had not been before. W. G. Hoskins, in his *Age of Plunder* (1976), Chapter 6, gives a vivid account of the accumulation of capital resources derived from the disposal of church and royal lands and the speculation which followed, and which were tempting gentry as well as merchants and the goldsmith bankers of the period into placing some of their gains into enterprises, the security of which could not be assured, but which offered, or might offer, high profits not easy to obtain in the unsettled economic situation of established branches of commerce. Even if the Merchant Adventurers clung to the Antwerp cloth trade and did all they could to revive its fortunes after its catastrophic decline in the early 1550s, some of its members and other merchants outside its circle showed willingness to take risks in other directions, even though they too might consider that cloth would continue to be England's main offering in new areas and markets.

Michael Lok and other London merchants could find capital to send English ships and goods to the eastern Mediterranean from 1551 onwards with some profit. Thomas Wyndham had both London and

Bristol merchant backing, as well as assistance from some of the south-western gentry, when he began a profitable trade with Morocco in 1551, which was to become a valuable new, though intermittent, commercial outlet from then onwards, but Wyndham's attempts to extend English commerce to Guinea and Benin in 1553 proved disastrous for himself and his men, though William Towerson and others followed with more caution and greater profit from 1555. Cabot had much to do with inspiring these ventures. He failed in the more ambitious task of getting the Duke of Northumberland to attempt a South American venture in 1551, but his continuous harping on the profitable consequence of penetrating northern waters, to the north-west, to the north, or to the north-east, eventually bore fruit in a major expedition of 1553. Richard Chancellor, an experienced pilot, and Sir Hugh Willoughby, a dashing gentleman adventurer, were backed by a syndicate of London merchants, including many of the Merchant Adventurers, to make a voyage in three ships to the north, in hopes of reaching Asia.

Chancellor took them safely round the North Cape but the ships were separated and it was Chancellor who took his vessel safely into the White Sea and found the Russian settlement at St Nicholas which provided him with an entry to the dominions of the young tsar, Ivan IV, and to the beginnings of a branch of commerce which had not hitherto been anticipated. Willoughby, missing the entry, perished with his men in the harsh northern winter. The return of Chancellor with trading concessions from the Tsar of Muscovy led to the chartering of the Muscovy (or Russia) Company in 1555 with a substantial capital and high hopes, and the building up of a substantial trade with Russia by the northern route, supplemented for a time after 1558 by trade through the Baltic to the Russian-held port of Narva. The market for cloth and tin in exchange for furs, flax and wax was conventional enough, but it created hopes of linking up the eastern Mediterranean and Russian commerce by an approach through Russia to the Middle East and the tapping of Asiatic sources by way of Persia as well as by contact with the Turkish empire. Cabot did much to inspire all this and was greatly honoured for his work, but something of this type of expansion would have taken place in any event during this decade. It did not add up to a great deal in terms of imports and exports or even in total profits, but it was a seminal period and indicated that English pilots could face the non-traditional routes with some expertise. The world map printed in London in 1549 under Cabot's auspices had, indeed, enlarged the horizons of English enterprise, even if the Americas and Asia remained largely unknown to them by direct experience. None the less, Richard Eden, in books published in 1553 and 1555, had given his readers substantial glimpses of the new discoveries and their potential in the East and in the west, while the new navigation manuals being published in the Iberian countries were beginning to filter into England and to place before merchants and pilots alike some of the more novel techniques of sailing in distant waters.

In 1555 Richard Eden had praised Spain to the heights for developing her empire and for bringing so much gold and silver, among other things, into Europe; but he had also called attention to much that was still unexplored: 'The Spaniards have shewed a good example to all Christian nations to follow.' Besides what Spain and Portugal had found,

> there yet remaineth another portion of that mainland reaching towards the northeast, thought to be as large as the other, and not yet known but only by the sea coasts, neither inhabited by any Christian men, whereas . . . in this land there are many fair and fruitful regions, high mountains and fair rivers, with abundance of gold and divers kinds of beasts. Also cities and towns so well builded and people of such civility that this part of the world seemeth little inferior to our Europe, if the inhabitants had received our religion . . . How much therefore is it to be lamented, and how greatly doth it sound to the reproach of all Christendom, and especially to such as dwell nearest to these lands as we do, . . . that we have no respect neither for God's cause nor for our own commodity to attempt some voyages into these coasts, to do for our parts as the Spaniards have done for theirs, and not ever like sheep to haunt one trade.

He celebrated the enterprise of those merchants who had contributed to the opening of trade with Muscovy, Barbary and Guinea, but did not succeed in encouraging any novel western voyaging. At the same time, as disillusionment with the Spanish connection had grown, and by 1558 had turned into a deep hostility among many in both mercantile and gentry circles, his words may well have come to mind and embedded in that hostility the intention to oppose and to emulate Spain in the west if and when opportunity to do this could be found.

The accession of Queen Elizabeth marked a considerable watershed in English history, but it did not have significant immediate effects on English overseas activity. The Netherlands cloth trade had picked up in the later 1550s, though it was not ever again to recover its earlier level: trade with Spain had flourished and was to continue to do so for some years. English merchant families living in Spain continued their Catholic practices, while their relatives and associates in England conformed to the Elizabethan Church. English exports to and from the New World by way of Spain had continued to grow, though they were hampered by heavy taxation. Direct trade with Lisbon for oriental produce was also improving, though much was still acquired in Antwerp and some from Rouen, while Portugal did her best through diplomacy and force to stop direct English trade with west Africa.

The reform of the coinage in 1560 made England more reliable as a trading partner. The war with France, begun in Spain's interest under Mary, ended in 1559, but it left behind a legacy of English pirate ships as well as a body of adventurous seamen and ex-soldiers who were to make the first forays into Spanish waters in the New World. Elizabeth was anxious to remain on good terms with Philip II, at least until her regime was well-established and the danger of a French takeover in Scotland obviated. But from the beginning of the reign some of her ministers and courtiers were inclined to turn a blind eye towards, or even to encourage, aggressive new ventures against Spain such as French privateers had been making in the Caribbean since the 1520s.

The basic uncertainty of longer-term Anglo-Spanish relations must be viewed in the light of the position of Spain in the Low Countries, both in the degree of tighter control over local autonomy by Philip II and the growth of religious persecution, since England continued to depend for by far the major part of her external commerce on the Antwerp cloth trade, which became a matter of major questioning in the mid-1560s, especially after the closing of the port, temporarily, to English cloth in 1564. George Needham, writing just after this episode (as brought to light in G. D. Ramsay's *The Politics of a Tudor Merchant Adventurer* in 1979), gave an authoritative account of the extent of this trade in the hands of the Merchant Adventurers and of the need for them to find alternative distributing centres for English cloth (he favoured Emden in particular) to the monopoly position of Antwerp, especially as there was a growing German demand for unfinished English cloth and for the heavier dyed and finished varieties which were also emerging. It is essential to conclude that the cloth trade as described by him at this period was the principal factor inhibiting new overseas enterprises, though it did not prevent them altogether. The figures for trade with Antwerp in 1564 (which we can take as informed guesses by a well-informed reporter) are:

80,000	white [unfinished] cloths, worth	£600,000
40,000	coloured cloths, with kerseys and other coarse cloths	£300,000
	Wool and wool fells	£100,000

These made up a total, according to him, of £1,020,000, out of which gross profits of 27 per cent amounted to £274,000, almost equivalent to the queen's total revenue.

This indicates very clearly how closely England's economy and policies were tied to the cloth trade. No wonder – since the Spaniards not only closed it down for a time in 1564, but did so again during the years 1569–73 – that serious attempts were made to find other staple ports, Emden, Hamburg or wherever, through which cloth exports to Germany and other parts of continental Europe could be canalised. Moreover, the situation both underlined the need for new markets, notably to places where woollen cloths could be sold, but also the need for a switch, slow and hesitant, to take place because of the industry's conservatism and inefficiency, from unfinished white cloth, saleable only where a finishing industry existed or could be established, to coloured, that is, dyed and finished cloths, especially fabrics lighter than the blue broadcloths and red Suffolks which made up the second category of cloth exports.

The traditional coloured cloths could indeed be sold by the Muscovy Company in Russia, even if they were too expensive for the Russians to take in large quantities, as well as tin, and re-exports from the Netherlands. Metal trinkets and such like rubbish could be sold to Lapps and Samoyeds on the north coast for furs and oil; from St Nicholas (or Archangel), furs, wax and flax were the principal exports. Trade with Narva gave the English a further entry into the Baltic which had seldom been exploited directly earlier as it was dominated by the Hanseatic League, a syndicate of German towns which had a privileged 'factory' or warehouse in London. The prospecting expeditions of Anthony Jenkinson down the Volga to the Caspian and beyond it to Bokhara (1557–9) were genuine voyages of exploration. Relations with Ivan IV were not equable. He gave them privileges and took them back again, but a fair flow of goods between the two countries continued. Jenkinson renewed his prospecting – this time, in 1562–4, to Persia, where he was able to deliver letters to the shah, Tahmasp I, from the English queen. He was given presents but no general licence to trade, though he found Indian merchants who desired trade with England and obtained silks and other precious goods from the northern provinces, so that he was able to bring some spices as well as silks on the long trail back to England. Contacts, if intermittent ones, were revived by Arthur Edwards in 1566, and some continuity was maintained down to 1580 when the Persian trade was finally abandoned as too precarious. But it had an importance beyond its financial returns in seriously turning English attention to the desirability of trading directly with Asia. The attempt to continue eastward exploration by way of a North-east Passage was continued in 1556 and subsequently, but with only enough success in pushing a little farther not to eliminate all hope of finding a passage by further voyages. The company was never highly profitable and found it difficult to continue to raise capital for successive enterprises and to find resources for its agencies in Russia.

The most revealing insight into the expansion of English commercial and exploratory activities in this early phase is contained in the summary of his travels and services from 1546 onwards, compiled by Anthony Jenkinson after he had retired from the services of the Muscovy Company in 1572 (the place names being given modern forms):

First I passed into Flanders, and travelled through all the base [low] countries, and from thence through Germany, passing over the Alps, I travelled into Italy, and from thence made my journey through Piedmont into France, throughout all which realm I have thoroughly journeyed.

I have also travelled through the kingdoms of Spain and Portugal; I have sailed through the Levant Sea every way, and have been in all the chief islands within the same sea, as Rhodes, Malta, Sicily, Cyprus, Crete, and divers others.

I have been in many parts of Greece, Morea, Achaea, and where the old city of Corinth stood.

I have travelled through a great part of Turkey, Syria, and divers other countries in Asia Minor.

I have passed over the mountains of Lebanon to Damascus, and travelled through Samaria, Galilee, Philistine or Palestine, unto Jerusalem, and so through all the Holy Land.

I have been in divers places of Africa, as Algiers, Cola, Bona, Tripoli, the Golet within the Gulf of Tunis.

I have sailed far northward within the Mare Glaciale, where we have had continual day and sight of the sun ten weeks together, and that navigation was in Norway, Lapland, 'Samogitia' and other very strange places.

I have travelled through all the ample dominions of the emperor of Russia and Muscovy, which extend from the North Sea [the Arctic Ocean] and the confines of Norway and Lapland, even to the Caspian Sea.

I have been in divers countries near about the Caspian Sea, Gentiles and Mohammedans, as Kazan, Crimea, Ryazen, Cheremissi, Mordva, Votiakin, Nogai, with divers others of strange customs and religions.

I have sailed over the Caspian Sea and discovered all the regions there about adjacent, as Chircassi, Comul, Shamkhal, Shirvan, with many others.

I have travelled forty days journey beyond the said sea towards the Oriental India and Cathay, through divers deserts and wildernesses and passed through five kingdoms of the Tartars and all the land of Turkmenskoya and Chagatai and so to the great city of Bokhara in Bactria, not without great perils and dangers sundry times. After all this in Anno 1562, I passed again over the Caspian Sea another way and landed in Armenia at a city called Derbent, built by Alexander the Great, and from thence travelled through Media, Parthia, Hircania [Shirvan] into Persia to the court of the Great Sophy, called Shah Tahmasp, unto whom I delivered letters from the Queen's Majesty, and remained at his court eight months, and returning homeward, passed through divers other countries. Finally I made two voyages more after that out of England into Russia, and one in the year 1566 and the other in the year 1571. And thus being weary and growing old, I am content to take my rest in mine own house. . .

There had been money to be made in the eastern Mediterranean trade since the 1550s, but there were also risks to be run, involvement in the great Turkish-Spanish struggle, seizure by North African pirates and the like, so that expansion, though very attractive to the small group of London merchants engaged in it, of whom Michael Lok appears to have been the leading figure, on a larger scale was not very likely. But two things were promising: the Muscovy Company's penetration into Persia, which might in the end bring commerce through from there to the Mediterranean instead of by the long way round by the White Sea or Baltic (though this was to prove a failure within a few years), and, more cogently, the amount and variety of materials from the Spiceries reaching the eastern Mediterranean, which modern research has shown had never been completely cut off by the Portuguese and which was, in the third quarter of the century, rapidly increasing once again. The gradual weakening and eventual breakdown of the Persian trade turned the Muscovy Company to take up again the search for a North-east Passage in the still strongly held belief that access to China that way (especially now that news of a Spanish presence in the Far East had become known) might bring the riches which had so far virtually escaped from their grasp. This led in the end to the gallant attempt of Pet and Jackman to penetrate the sea south and east of Novaya Zemlya in 1580, only to be stopped, as all others were to be in this century, by a wall of ice. Thereafter the Muscovy Company gave over its explorations in the north-east, and they were taken up by the Dutch with similar aims in the last decade of the century. The Mediterranean traders, however, turned their attention to the possibilities of getting to the Spiceries by sea.

The African trade had proved profitable between 1555 and 1557, even if it had involved conflict with the Portuguese, so that under Spanish and Portuguese pressure it was prohibited for several years, though there had been some slight hope, while the Spanish connection lasted, that there would be some loosening of the restrictions which excluded the English from the Spanish Indies, but this was not achieved. After

Elizabeth was reasonably firmly established on the throne, John Hawkins, son of the Brazil pioneer, made the first breakthrough into the Spanish Americas. The West African trade restarted and London merchants as well as his father-in-law, Benjamin Gonson, treasurer of the queen's navy, backed Hawkins's new venture. This was to take or buy slaves in Portuguese Africa and then trade them across the Atlantic to the Caribbean, obtaining Spanish colonial products in return. It appears that the queen knew of the venture. The Spanish empire was short of slaves and it appeared just possible that they might accept those brought by the English as legitimate products of the trade, and so might agree that the English should receive payment in goods, possibly by sending the return vessels to Spain. Hawkins was careful to appear in 1562–3 as a trader not as a pirate, and as such he disposed of his cargo profitably in the Caribbean islands. To test official Spanish reactions, he dispatched one of his vessels, containing goods obtained in payment, direct to Spain. If it was not confiscated then he had some chance of obtaining a contract (*asiento*) for the supply of at least some of the slaves required by the Spanish colonists. In fact the authorities at Seville seized the ship, and condemned it and its goods, while orders were rapidly dispatched to officials in the Caribbean ports forbidding them to trade illegally with the English. Hawkins had at least half anticipated this and had himself returned with most of the goods he collected direct to England.

Hawkins and his backers, and they now included the queen, were prepared to press matters a little further. He was sent out once again with a small squadron, including one of the queen's ships on charter, and with help from a number of her ministers and courtiers. Slaves were obtained from African salesmen (some taken on the previous occasion had been seized); again, in spite of official prohibitions, trade was good, though Hawkins made a show of force where there was any sign of reluctance to accept this terms, which were higher in 1564–5 than on the previous occasion. He returned after a profitable voyage to England without having been molested either at sea or on land. He had established that there was an unsatisfied demand for slaves by the Spanish colonists and that they were willing to pay for them in American commodities, even including some silver. He was fortunate, however, that he was not caught by Pedro Menéndez de Avilés, who, having wiped out a French settlement in Florida, had used his fleet to scour the Caribbean for French and English intruders.

A further venture into the Caribbean would clearly be directly provocative, but curiously enough, Elizabeth, normally cautious, was prepared to risk violent Spanish reactions in backing, along with many courtiers, a third voyage. Hawkins set out in 1567 with six ships, including two of the queen's. This time he encountered and captured off the African coast several Portuguese vessels and crossed the Atlantic with some 550 slaves. This time he met more resistance from Spanish officials and settlers, but by threats and some force, he disposed of them all between Burburata, Rio de la Hacha and Santa Marta, though with relatively much less profit. His ancient flagship, the *Jesus of Lubeck*, a royal ship since the time of Henry VIII, could not stand up to Caribbean storms or worms and was in a sinking condition when he put in for repairs to Vera Cruz, or rather the harbour on the island of San Juan de Ulúa, where he took over without resistance the defences of the island, and anchored the rest of his ships in the harbour. He was unlucky, since almost at once the outward-bound *flota* arrived from Spain, under the command of Martin Enriquez, newly designated viceroy of Mexico, whose vessels promptly hemmed in the English ships. Enriquez temporised with Hawkins in face of the English land battery and exchanged hostages. But he prepared an attack which took the island by surprise and seemed to have Hawkins at his mercy. However, Hawkins in turn, turned all his firepower on the Spanish fleet and did much damage, but he was obliged to see one after another of his ships sunk or boarded, until only three of eight (including two prizes) were left and the *Jesus* was sinking. He piled his remaining men and stores into the *Minion* and *Judith*, which were still intact, and cut his way through the blockade. He had 265 men left, 200 of them on the *Minion* and 65 with most of the remainder of the stores on the *Judith*, of which Francis Drake was in command. The two vessels lost company, Hawkins claiming Drake deserted him, and he was faced with an impossible situation. With so many men and so few stores all must perish; he ruthlessly, if necessarily, landed a hundred of them on the coast of Mexico to take their chance, and sailed home with the rest, losing many of them on the way, but reaching Plymouth before all provisions were gone. Between Drake's cargo and his own, which included some bullion and pearls, he partially recouped the losses of the investors, but at the cost of a serious diplomatic incident. He not only brought to an end all hope of peaceful access to the Caribbean but nearly brought about a war with Spain. The Spanish empire was, indeed, vulnerable, but it was also very powerful when its force could be brought to bear on intruders. The Hawkins voyages, however, displayed an altogether new level of transatlantic activity on the part of the English. Philip II learned, moreover, that his power to stop or at least impede the English cloth trade by closing the port of Antwerp could be met by a show of aggressive reprisals. The queen's part in the enterprise, though it ended in an English defeat, indicated that she wished Spain to understand that she was by no means helpless at sea.

Hawkins's voyage coincided with the development of the Netherlands revolt and Philip's attempts to suppress it, while England's interest, though Elizabeth was reluctant to admit it, lay on the side of the provinces which were defending their liberties and, in places, the Protestant religion. Philip II could and did close the port of Antwerp to English cloth, though this was partly evaded, as in 1564, by the transfer of the English staple outside Philip's jurisdiction, while Elizabeth also seized (or 'borrowed') at Plymouth, money loaned to Philip by Italian bankers to pay his troops in the Low Countries. In England, the Crown had to deal with the northern rebellion of 1569, the intrigues of Mary, Queen of Scots, a prisoner (or hostage) in England since 1568, the Ridolfi plot of 1571 in particular, which aroused clamour for Mary's execution; and these involved in turn the ending for the time being of the trade, important to both parties, with Spain herself. The crisis of 1568–73 could have led to war, but Elizabeth's diplomacy succeeded in diverting Spanish concentration on England by minor, indirect aid to the insurgents in the Netherlands and by establishing links with the treacherous Catherine de Medici, so that Philip might consider France not unlikely to move against him. He was gradually brought round to acceptance of the need to compromise the issues at stake, since Antwerp and Seville were suffering from the stoppage of trade. A truce was made in 1573, followed by a treaty in 1574.

In the meantime, Hawkins's companion at San Juan de Ulúa, Francis Drake, had found a following among the west-country men for acts of pillage and revenge against Spain. Philip had had to admit in the treaty of 1559 that France would not deal with the pirates who plundered the Caribbean and he must do it himself: he now learnt the same thing with regard to the English. We know little about Drake's two voyages in 1570 and 1571, the first with the *Dragon* and *Swan* (except that on their way home they made a surprise raid on Spanish Florida) and the second with the *Swan* alone. They were intended to spy out the land for later expeditions, but in the meantime were simply piratical raids during which Drake made valuable contacts with more experienced French pirates who had for more than a generation been preying on the inter-colonial shipping and the more isolated ports in the Caribbean, though finding at times that trade, however illicit, paid better than simple piracy. Drake returned with a good deal of knowledge about how the Spaniards brought their silver across the isthmus of Panama to ports on the Atlantic side. For his expedition of 1572, he was able to get not only the backing of the Hawkins firm but that of the influential, London-based Winter family. His first important campaign was thus to attempt to seize treasure trains on their way from Panama to Nombre de Dios. His knowledge that there were potential allies on land in the shape of escaped slaves (*cimarones*) and at sea French pirates was important. His first attempt was to enable him to penetrate the

Isthmus and sight the Pacific, but to miss the mule-train and bungle an attack on Nombre de Dios. After wintering, and making an alliance with Guillaume Le Testu, a brilliant cartographer and an able commander, he was at last successful, with some aid from the escaped slaves, in seizing one consignment of silver after fighting in which Le Testu was killed. His share of the bullion (some gold as well as silver) which he brought back to England was conservatively valued at £30,000, but was probably worth much more. It provided dividends and made Drake a rich man, while it also was to continue to provide incentives to subsequent English voyages to the Caribbean over the next decade. For the time being, his return was a grave embarrassment to the queen, who was busy patching up her truce with Spain, and, indeed, the treaty of Bristol in 1574 provided for mutual reimbursement of losses suffered by each party. But it was not easy to lay hands on Drake's spoils, and he was pushed off to Ireland, out of the way, to assist the Earl of Essex in punitive campaigns against the island Scots in north-east Ulster.

Even if the undeclared war was brought to an end and Anglo-Spanish trade rapidly revived, along with the traditional cloth trade to Antwerp (now somewhat disrupted by continuing disturbances in the Netherlands), English overseas enterprise had entered a new phase. Trade by force of arms, as we may perhaps call the Hawkins ventures, gave place to piracy and plunder, and this was to continue, with checks from time to time for diplomatic reasons, for more than another decade. During this time, however, England gained some fresh opportunities for purchasing overseas products in Spain and selling her more of her own goods to send to the Indies. Moreover, she also began to detach some of her Newfoundland fishing vessels to go direct to Spain and sell their catches and bring back Spanish goods to England, while she was able to develop a substantial carrying trade in Baltic corn and maritime stores with the Iberian peninsula. The atmosphere between the two countries was one of continued suspicion and dislike and Spanish officials and officials of the Inquisition made things difficult for English traders in Spain even while English pirates continued to prey on the Indies.

Lord Burghley, the cautious lord treasurer, was in 1574 somewhat complacent about the rapproachment with Spain: other powerful figures at court, Sir Francis Walsingham, secretary of state, the Earl of Leicester, Lord Lincoln, the lord high admiral, and Sir Christopher Hatton among them, were not. Pro-Protestant feelings in regard to the Netherlands struggle and a feeling that the Spanish empire was ripe for the picking and would in any case be diverted from the Netherlands to some extent by English activity in the west influenced them to take action against Spain. Huguenot La Rochelle and other French ports were reaping a rich harvest by their depredations on Spanish shipping:

west-country men had close ties with some of them and could co-operate or compete. The expansion-minded group had two specific objects in mind, the first being exploration and route-finding in areas where Spanish and Portuguese power had not reached or at least was not strong. Lord Burghley was ready to associate himself with plans to reopen the viability of the northern passage to east or west, and even to consider exploration in the South Atlantic below the limit of Spanish settlement. While too, perhaps, the North American coast might be found to contain products of value. Such ventures if they succeeded would enhance and revive existing English trade. There was some slight hope of colonisation prospects, but these did not emerge for several years. There were, on the other hand, projects for aggressive action in which Walsingham was the leading spirit. These included stepping up trade in Portuguese West Africa, though not now for slaves but rather in hope of getting gold and ivory, the loosing of a more or less continuous string of piratical enterprises against the Caribbean, which private enterprise in the west country, if nourished by capital investment from London merchants and from courtiers, would be only too willing to carry out, together with plans to steal the Spanish and Portuguese fishing fleets at Newfoundland.

If Burghley remained doubtful about backing any enterprise which would drive Spain and Portugal to co-operate in measures for the aggressive defence of their empires, the attitude of the queen was ambiguous. She did not want a war with Spain; on the other hand, she was willing to go some way towards discommoding Philip II, especially if she might profit financially from her subjects' actions. A little goading and a lot of profit might be regarded as her policy so far as she had one, and she was led into backing Drake's enterprise in 1577 by such objectives. But the initiatives from 1575 onwards, which seems to be a reasonable year from which to date expansionist plans, did not necessarily come from court or Crown. There was certainly a new risk-taking attitude among merchants in London and the outports who were not bound up with the Spanish trade or too pessimistic about the long-term effects of the Netherlands struggle. Militant landed gentlemen, often with mercantile connections and perhaps some involvement in shipowning and in coastal piracy, appear to have emerged as an effective ginger group prepared to act as the aggressive court party wished. We do not know as much as we would like about the precise make-up and inspiration of this body of opinion; some initiative came from merchants who were rising outside the charmed circle of the Merchant Adventurers and wished to make money and their mark, but conservative interests in the City of London also put up a good deal of money in the years between 1576 and 1585 for expansionist ventures, much of it being lost, and only a small number of ventures, Drake's especially among them, returning the kind of profits on which high-risk speculators counted.

Ever since Giovanni da Verrazzano's voyage of 1524, the notion had been current in England that North America was very narrow, that there was a passage through the Arctic seas at relatively low latitudes, and that the west coast of North America fell away rapidly so that access to temperate areas of the Pacific coast was relatively easy, with the implication that access to Asia by passages through or around North America would prove simple. This was known in England through a map presented to Henry VIII about 1525 by one of the Verrazzano brothers, by the productions of the Dieppe school of cartographers, of whom Jean Rotz was in Henry's service from 1542 to 1547, and also from the world maps of such academic geographers as Gemma Frisius, which were current in the 1540s and for long after, showing an open polar sea. It is not surprising therefore that Englishmen, whose way to the east was blocked by the Iberian nations and whose lack of success in finding a North-east Passage had been discouraging, turned to the concept of a North-west Passage which would bring them rapidly through sub-polar seas to the supposed Strait of Anian (another creation of the academic geographers) and so to the Pacific, to Cathay (China) and to the Moluccas, which it was beginning to be known by 1570, the Spaniards had reached from their western territories in Central America. Michael Lok, a pioneer of the revived Mediterranean trade and much concerned with Muscovy, turned in the 1570s to attempt to do something about the exploration of a North-west Passage. The young soldier-scholar, Humphrey Gilbert, had already in the 1560s argued the case for the existence of such a passage and had revised a treatise on it, to have it published by a friend as *A discourse of a discoverie for a new passage to Cataia*, in 1576. By that time Lok had already aroused the interest of a number of London merchants, had written his own theses on the project, and was busy putting the expedition in hand.

He had engaged Martin Frobisher, a gentleman adventurer with some experience at sea, to take two small ships led by the *Gabriel*, which he would command, to look for a passage north of 60°. He duly found an entry to what we know as Frobisher Sound, penetrated it for some 180 miles, he claimed, and decided it was the North-west Passage. The Eskimo man he caught and brought home was said to have the same appearance as the Samoyeds which Muscovy Company men had seen on the shores of the North-east Passage, and so he seemed proof that the route to Asia was open. Lok got his licence from the Muscovy Company to venture to the north-west enlarged into a chartered Cathay Company and received a wide range of subscriptions and promises of more from the queen, Lord Burghley, courtiers, gentlemen and merchants. Before the second expedition was ready, gold was found, an alchemist said, in a piece of rock brought from the terrain in the first voyage, named Meta Incognita by the queen, and the search for the passage turned into a gold rush. Frobisher, now commanding one of the queen's ships, the *Aid*, and with enough shipping to bring back 200 tons of ore, returned to mine and, according to instructions which he did not attempt seriously to follow, trace the passage to its opening in the Pacific. The hard rock of Kodlunarn Island at the mouth of the supposed strait was hacked out and brought off to England, without the end of the inlet being discovered (Frobisher probably went as far as the unmelted shore ice and then returned without saying it did not appear to go anywhere). The excitement which greeted the return of the vessels and the care taken to store the ore in Bristol and London (the three Eskimos brought to Bristol did not long survive) demonstrated the apparent success of the venture. The long series of laboratory experiments which followed seemed to establish that gold was there, but the iron-hard rock of the Canadian north defied all attempts to smelt it. A body of commissioners decided that there was gold in it and that blast furnaces should be built at Deptford to smelt the ore and to bring several thousand tons more back with the aid of a great expedition of fifteen ships in 1578. Moreover, portable buildings were taken in which it was believed 200 men could winter so as to get still more ore before the summer of 1579. The men, with incredible labour, succeeded in filling some ten ships with ore. Fortunately one, carrying part of the over-winter housing, had foundered on the way out, and though a party offered to stay on, Frobisher wisely vetoed this. On the way out his own ship had failed to make sufficient northing and he found himself in what really seemed to be a passage. Frobisher, in his haste to get to Meta Incognita, did not pursue these 'Mistaken Straits', apparently Hudson Strait, but he could point to the existence of this passage when it had become clear that Frobisher Bay was found to be what it was, a mere inlet. But disaster more terrible than shipwreck met the expedition on its return. Furnaces had eventually smelted the ore and found there was no gold whatever in it; mica and iron pyrites had misled the commissioners and unskilful or disingenuous experts had lied or misled themselves. All the labour and money, and a number of lives, were lost on all three expeditions, leaving Lok to pick up the mess. And what a mess! Paid subscriptions, Lok's large private fortune, the queen's adventure – all had gone, some £70,000-worth, and nothing but some odds and ends of ships and equipment to pay the seamen and countless creditors. The first big overseas gamble England had ever made, at least in the west, had been a genuine disaster. It was to make the London merchants wary of mineral finds anywhere in the overseas world for another generation or more. Frobisher got out of it with more credit than perhaps he deserved. He was a poor seaman, but fortunately the masters who served under him, and cursed him from time to time, were generally competent. The disaster, except for Lok, might have been worse than it was: at least the mining party did not freeze to death as it would almost certainly have done had it been left. The Frobisher expedition threw little light on the North-west Passage, except to maintain expectations on the part of a few enthusiasts that there might be a passage through the 'Mistaken Straits'. The episode showed that the mobilisation of venture capital was now possible on a considerable scale and that the mercantile marine was effective on long voyages; but the lack of technical expertise in the metallurgical industry shows how backward England was in this sphere, and the gullibility of the officials and 'experts' indicates that the demand for bullion and its romantic attraction overrode more realistic expansionist projects. At the same time, the expeditions supplied valuable experience in preparing and organising such large-scale expeditions and in carrying them out under unfavourable physical conditions, while the news of the expeditions and of the Eskimos they encountered gave English exploration and expansion a European currency for the first time in the sixteenth century.

Drake's venture in 1577 was something else again. John Oxenham had gone out in 1576 to try to repeat Drake's isthmus raid, but was caught by the Spaniards, who were by no means complaisant about attacks on the life-line of bullion which linked Peru and Panama, by a long sea and land route, with Spain. But Drake now had the backing of Walsingham, Leicester, and Hatton at court and some countenance, and investment, by the queen. The *Pelican* (150 tons) and the four small vessels which accompanied her from Plymouth in November 1577 were going, officially (it is now generally agreed), to prospect the possibilities of English bases in unoccupied lands from the Rio de la Plata southwards and, after passing the Strait of Magellan, to continue the reconnaissance up the coast of Chile. Unofficially, as Drake's closest supporters well knew, he was determined to try to scrape up as much as he could of the bullion which the Spaniards carried peacefully up the Pacific coast to Panama – in revenge for 1568, as he was to say many times, but in fact simply to make himself rich by any means whatever, though he was anxious not to be branded as a killer and so he maintained a correct, even courteous, attitude to his victims, some of whom almost seemed to consider it a privilege to be robbed by so courteous a person. (French pirates in the Caribbean were much tougher; they killed their victims when they felt like it in revenge for the slaughter of so many of their fellows.) On the way down the African coast and at the Canaries, Drake plundered small Spanish fishing boats and large Portuguese vessels alike for stores for his voyage. He took the Portuguese vessel he renamed the *Mary* to add a second ship of some size to his fleet (the *Pelican* was his only ship of over 100 tons). He did his survey work thoroughly, forming a poor opinion of the Plate estuary, and found little to commend itself to him in Patagonia. A rest at Port St Julian did give him a chance to quell a threat of mutiny, led by Thomas Doughty, which would have prevented him from making the passage of the Straits. He also stocked up with seabirds and seals for the voyage onwards. His passage was too early in the year (he should have waited another month or two) so that, after an easy transit, he met the westerlies head on in the Pacific. He barely survived the storms that blew him southwards twice after he had clawed his way to the north. In the end he reached the coast of Chile with only his own ship, the *Pelican*, now renamed the *Golden Hind*. He soon found that Spanish occupation of Chile extended farther south than had been surmised in England, but he was impressed by the fine climate. He had an unfortunate clash with Indians hostile to Spain and he soon had Spanish resistance, of a sort, also to contend with.

From Valparaiso, where he took his first plunder, onwards, Drake ranged the coasts all the way to Gautulco in Mexico, a stretch of water where no marauding ship had even been and where there were insufficient weapons on sea or land to stand up to sharp attacks by his well-trained men. At Valparaiso, a tiny settlement, he sacked the place and took some gold and supplies from a large vessel which he added to his solitary surviving ship, and also put together the last of the knocked-down pinnaces which had survived the buffeting of the *Golden Hind*. In Arica there was silver on board one ship and in another wine, which he also took with him, but abandoned both Spanish ships very soon. He hoped for something quite different from Callao from which the silver was shipped to Panama, but it was almost all still housed in Lima, which he could not hope to attack – a disappointment comparable with some of those of 1572–3 but on a larger scale. He cut loose the empty ships at Callao: vessels hastily armed to chase him soon turned back when they learned of the heavy armament carried. One ship he overpowered on his way north provided him with silver, some gold, and jewels. Thus far his actions were very much of a piece with his Caribbean raiding, except that most of the vessels taken carried at least a certain amount of bullion. But ahead of him he learned there was a ship full of silver. He caught up with her, *Nuestra Señora de la Concepción*, only a little north of the equator. She was a stinker, her crew said afterwards, and was known as 'Shitfire'. After a token resistance he took from her 362,000 pesos-worth of bullion, silver and gold (106,000 pesos of which belonged to the Crown), together with much unregistered loot (which may have amounted to as much again). This was something altogether outside the range of previous piracy, an empire's ransom. He later picked up a small bark which he decided to keep and got on her charts for the Pacific crossing and vital information from a pilot who, however, refused to serve him. Another small captured vessel provided him with Chinese silks and porcelain, of which he took what he could, including four crates of the latter. This was being distributed in flagrant contempt of the regulations regarding the Manila galleon which had since 1573 been annually bringing to Acapulco, for trans-shipment to Spain, oriental goods from Manila. He raided Guatulco but took little but water from it. He had now 'made his voyage' in a sense quite unparalleled by any English seaman.

How to get back? The Straits were too risky. The talk of a Strait of Anian which might bring him round North America to meet with Frobisher was worth trying only if it opened in reasonably low latitudes. He had to sail far out into the ocean to get a wind, but by 48° N. he was already in cold, wild seas. His men made him turn back, probably with little difficulty, and he reached the western North American coast at about 43°, the first English explorer, as he had now become, to do so. He coasted down to 38° and found a good enough harbour to careen and repair his ship (probably using the small bark for timber), rested his men, fraternised with the Coast Miwok Indians, and collected salt meat. This was apparently on Drake's Bay. He named the area New Albion to flatter the queen. In late July he set out across the Pacific. He was rather far north for this, but fortunately found the wind and currents easy. The idea of going home by way of Moluccas had been canvassed before they entered the Straits and so was a natural if daring experiment. His passage to Palau (most probably) was followed by a visit to Mindanao and then to the Moluccas. At Ternate the sultan, Babú, hailed him as counterweight to his Portuguese enemies. Knowing there were Spaniards in the Philippines, the appearance of the ships of still another European nation was not so surprising as it might otherwise have been. The sultan sold Drake some six tons of cloves and promised exclusive trade agreements to Drake's successors, if there were any, in return for help against the Portuguese.

Sailing off into unknown waters, Drake met near disaster, grounding on a rock on the Celebes coast. He jettisoned cloves, guns and other non-essentials, but it was a change of wind at low tide which released the *Golden Hind* with little damage. He was lucky thereafter, succeeding in passing the strait to the west of Timor and being well received in southern Java, where he was able to give handsome presents in return for some essential food and help in getting the ship ready for her longest voyage. His long, arduous passage was uneventful, and eventually he passed the Cape, but lack of water forced him to try a landing without success in finding any. Rain saved him until he got to Sierra Leone, when he watered and then sailed back by a familiar track, entering Plymouth Harbour on 26 September 1580, having been gone almost three years and having covered perhaps 50,000 miles. How much treasure there was in his ship has never been conclusively established. Some was placed for safety in a castle on shore; the queen allowed Drake £10,000 before anything was brought to London, and he paid his men off handsomely as well (what he and they concealed is anyone's guess). He himself carried some gold and jewels to London where he met the queen in November and after that much more was brought to the Tower. Spanish protests at the robbery had to be met. The queen temporised for a long time and finally agreed that some claims of private men could be satisfied, but that Philip owed her much for complicity in the Smerwick invasions of 1579 and 1580. The agent for the Seville merchants, Pedro de Zubiaur, was in England as late as 1584, still bargaining, though with what result is not clear. In the meantime the queen was enriched, investors got very large dividends; and by April 1581 the queen could come aboard the *Golden Hind*, by now in the Thames, and knight Drake. The economic importance of the great plundering expedition was scarcely less considerable than the remarkable seamanship displayed by the commander. The bullion formed a nest egg which the state could use, and it enriched a privileged class of investors, including courtiers, and of course made Drake a very rich man, but it also released capital to pay for future ventures. It broke the depression caused by the losses of the Company of Cathay and rendered speculation, especially in privateering, but in colonisation as well, possible and attractive. That it was also a stage in the open war with Spain, which had loomed for so long, is also clear. Piracy against Spain was now normally legitimised by Drake's success and the queen's acceptance of the major part of his spoils. The circumnavigation is thus a turning point in overseas enterprise, an effect with which it is not invariably credited.

We have in John Browne's *The marchants aviso* (1589) an instruction book based on materials of about 1580 on the conduct of commerce in the Iberian and French trades, compiled for Bristol merchants. It shows how well they were briefed on the spices and sugar which were obtained at Lisbon and Seville:

Pepper.
Note that of pepper, the greatest and largest is best, and that which is cleanest without much dust. The which you shall try the cleanness of it by taking up a handfull of it somewhat low in the bag, for the dust will appear on your fingers after letting down the pepper. The russet-coloured pepper is best, and what which is sound, the which you may prove the soundness of it by rubbing it hard betwixt your hands. If it be very black of colour and the dust of it moist and sticking to your fingers then hath it taken wet and is not so good . . .

Ginger.
Note that of ginger, the greatest and largest are best, and which are of yellow or fair russet colour and sound, weighty and hot on the tongue.

Sugar.
Note that of sugar, the fair and white colour is best, and which is hard, and without brownness in the heart of the loaf, the which brownness of it is seen by having the loaf broken in the midst or otherwise if the whole head of the loaf round about the brown and dark-coloured.

Cloves, mace, cinnamon, nutmegs, calicos, salt, cochineal, olive oil, soap, woad, iron, train oil and wines were also covered in similar detail. Clearly, the English merchants were both closely in contact with the overseas trade products of the Iberian empire and knowledgeable about their character in detail. When the book was published this trade had virtually ceased, but plans were on foot to establish a direct trade to the Indies, though not much was done before the war ended fourteen years later. In the interim, most of these products, apart from those obtained from France, which included some Iberian and overseas produce, were taken on the high seas by privateers, but the prize goods could be expertly assessed on the basis of experience like that gathered in Browne's little book, which was reprinted in 1590, 1591, 1607, 1616 and 1640. (A modern edition was edited by Patrick McGrath in 1957.) But Drake's achievement seemed to put the direct acquisition of these commodities, or most of them, within sight of attainment and at much less cost than they had been bought in the Iberian lands.

During the 1570s, English activity in Newfoundland and adjoining waters had led to the increase of cod-fishing vessels there from a handful to fifty by the year Drake sailed. This was one factor in turning English interest to North America. A second was the sudden switch of Sir Humphrey Gilbert from plans for English exploitation of Irish lands to the concept that North America lay open to English occupation, and land was to be had there for the taking, without resistance from Spain and with negligible, if any, danger from primitive native inhabitants. A third factor was that Richard Hakluyt, a lawyer who had built up a practice as a consultant to the Muscovy Company, the African traders, and speculators who projected voyages to the East, came out in favour of settlement in North America on economic grounds. Settlement in latitudes comparable with those of Western Europe could produce all the produce England got from the Iberian lands, France, the Baltic and at home. There might be minerals too, but he was cautious about these. The natives, he was sure, would buy English cloth. A final factor, though when precisely it entered English thinking is not clear, was to establish shore bases from which ships raiding in the Caribbean could be supplied. The drift towards colonising experiments was slow to develop, though it was attractive to Walsingham for strategic and anti-Spanish reasons, and to the cautious Lord Burghley for its promise of replacing, especially, the Baltic as the source of English naval stores and would help the fishing industry in which he greatly believed. Whether anything would have come of it rapidly without the intervention of one man, Sir Humphrey Gilbert, is hard to say. In June 1578 he received a patent, the full implications of which Queen Elizabeth is unlikely to have appreciated, entitling him to found colonies and establish English jurisdiction anywhere there was not already an established European colony. This was an extraordinary blank cheque, but he took it to mean (and it was evidently meant to mean) that he had the first choice of places to transport colonies to in North America and could license others to do the same in other parts of that vast area, to which, in effect, England was claiming prior rights of discovery.

The lawyer Richard Hakluyt, who had been advising merchants on new trading opportunities for some years, considered that by 1578 he knew enough about North America to give some general advice about colonising there. In notes probably prepared for Gilbert he laid out a coherent plan:

That the first seat be chosen on the seaside so as (if it may be) you may have your own navy within bay, river or lake, within your seat safe from the enemy . . . This seat is to be chosen in temperate climate, in sweet air, where you may possess always sweet water, wood, seacoals, or turf, with fish, flesh, grain, fruits, herbs and roots, or so many of those as may suffice every necessity for the life of such as shall plant there . . . The people there to plant and to continue are either to live without traffic, or by traffic and by trade of merchandise. If they shall live without sea traffic . . . so will they be forced of themselves to depart . . . And by trade of merchandise they cannot live except the sea or land may yield commodity for commodity. And therefore you ought to have most special regard of that point . . . And for that in the ample vent of such things as are brought to you out of England by sea standeth a matter of great consequence. It behoveth that all humanity and courtesy and much forbearing of revenge to the inland people be used, so shall you have firm amity with your neighbours, so shall you have their inland commodities to maintain traffic, and so shall you wax rich and strong in force . . . And in your planting the consideration of the climate and the soil be matters that are to be respected . . . Or if the soil and climate be such as may yield you the grape as good as that of Bordeaux . . . Or if you find a soil of the temperature of the south part of Spain or of Barbary in the which you find the olive tree to grow, then you may be assured of a noble merchandise for this realm . . . Or if you should find the berry of cochineal . . . you win a notable thing fit for our state of clothing . . . Or if great woods be found, if they be of cypress, chests may be made; if they be of some other kind of trees, pitch and tar may be made; if they be of some other then they may yield resin, turpentine, etc., and all for trade and traffic . . . Since every soil in the world by art may be made to yield things to feed and to cloth man, bring on your return a perfect note of the soil without and within, and we shall devise, if need require, to amend the same and to draw it to more perfection.

It was clear, therefore, that serious thought was being given to the technique and economics of colonisation, even though the advice given above, and to be given in many other tracts over the next ten years, was a similar mixture of common sense, wishful thinking and substantial ignorance of conditions at the points of contact where would-be settlers actually encountered North America.

There had been an unparalleled growth in coastal piracy affecting all the approaches to the British Isles in the period since 1568. Finally, in 1577, the government clamped down and arrested and executed a number of pirates. This left many small outports without the profitable prize marts the pirates maintained. Other pirates had official protection, since even the younger sons of high officials were involved. There was therefore a strong tendency to diversify, to employ the talents of the pirate seamen in less dangerous areas. This helped to feed piracy in the West Indies, which gradually developed into an industry, small but increasing. It also drew owners of men-of-war behind the new colonising promoters. When Gilbert raised his first colonising fleet in 1578, there were many offers of former, or 'resting', pirates to go with him, so that he had little difficulty in raising ten armed ships, his objective being apparently to reconnoitre the North American coast by way of a profit-making cruise through the West Indies at the expense of the Spaniards. When it came to the point and the vessels were at sea, most of the ships deserted him and went off to attack shipping indiscriminately on the Spanish coast and at the mouth of the Channel. He, himself, had the bad luck to be driven back by storms, and only the crank old *Falcon* got past the Canaries but had to creep home in a leaking condition. The pirates, though a few were punished, went back to their old trade and colonising as an investment slipped back in credit. Gilbert revived it again from 1580 onward by selling off parts of the North American coast and mainland, sight unseen, to all takers. His biggest coup was to get Walsingham's support to let loyal Catholic gentry escape the crippling new penalties for not attending the Anglican service by letting them go to America. Round them, in a skilful promotion scheme, he built up groups of English gentry, desirous of getting estates for their younger sons, merchants, town corporations (Southampton now a decaying but once prosperous port was to have special concessions), and all this was to come to the boil in 1582 by the middle of which some 20 million acres on paper had been handed out. But there were too many promises and not enough ready money.

Gilbert's reconnaisance fleet was unable to get away from Southampton in 1582, and a bigger expedition initiated by the Catholics never got to sea either that year. Only in June 1583 did his ships leave Plymouth, the plan being to work down the coast from Newfoundland to 'Norumbega', the future New England, where the land was to be allocated to the various subscribers. Gilbert, when he reached St John's, partly changed his mind. He would annex the island, take control of the international inshore fishery, and allocate to himself a great block of territory covering much of eastern Canada. But before doing more he must go down the coast to secure his supporters their lands. On his way, at Sable Island, one ship was wrecked, two others had left him, and with only two small vessels remaining he had to turn homewards, the smaller one being overwhelmed at sea, so that the *Golden Hind* under Captain Edward Hayes alone got home without him.

The colonising movement may have been a small one, but it took up much space with its publications and publicity. Sir George Peckham, the leading Catholic promotor, did his utmost late in 1583 and early in 1584 to go ahead with at least part of the plan, but had to give it up. Christopher Carleill, with Walsingham's support, set out in the summer of 1584 for, apparently, Acadia (the modern Maritimes), but unaccountably turned his ships and men over for government service in Ireland. By that time a more astute personality had come on the scene. Walter Ralegh, Gilbert's half-brother, had made a name and money at court, and in February had Gilbert's patent assigned to him (excepting Newfoundland). He sent out a successful reconnoitring party to south-eastern North America in 1584. They kept clear of piratical attachments and located what seemed to be excellent land for settlement on and behind the Carolina Outer Banks, where Indians were friendly and not too numerous. Reports they brought back and the words of two Indians, crammed with appropriate English sentences and sentiments, brought support at court and in the west country for an experimental colony. Sir Richard Grenville brought five ships out to Roanoke Island in 1585, stopping long enough in the Caribbean to seize some ships as well as buy livestock and taking a valuable Spanish ship coming from the Indias on his way home. One purpose of the colony was to explore and assess the practicalities of settlement, but another was to provide a base, if possible, for extended operations against Spain in the West Indies.

When Grenville got home, it was to find that at last Spain had reacted against continued English provocations, alike at sea and in the Netherlands, and had virtually, if not formally, gone to war, by an embargo on all English shipping in Spanish ports in May 1585.

Arthur Barlowe had brought back an idyllic account of the North Carolina Outer Banks at which the expedition arrived in July 1584:

> The second of July we found shoal water which smelt so sweetly and was so strong a smell as if we had been in the midst of some delicate garden, abounding with all kind of odoriferous flowers, by the which we were assured that the land could not be far distant, and keeping good watch and bearing but slack sail, the fourth of the same month we arrived upon the coast which we supposed to be a continent and firme land . . . We viewed the land about us, being whereas we first landed, very sandy and low towards the water side, but so full of grapes as the very beating and surge of the sea overflowed them, of which we found such plenty, as well there as in all places else, both on the sand and on the green soil on the hills, as in the plains, as also climbing towards the tops of the high cedar, that I think in all the world the like abundance is not to be found.

Not only the land but the people were friendly and hospitable: 'for a more kind and loving people there cannot be found in the world, as far as we have hitherto had trial.'

But the 1585 expedition was not to take such reports at face value. With Thomas Harriot to survey and John White to paint, a comprehensive picture of the country was to be drawn, one that would enable a considered assessment of its prospects for permanent settlement to be made. Already in 1582 or 1583 instructions for such a survey had been drawn up, which were no doubt duplicated, and elaborated in 1585: springs, islands, fish, birds, beasts, metals, herbs, native cultivation methods, the customs of the indigenous people, their languages (and the compilation of vocabularies), bays, havens, rivers, places to make salt, latitude observation, compass-bearings were to be noted and attempts made 'also to draw to life all strange birds, beasts, fishes, plants, herbs, trees and fruits, and bring home of each sort as nere as you may'. The instructions went on: 'Also draw the figure and shapes of men and women in their apparel as also of their manner of weapons in every place as you shall find them differing,' while a detailed map was to be made by survey on the ground. All these things were to be attempted in 1585–6: preparations for permanent colonisation were indeed to be seriously begun.

If overseas ventures, more spectacular than profitable except for piracy, had dominated the public scene, older trades had maintained themselves. The official figures for cloth exports from London (fallible as they are) showed impressive figures for the eleven years of 1574 to 1585. This was partly the result of the flexibility of the Merchant Adventurers in shifting their headquarters to German soil, Hamburg and Bremen at various times, and going ahead with the building of a central European market, and a continuing overland Italian one for English woollens. Trade with the southern Netherlands was frequently interrupted and Antwerp fades out, even if the Merchant Adventurers held meetings there until 1581. Trade with the emerging northern provinces was developing since Amsterdam was growing, in spite of the war, into one of the great distributing centres of Northern Europe. But there were other developments also. The Muscovy Company, it is true, had some set-backs: its Persian markets came to nothing; Narva fell to the Swedes in 1581, but a substantial if not highly profitable trade continued by way of Archangel with Russia itself. More progress was being made in the Baltic. First of all Danzig continued as the outlet for Polish corn (rye usually rather than wheat) and the inlet for English woollens. Then, in 1579, came the incorporation of the Eastland Company – a regulated company not, like the Muscovy Company, a joint-stock one – and then the staple moved to Elbing, where very substantial growth in the trade to England of naval stores as well as grain took place. Shipbuilding, for the queen and for many private merchants was demanding more and more in the way of timber, masts, pitch, tar, hemp, flax, canvas and such like. The Mediterranean trade also received a considerable fillip as trade became easier after Spain and Turkey ceased to wage war on each other in the mid-1570s, though the North African states, loosening the hold which the Ottomans had on them, interfered by piracy from time to time with trans-Mediterranean shipping. From 1576 onwards, English ships were able to go more freely to the eastern Mediterranean so that the establishment of formal relations with the Porte in 1580, and the sending out of William Harborne to put trade and diplomatic relations on a formal basis, meant that by 1582 the Levant Company, a regulated company from 1589, could be chartered to organise at a higher level what was now an important channel for spices as well as Mediterranean products to come to England, while cloth, tin, lead and other traditional exports found markets within the Turkish dominions. The two shadows on this were the rise of Algerine piracy and the possibility of Spain, as relations worsened, restraining or stopping foreign traffic coming through the Straits. Up to 1585 neither of these events had taken place.

Over the thirty-five years from 1550 to 1585 it is clear that the export trade and the expansion of the range of English exploration and commerce had gone on rapidly in spite of adverse political conditions for England in Europe. At the same time it has been repeatedly and correctly stated that external trade represented only a small proportion of English economic activity in this period. Domestic production, marketing and consumption accounted for a much higher proportion of industry and commerce than it was to do later on. Population too was expanding and was by the end of the period over 3 million creating problems of employment and providing incentives to expand domestic and overseas trade and to turn towards colonisation as one possible solution for underemployment. Joan Thirsk's *Economic Policy and Projects* (1978) has shown the range of new products and industries begun during this period and their interrelationship with the growth of a consumer society. This development accounted for the partial solution of what might have otherwise proved more serious internal economic dislocation. It also meant that England was beginning to have a much wider range of manufactured products to offer to the outside world and that consequently the possibilities of attracting new markets (outside traditional woollen-cloth consuming areas in particular) was improving. At the same time, the consumer society, expanding from a narrow base in the south-east, was beginning to demand more overseas produce, thus helping to prime overseas trade. The share of foreign shipping in English ports was falling as the English mercantile marine advanced in numbers and strength. Not only men-of-war but peaceful trading vessels were much more numerous. At the same time, by 1585, except in the Newfoundland fisheries, no inroads had been made in trade with the New World, no colonies had been established, no direct trade with Asia by sea had come into being. The achievements in these areas had been experimental only and were, in some of these, unable to bring results until a considerably later period.

CHAPTER 2

The Making of a Navy

When faced with a crisis in foreign relations, Henry VIII, like many of his royal predecessors, looked to the sea as the wall of England. Whereas his predecessors had called upon the merchant ships and seamen of the realm to man the wall, Henry's first line of defence was a fleet of purpose-built heavy warships. His programme of naval armament was impressive. From his father, Henry VII, he had inherited an establishment of five royal warships. During his reign (1509–47) the establishment, exclusive of row barges, was increased by the building of forty-seven warships, the purchase from various sources of twenty-six and the capture of thirteen. Henry's additions to the fleet include some famous names: the floating fortress, *Henry Grace à Dieu* or *Great Harry*, of 1,200 tons; the *Mary Rose* of 500 tons, built in 1509, rebuilt in 1536, doomed to capsize off Portsmouth in 1545 and to become in the twentieth century the object of archaeological investigation in the mud where she and her crew lay for over 400 years; the *Jesus of Lubeck* of 700 tons, purchased in 1545 from the Hanseatic League and destined to achieve a permanent place in the history of maritime misfortune at San Juan de Ulúa as John Hawkins's flagship on the third slaving voyage. Of the new ships, one was of 1,200 tons, eight of 500 to 900 tons, thirteen of 400 to 450 tons and nine of 300 tons. These vessels were the prototype broadside sailing warships.

The peaks of the shipbuilding effort coincided with the French wars of 1512–14 and 1522–5, the threat of an anti-English Franco-Habsburg alliance in 1539 and the French war of 1544–6. This does not mean that Henry's interest was spasmodic. Continuity of interest is reflected in the history of the shore installations, some of which were to have long and indelible associations with the Royal Navy. Portsmouth dockyard, founded in 1496 by Henry VII, was enlarged and repaired in the early years of the reign and again in 1523–6. In 1527 land was purchased there by the Crown to allow for its further enlargement. The foundation of yards within the Thames, which was favoured by Henry

VIII over Portsmouth as being less vulnerable to enemy attack and nearer to the seat of government and supplies of all kinds, including ordnance, took place during the reign. The history of Woolwich, where the *Henry Grace à Dieu* was built, dates from 1512 with extensions in 1518 and 1546. In 1518 work was begun, probably at the site of an earlier installation, on the construction of Deptford dockyard, which grew steadily into the most important yard of the kingdom by 1547. Activity at Erith in the 1510s and early 1520s suggests a plan, later abandoned, of constructing a dockyard there. In the last year of Henry VIII's life, money was allocated for the hire of a storehouse at Gillingham which is the first hint of an intention to establish yards within the Medway River.

The increase in the number of royal ships and royal yards led to an increase in the number of royal administrative officials. Henry VIII's administrative inheritance was the creation of an age when there had been no clear-cut distinction in northern waters between the warship and the merchantman: an age of intermittent naval establishments when the sea forces of the realm in time of war had been largely made up of hired or impressed merchantmen. It consisted of two officials: the lord admiral and the clerk of the ships. The functions of the lord admiral must not be confused with those of the later first lord of the admiralty. The office of lord admiral was a feudal office of prestige and profit under the Crown, monopolised by the aristocracy and remote from naval affairs. One of Henry's innovations was to thrust this dignitary into the heart of things by ordering him to lead the fleet at sea. This innovation casts an interesting light on contemporary concepts of maritime war, for it shows that, provided a man had the appropriate social qualifications for a post of authority in the armed services, lack of naval experience was no obstacle to appointment as commander-in-chief. The first such appointment was that of Sir Edward Howard, who was killed in a grapple with a French galley on 25 April 1513. Despite this inauspicious beginning, the practice was not allowed to lapse. John Dudley, Viscount Lisle, better known by his later title of Duke of Northumberland, commanded the fleet in 1545; William, Lord Howard of Effingham, was sent to sea against the French by Queen Mary in 1557; Charles, Lord Howard of Effingham, later Earl of Nottingham, led the national sea forces against the Spanish Armada in 1588. For a society which lacked even the rudiments of a naval profession, there was no obvious substitute at sea for aristocratic leadership. Although it tended to bring the lord admiral into the limelight as head under the government of the naval service, the association of the office with high command tended also to isolate him from day-to-day administrative business.

In the early Tudor period, routine administration was the

responsibility of the clerk, sometimes called the keeper, of the ships. The office, which dated from the thirteenth century, had been created by King John as a means of mobilising more effectively merchantships of the realm for defence against France. In 1509, Robert Brygandine, clerk of the ships until his retirement about 1523, was the sole administrative official; but he did not remain so for long. Although no systematic enlargement of the administration can be detected, *ad hoc* appointments were made from the early years of the reign to meet new organizational demands, often under the pressure of war. Sir Thomas Wyndham, for example, appears as 'treasurer of the army by sea' in 1513–14. John Hopton, a gentleman usher of the chamber and a shipowner, was given administrative charge in 1513 of a fleet carrying troops to Calais. In 1514 he was made keeper of the storehouses at Deptford and Erith with a status presumably equivalent to that of Brygandine, for in 1517, when he contracted to enlarge the pond at Deptford, he was called 'clerk comptroller of the ships'. Another leading Henrician official, Thomas Spert, who was later described on a seventeenth-century monument in the church of St Dunstan, Stepney, as 'comptroller of the navy', is first officially mentioned in the 1520s as having been given at Portsmouth 'the rule of all the foresaid ships, masters and mariners with the advice of Brygandine'. Hopton's functions were divided after his death in 1524. Spert was appointed clerk comptroller of the navy and William Gonson, warden of the Grocers Company and owner of the first English ships to sail to the Levant, was made storekeeper. Over the next twenty years – he died in 1544 – Gonson became the dominant naval official. He equipped and commanded ships at sea and, more significantly, assumed financial responsibilities on a scale which suggests the centralisation of naval finance and the allocation by the crown of sums of money for general naval purposes. The transformation of his office from a keepership into a treasureship is reflected in the description of his successor, John Winter, as 'treasurer of the sea', 'paymaster of the sea' and 'treasurer of sea marine causes'. Gonson's earlier functions were allocated to a new official, the keeper of the king's storehouse. Other officials to emerge in the 1540s were the surveyor and rigger, the master of naval ordnance and the vice-admiral, whose probable functions were to serve as a link between the lord admiral and the civilian administrators and to preside over meetings.

Haphazard though its growth may have been, naval administration had become by the mid-sixteenth century a continuous and, despite the other interests of its officials, professional activity. This was recognised by two memoranda of 1545 and letters patent of April 1546 wherein are listed names, offices, fees and clerical establishments. In the letters patent, Sir Thomas Clare was named lieutenant of the admiralty, a new term for the vice-admiral of 1545; Robert Legge, 'treasurer of our marine causes'; William Broke, comptroller of the ships; Benjamin Gonson, son of William, 'surveyor of all our ships'; Richard Howlett, clerk of the ships; William Holstocke and Thomas Morley, assistants to the other officers; Sir William Woodhouse, 'master of the ordnance of the ships'. The first extant documentary reference to the 'king's majesty's council of his marine' is dated March 1545. Here without doubt is the future Navy Board – the term itself was first used in the seventeenth century – the body which from the days of Henry VIII to those of William IV was the administrative cornerstone of the navy.

The king and his advisers, the new naval officials, the shipwrights and dockyard workers, the lords admiral and the men who served under them were pioneers of a new age in history: the age of the broadside sailing warship. Its construction marked a decisive break with the past. Hitherto the only specialised warship known to Europeans was the *navis longa*, the oared galley which had since classical times been the spearhead of the Mediterranean war fleets. The merits of the galley had long been known to the English, but navigational conditions in the English Channel, and the northern seas in general, were a decisive objection to making the defence of the realm dependent upon low-lying vessels driven by oars at a maximum speed over short distances of seven knots and at an average speed of three knots. The strength of the tidal forces in the Channel and North Sea deprived the galley of its great operational advantage over the sailing ship, freedom of movement whatever the direction of the wind and in calm weather. Then, again, long, narrow, low-lying craft were not designed to cope with the high winds and heavy seas likely to be encountered at any time of year in the waters around the British Isles. Because of these technical limitations, it had never been possible to justify the expense of building, maintaining and manning a specialised galley fleet. Largely for experimental reasons, with an eye to their possible employment in coastal waters, Henry VIII, like some of his predecessors, dabbled in the construction of galleys. He never doubted, however, that the sailing ship was and would remain the backbone of the English sea forces.

The history of the English sailing-ship navy in the sixteenth century is best understood as a history of trial and experiment in searches for solutions to unfamiliar problems caused by technical change. Only at the beginning of this century did it become possible with some effort of the imagination to think for the first time in history of the sailing ship as an effective warship. Even as recently as a generation earlier such an idea was hardly conceivable. Advances in European ship design – increased numbers of masts, improvements to the sail plan and to the rigging and gear, stronger and better designed hulls – had done much to liberate the sailing ship from the more obvious limitations upon

its manoeuvrability and speed still recognisable in the first quarter of
the fifteenth century and to make possible European conquest of ocean
routes. But these liberating factors revolutionised neither sea warfare
nor the character and structure of the national sea forces. Improved
performance by itself added little to the sailing ship's fighting capacity.
Without a distinctive weapon, it remained an unarmed platform for
conflict between armed soldiers in grappling and boarding operations.
As such it was indistinguishable from, and interchangeable with,
contemporary merchantmen, whose enrolment along with their crews
in time of war provided the Crown with the bulk of its sea forces. The
conversion of merchantmen for war service by the building on the decks
of superstructures known as castles in an effort to give the fighting men
the advantage of height in combat did not create a distinction. Castles
became a feature of fifteenth-century shipbuilding, entered English
nautical terminology and are still recalled today when we speak of the
forecastle or fo'c'sle of a ship.

Already, however, the weapon which was to make it difficult to think
of the navy as coterminous with the shipping of the realm was emerging.
Hesitatingly at first, and uncertainly, artillery was placed on board the
sailing ship. The early use of naval artillery, not to be confused with
the use of individual guns by the fighting men, is obscure partly through
want of adequate evidence and partly through the inexactitude of the
terminology of artillery as it has come down to us. Cannon were
probably fired, though with little effect on its outcome, in an
engagement between four Genoese carracks and an Ottoman galley fleet
off Constantinople in 1453, and again off Zonchio in the eastern
Mediterranean in a Venetian-Ottoman encounter in 1499. The evidence
suggests that both sides used artillery at Zonchio and that the heaviest
guns were fired through ports cut in the sides of the ships. It also
suggests that neither the Venetians nor the Ottomans had any concept
of a sea battle as a running artillery duel fought at range, for Zonchio
was a grappling combat in which three carracks, two Venetian and one
Ottoman, were destroyed in close encounter through fire spread by
burning pitch. The first demonstrations of the effectiveness of artillery
at sea were given by the Portuguese in the early sixteenth century against
weakly armed Muslim fleets, which they easily outgunned, in the Indian
Ocean. The experience gained by the Portuguese gave them an edge
over other European powers in the tactical use of the sailing warship,
and may have taught them that, no matter how formidable the defensive
qualities of the lofty and heavy carrack type of vessel, advantages in
attack, and for that matter in defence, might lie with smaller, more
manoeuvrable vessels.

Recognition at the turn of the fifteenth and sixteenth centuries that
artillery had become a weapon of the sailing ship worked its way through

the English navy under Henry VII, whose shipbuilding programme, though numerically modest, was technically ambitious. It used to be assumed that the guns on board Henry VII's warships were light pieces. A more recent review of the admittedly baffling evidence seems to point to the conclusion that heavy pieces of artillery were mounted in the waist and less heavy pieces in the upper works of warships built in the 1490s. The piercing of the ships' sides at the level of the lower deck for a few heavy guns must also have been under consideration, for all English warships of more than 300 tons, built or rebuilt in the years 1509 to 1515, were so treated. These guns were intended for point-blank fire against enemy's hulls just above the waterline: an advance which was made possible by the adaption of the hinged port borrowed by the English from foreign designers. The idea, imported from the Mediterranean, must also have taken root that the most powerful species of warship under sail was the high-charged ship of the carrack type with a towering forecastle. This forced upon the Crown a reappraisal, to which Henry VIII's programme of building and purchase was a response, of the role of the state in the provision of naval defence. With the emergence of the heavy carrack as 'the vanguard of the order of battle' – the terminology is that used by Lisle in the fighting instructions of 1545 – the character and structure of the national sea forces underwent changes. Armed English merchantmen certainly had a place in the Henrician fleet. But there were few English merchantmen of a tonnage commensurate with a place in Lisle's vanguard. Many years later, in 1572, the merchant marine was reckoned to include only fourteen ships of 200 tons or more. The result of this evident disparity between the ships of the vanguard and those of the native shipping industry was the creation by Henry of a distinctly regular element which owed its existence to the action of the state.

The regular element was henceforth to have a continuous history. There was no sale of Henry VIII's warships in the years of financial difficulty following his death as there had been of those of Henry V. Traditional patterns of behaviour, almost incomprehensible to us who are accustomed to think of the Royal Navy as a professional specialised force, continued however. During the peace years of Edward VI's reign, royal ships were chartered to mercantile syndicates, with which naval officials were prominently associated, for trading ventures. Thomas Wyndham, the master of naval ordnance, led syndicated voyages to North Africa in 1551–2 and in 1553 he sailed with two royal ships, the *Primrose* and *Moon*, to the fever-stricken Gold Coast in search of gold, pepper and ivory. William Winter, surveyor of the ships, and Benjamin Gonson, treasurer of the navy, were associated with a commercial enterprise to the Levant for which the *Jesus of Lubeck* and the *Matthew* were rented from the Crown. There is evidence of the *Mary Willoughby* and the *Gerfalcon* being employed in the Spanish trade. The survival of assumptions and attitudes from the age of interchangeability between warships and merchantmen should not surprise us. Examples of it can be found under both Henry VIII and Elizabeth I. Much less should it shock us, when combined with evidence of a reduction of naval expenditure in time of peace, into detecting sinister designs upon the fleet during the reign of Edward VI (1547–53).

Other evidence, also emanating from the time of Edward VI, seems indeed to point in an opposite direction. A sure sign both of concern for the security of the royal ships and of recognition of their distinctiveness is the provision of segregated anchorages and bases. Edwardian activity in the Medway was motivated by these factors. During 1548–50, money, additional to the small sum allocated by Henry VIII in the last year of his life, was spent on an expansion of storehouses at Gillingham and Rochester and payments of £3,270 were made for victualling, presumably of a work force. Arrangements for the laying-up of the ships within the Medway can be traced in the Acts of the Privy Council. On 8 June 1550, the lord admiral was instructed that

> all the king's ships should be harboured in Gillingham Water, saving those that be at Portsmouth, to remain there till the year be further spent for avoiding of all inconveniences, and that all masters of ships, gunners and pursers be discharged except a convenient number till the danger of the year be passed, and afterwards to be ordered as it hath been accustomed in time of peace.

On 14 August the lord admiral was further instructed 'to remove the king's majesty's ships from Portsmouth to Gillingham Water, where he shall take order that they may be caulked and grounded'. A week later orders were sent to 'William Winter, surveyor of the ships, to repair to Portsmouth, there to take charge of the king's ships appointed to be removed to Gillingham Water and further to follow such orders as the lord admiral should prescribe unto him'. Although Deptford remained the chief centre for shipbuilding and heavy repairs, the Medway became increasingly prominent as the sixteenth century wore on as a home of the navy. Having the advantage of greater spaciousness than was to be found in the Thames, and being more suitable for the grounding and graving of ships because of its mud banks and large rise and fall of tide, it had become by the 1560s the chief anchorage of the fleet. In 1564, twenty-three large warships were moored below Rochester, compared with six at Portsmouth and none in the Thames. Until 1567, contemporary records talk of Gillingham or Gillingham Water. In this year the famous name of Chatham was first used. In 1570, Chatham acquired its first mast pond and was identified in unmistakable

fashion with the navy by the acquisition of a house, the Hill House,
furnished for the use of the lord admiral and the officers of the board
created by Henry VIII. The anchorage, which extended down river from
Rochester bridge to Upnor, was defended by fortifications at Upnor
and Sheerness, both of which were planned under Edward VI.

A government responsible for the foundation of what was to become
in the seventeenth century the great Chatham dockyard was hardly
neglectful of the navy, whatever the peacetime reductions in
expenditure. Another Edwardian development was the acquisition by
the navy of a permanent victualling officer in 1550, when Edward
Baeshe, who was to serve until 1583, was appointed general surveyor
of the victuals at an annual fee of £50. Economies at the expense of
the ships moored in the Medway must therefore be seen in their proper
perspective as evidence of financial weakness rather than of
discontinuity of policy and of the dependence of regular armed services
upon healthy public finance. The financial connection was underlined
in 1557 when, following the mobilisation of the fleet in Mary Tudor's
French war, an attempt was made to formulate the principles of a state
naval policy with particular reference to the role therein of William
Paulet, Marquess of Winchester, who was lord treasurer of England
from 1550 to 1572. The Privy Council's crucial decision of 7 January
1557 concerning the lord treasurer was that 'the whole marine affairs
are referred unto him'. The responsibility entailed was elaborated in
an order for the regulation of annual expenditure on the fleet.

> Where heretofore the Queen's Majesty hath been sundry times
> troubled with the often signing of warrants for money to be defrayed
> about the necessary charges of her highness's navy and being desirous
> to have some other order taken for the easier conducting of this
> matter hereafter, did this day upon consultation had with certain of
> my lords of the council for this purpose desire the lord treasurer with
> the advice of the lord admiral to take this matter upon him, who
> agreeing thereunto was content to take the charge thereof with these
> conditions following. First he required to have the sum of £14,000
> by year to be advanced half-yearly to Benjamin Gonson, treasurer
> of the admiralty, to be by him defrayed in such sort as shall be
> prescribed by him the said lord treasurer with the advice of the lord
> admiral.

That part of the order which itemises the areas of expenditure is
important for the clues it offers to the identification of the government's
practical aims. The lord treasurer was to

> cause such of her Majesty's ships as may be made serviceable

with caulking and new trimming to be sufficiently renewed and repaired; item to cause such of her Highness's said ships as must of necessity be made of new to be gone in hand withal and new made with convenient speed; item he to see also all her Highness's said ships furnished with sails, anchors, cables and other tackle and apparel sufficiently; item he to cause a mass of victual to be always in readiness to serve for 1,000 men for a month to be set to the sea upon any sudden; item he to cause the said ships from time to time to be repaired and renewed as occasion shall require; item when the said ships that are to be renewed shall be new made and sufficiently repaired and the whole navy furnished of sails, anchors, cables and other tackle then is the said lord treasurer content to continue this service in form aforesaid for the sum of £10,000 yearly to be advanced as is aforesaid; item the said Benjamin Gonson and Edward Baeshe, surveyor of the victuals of the ships, shall make their several accounts of the defrayment of the said money and of their whole doings herein once in the year at the least and as often besides as shall be thought fit by my lords of the council. (Quoted by M. Oppenheim, *A History of the Administration of the Royal Navy, 1509–1660*, p. 112.)

This is one of the key documents appertaining to the regulation of naval affairs in the sixteenth century. It points to the privy council, of which the lord admiral and lord treasurer were members, as the governing body of the service. It is also clear that, though these two officials were associated in that the latter was to act 'with the advice of the lord admiral', the lord treasurer was established as the effective supervisory head of the navy. It is not too fanciful to see Winchester and his even more remarkable successor Sir William Cecil, later Lord Burghley, as ministers of the marine. The lord admiral, as supreme commander, was the executive officer through whom instructions for the fleet were passed, and he retained his medieval responsibilities for the functioning of the High Court of Admiralty. As for the admiralty mentioned in the document, this is evidently the managerial council of civilian officials created by Henry VIII. It will save confusion if we anticipate the nomenclature of the seventeenth century and call it the Navy Board.

The continuous history since Tudor times of a regular element in the national sea forces does not mean that the Tudor state was able to dispense with the services of auxiliary and irregular elements. Despite an emerging differentiation between the specialised warship and the armed merchantman, merchantmen of upwards of a hundred tons were considered suitable for fighting purposes in all sixteenth-century plans for naval mobilisation. The Tudor monarchy inherited from the past the idea of a flourishing mercantile marine as a pool of ships and seamen, and hence as an essential component of naval power even in the changed circumstances of the sixteenth century. Legislation designed to encourage English shipping by protective restrictions at the expense of foreigners was continuously renewed, tightened up and, in so far as was possible, enforced more stringently throughout the Tudor age. The Elizabethan Navigation Act of 1562, 'touching certain politic constitutions made for the maintenance of the navy', was one of the most comprehensive of the century, with clauses designed to assist the native fishing industry and the coastal trade and to limit the carriage of both exports and imports on board foreign vessels. Besides increasing the opportunities of the English mercantile and fishing fleets through discrimination against foreign competitors, Tudor governments gave encouragement to the English shipbuilding industry through a system of rewards. Henry VII had renewed a practice, probably dating from the mid-fifteenth century, of awarding a bounty of five shillings per ton for ships of a hundred tons and upwards. His successors followed suit. Under Elizabeth I, when the names of certain families, such as the Drakes, the Hawkinses of Plymouth, the Fenners of Chichester, make regular appearances in the exchequer warrants, payments became a much more common occurrence than ever before. And the government's sense of purpose was underlined by the requirement that recipients of the bounty must give surety not to sell their ships to foreigners.

The Elizabethan government endeavoured to keep up-to-date records of available ships. In 1559, the Navy Board was instructed to inquire into the state of the national sea forces and report thereon. Its report, the 'book of sea causes', which was mainly the work of Edward Baeshe and William Winter, son of the late John, who held office both as surveyor of the ships and master of naval ordnance, considered the requirements of the kingdom. It recommended a regular establishment of twenty-four 'great ships' ranging from 200 to 800 tons as well as eight smaller craft designated as barks and pinnaces. It also reported, perhaps optimistically, the availability for service of forty-five merchantships with an average burden of some 190 tons, 'which may be put in fashion of war', and twenty more suitable for service as victuallers.

Lists of merchantmen suitable for service as fighting auxiliaries were thereafter prepared from time to time for the information of the Privy Council. The list of February 1577 appears to be the most complete. It records 135 merchantmen of upwards of a hundred tons. London, described as 'the river of Thames wherein is curtained Malden, Colchester, Brightlingsea, Lea, Faversham, Rochester and the creeks belonging', led the way with forty-four, the nine largest of which ranged from 200 to 350 tons. Of the outports, Newcastle-upon-Tyne was prominent with fourteen, all of which measured from 100 to 180 tons. The expected contribution of Harwich and Ipswich was eleven, the largest being 150 tons. The county of Devon was well to the fore. The list of fighting auxiliaries belonging to its ports shows one of Barnstaple, four of Dartmouth, four of Exmouth and six of Plymouth. The largest was a Dartmouth ship of 350 tons. A Plymouth ship of 150 tons was already on the threshold of immortal fame. She was the *Pelican*, afterwards the *Golden Hind*, which carried Francis Drake around the world in 1577–80.

In 1582 Burghley ordered the lord admiral to make a survey of all merchantships of the realm complete with names and tonnage. He followed this up in 1583 with directions to the Navy Board, the regional vice-admirals, the lords-lieutenant of counties and the mayors of towns to make a census of the maritime population: a reminder that government as always was looking to the merchant service not only for 'merchantships of war' but for prime seamen to man the queen's ships. The information thus assembled was used by the Navy Board when it directed selected vessels to rendezvous with the queen's ships for service as auxiliary armed merchantmen, victuallers and dispatch vessels in the general mobilisations of 1587–8. The result in 1588 was a fleet to meet the Spaniards of thirty-four royal ships, sixty-four armed merchantmen, thirty-three supply ships and forty-three privately owned pinnaces for purposes of communication.

Here we see the sixteenth-century English state making, in the act of providing for its defence at sea, advances towards centralisation and unification. The possession of maritime power could hardly lead to the establishment of autocratic government, but its mobilisation certainly strengthened the centralising tendency of the Tudor monarchy. Maritime mobilisation and the fact-finding exercises which made it possible bound the regions more firmly to London through the activities of government agents responsible for the compilation of facts and the furnishing of ships to the royal fleets. The consciousness of being English and a sense of loyalty to the person of the Crown were undoubtedly alive in Elizabethan England, but distance from London and deplorable roads fostered regionalism and encouraged a spirit of independence from government which inclined men of all sorts, including those of the shipping industry, to define and promote their own interests without much regard for some consolidated national interest. The outports, however, no matter how distant by land from the seat of government, were accessible by sea to government agents as well as being partners with government in the elaboration of naval policy through participation in the bounty system. This not always harmonious partnership existed because the Tudor state lacked sufficient income to build the national sea forces into a full-time professional fleet controlled by government in the public interests and free from any obligation to private interests. It does much to explain the character and performances of the Elizabethan navy.

The link between the public and private sectors of Elizabethan sea power is to be found in the membership of the Navy Board. In making administrative appointments, Henry VIII had kept in mind the importance of recruiting men with practical experience of the shipping industry and, often enough, of service in the fleet. The influence of dynasticism, a potent force throughout its history in the sailing-ship navy, saw to it that these principles of selection and the families who owed their rise to them survived the death of the king. Treasurer since 1549 was Benjamin Gonson, son of William; surveyor of the ships since 1549 and master of the ordnance since 1557 was William Winter; clerk of the ships since 1560 was George Winter. These were the sons of John Winter, a sea-captain and merchant of Bristol, who had been appointed treasurer in 1544 and served as such until his death in 1545. Comptroller of the navy from 1562 until his death in 1589 was William Holstocke, who had served the Henrician navy in both active and administrative capacities. This quartet remained in office until 1577 when Gonson retired; the Winters and Holstocke all survived into the 1580s, William Winter and Holstocke both living long enough to see the defeat of the Spaniards in 1588. Waiting in the wings for many years to make his entry was the shipowner and merchant adventurer of Plymouth, John Hawkins. His opportunity came in 1577 when he succeeded Gonson, whose daughter Katherine he had married in 1559.

The remuneration of office-holders in sixteenth-century England was not such as to encourage them either to abandon gainful activities in which they might be involved or to distinguish sharply between the role of public servant and that of private citizen. The amalgamation of public and private interests in the case of the naval officials reveals itself in their involvement in commercial syndicates with ambitions to establish trade in distant waters where the resistance of foreign powers might be encountered. We have seen evidence of such involvement already in the syndicated voyages led by Thomas Wyndham to the Guinea coast of Africa in the 1550s. Deterred neither by the devastatingly high mortality rates nor the objections of the Portuguese government, a syndicate of London merchant adventurers, Sir William Chester, Sir William Garrard, Sir Thomas Lodge, Edward Castlyn, Anthony Hickman, and the naval officials, Benjamin Gonson and William Winter, chartered from the queen in June 1561 four royal ships, the *Minion* and the *Primrose* and the two pinnaces *Flower de Luce* and *Brygandine*, for a voyage formally described as being to those parts of Africa where the king of Portugal 'hath not presently dominion, obedience and tribute'. The command was entrusted to a companion of Wyndham on the African voyages, the London merchant and sea-captain John Lok. The *Minion* and *Primrose* featured in another agreement between the syndicate and the queen at the end of 1562 for further Guinea venture. In July 1564, there was a meeting at the house of Sir William Garrard to arrange a voyage to Guinea with the *Minion*, the *John Baptist*, an armed London ship, and the *Merlin*, which belonged to Gonson. Present at the meeting were

> these chief adventurers, Sir William Garrard, Sir William Chester, Sir Thomas Lodge, Anthony Hickman and Edward Castelin. Where it was agreed that Francis Ashbie should be sent to Deptford to Mr Gonson for his letters to Peter Pett (one of the principal royal shipwrights) to go about the rigging of the *Minion* upon the queen's majesty's charges, and so the said Francis to repair with the same letters to Gillingham with money to supply our charge there. (Richard Hakluyt, *The Principal Navigations . . . of the English Nation*, Vol. VI, 1904, p. 262)

Already by 1562 Sir Thomas Lodge, Gonson and William Winter, as well no doubt other members of the Guinea syndicate, had also entered into a business relationship with John Hawkins of Plymouth in a venture to ship slaves from the Sierra Leone area of Africa to Spanish settlements in the Caribbean and on the main. For the second of Hawkins's slaving voyages, which began in 1564, they were joined by Lord Clinton, later first Earl of Lincoln, the lord admiral of England from 1558 to 1585, by the Earl of Leicester, the Earl of Pembroke and possibly also by Sir William Cecil. Flagship on this and the ill-fated third voyage of 1567–8 was the 700-ton royal ship *Jesus of Lubeck*, a high-charged capital ship with lofty poop and forecastle which had been listed in Lisle's vanguard of the battle order in 1545. She was joined on the third voyage by the queen's ship *Minion*, another lofty vessel of some 300 tons, built in 1536.

We can therefore detect in the early 1560s a well-established predatory syndicate which included the regular navy, through the involvement of the lord admiral and Navy Board, the Privy Council, London magnates and, by implication at least, since royal warships were employed alongside private ships, the queen herself. Its aims of breaking into the Guinea gold and transatlantic slave trades were of the sort that could easily shade, ostensibly by way of reprisal in far-distant waters where foreign opposition might well be met, into quests for plunder. The regular navy, through the ambitions and interests of its own officials and of members of the court, was fast becoming identified with a role akin to that of the armed private marauder.

The English had already shown an aptitude for enemy commerce-raiding and a taste for piratical deviations from it under the privateering movement launched by Henry VIII in his French wars. During the 1540s, something like a maritime nation at arms, composed of landed families, naval officials and private shipowners, was emerging, dedicated to pillage as the most effective and profitable form of maritime war. It was kept alive by the growth of opportunities for profit either from plunder or illegal trading under arms in distant waters and by the untidy patterns of international rivalry which emerged in the second half of the sixteenth century. Indeed, a concept of maritime war as a continuous business offering, in prospect at least, glittering rewards to those venturesome enough to risk their capital and lives was fostered by widespread political instability in Western Europe. Civil wars in France, rebellion against Spanish government in the Netherlands and Philip II's absorption of the kingdom of Portugal gave rise to the appearance of various illegitimate authorities seeking international recognition. Associated in France and the Netherlands with the Protestant cause, they furnished seafarers of whatsoever nationality with licences to prey upon Spanish shipping. Thus the seas of north-western Europe, and beyond them the oceans of the world, became the hunting ground of loosely controlled packs of Protestant maritime guerrillas dedicated to revenge upon Spain, the survival of Protestantism and their personal enrichment. While retaining its own identity, the English privateering movement played a part, often through direct association, in this international movement, whose aspirations it shared. It was poised, when England and Spain came to the brink of formal war, to undertake a self-financing maritime offensive on behalf, and yet in a sense independently, of a state whose straitened financial resources made impossible the deployment of a regular navy sufficiently large and varied to seize the opportunities revealed in the recent period of guerrilla warfare.

The growth of this formidable, privately financed force to do for the state what the state was as yet unable to do for itself is inconceivable without parallel developments in the English iron industry. When Henry VIII launched his naval programme, expensive bronze guns were the order of the day all over Europe. The only English bronze-gun foundry, with an output quite inadequate for the demands of the fleet, was at the Tower of London. Henry was forced to contract for the manufacture of artillery with the great gun-founders of the southern Netherlands, including Hans Poppenruyter of Malines, who furnished the king with some 144 bronze guns of all calibres during the first twenty years of the reign. Dependence upon foreign manufacturers for naval ordnance was undesirable on many counts, not least that of expense, as Henry VIII became increasingly aware. A solution was near at hand, beneath the ground of sixteenth-century England's 'black country', the

Sussex Weald. Iron deposits here, worked at least as far back as Roman times, were already being exploited intensively when Henry recruited through his agent, William Levett, foreign and English gun-founders and iron-masters to cast iron artillery.

Cast-iron ordnance was in many respects inferior to bronze, being heavier, bulkier and more dangerous to handle. But an international rise in the price of raw copper from three times that of iron in the 1520s to nine times that of iron in the 1590s gave cast-iron ordnance the overwhelming advantage of costing only a third as much as bronze. The manufacture of iron ordnance in the foundries of the Weald, relics of which can be observed today, was on a scale from the 1580s approaching mass production. And in an age of rising prices, the cost actually fell from £10 to £12 a ton in 1565–70 to £8 to £9 a ton by 1600. The contribution of the availability of cheap-produced ordnance to the rise of English seapower in the sixteenth century can hardly be overrated. While the Mediterranean seapowers, Spain and Portugal included, struggled to keep up with the rising cost of bronze artillery, the English gained a decisive lead over them in the race to arm men-of-war, auxiliary merchantmen and privateers. Their success did not pass unobserved abroad. As early as 1578, Francisco de Alava, the *Capitán del Arma* of Spain, was urging the advantages of introducing the production of cast-iron guns, pointing out that while bronze guns cost 16 ducats per hundred kilos weight, cast-iron cost only 5½. For its part, the English government attempted to prevent the sale abroad of iron guns. A standing order against it was reinforced in February 1574 by a requirement that gun-founders should give bonds of £2,000 not to cast ordnance without licence and not to sell it to foreigners, and in June 1574 by a further requirement that all founders should send their guns to the Tower, there to be sold to English subjects and submit an annual return to the master of ordnance of the number of guns sold and to whom; a precaution against their sale abroad by legitimate English purchasers.

The experiences of private adventurers were a by no means negligible influence upon naval thinking in the sixteenth century. Popular images of low-built nimble English galleons, ablaze with 'ship-killing' guns as they routed a formidable but technically retarded enemy in 1588, are so much part of established historical folklore that it requires an effort to understand the complexities which accompanied their creation and surrounded their employment. We can only begin to understand if we take care not to lift the Tudor navy out of its own time and impose upon it strategic and tactical concepts which were first formulated by seventeenth- and eighteenth-century sea officers and sanctified by late nineteenth-century historians. Although we can with the advantage of historical hindsight see that by the mid-sixteenth century the armed sailing ship was the ultimate weapon of sea warfare, the idea of a specialised way of fighting was by no means self-evident to contemporaries. Sixteenth-century fighting instructions which have come down to us are almost entirely retrospective. Those of 1530, for example, assume the superior fighting capacity of heavy ships with massive upperworks and direct that

> in case you board (i.e. close with) your enemy, enter (i.e. board) not till you see the smoke gone and then shoot off all your pieces, your port pieces, the pieces of hail-shot [and] crossbow shot to beat his cage deck, and if you see his deck well ridden (i.e. cleared) then enter with your best men, but first win his tops in any wise if it be possible. In case you see there come rescue bulge (i.e. scuttle) the enemy ship [but] first take heed your own men be retired, [and] take the captain with certain of the best with him, the rest to be committed to the sea, for else they will turn upon you to your confusion. (J. S. Corbett (ed.), *Fighting Instructions, 1530–1816*, Navy Records Society, Vol. 29, p. 15)

Those of Viscount Lisle in 1545 reflect a change of emphasis by putting some premium upon seamanship.

> It is to be considered that the ranks must keep such order in sailing than none impeach another. Wherefore it is requisite that every of the said ranks keep right way with another, and take such regard to the observing of the same that no ship pass his fellows forward nor backward nor slack anything, but [keep] as they were in one line and that there may be half a cable length between every of the ships. (Corbett (ed.), *Fighting Instructions*, p. 22)

Nevertheless the evident tactical aim of Lisle's formation, which seems to have been drawn up in line abreast, was that the heaviest ships in the first rank of the vanguard should endeavour to break up the enemy's formation and clear the way for the second rank, the two ranks being 'appointed to lay aboard the principal ships of the enemy'. No more than in 1530 had the use of 'ship-killing' artillery at range a place in the fighting instructions. The consummation of battle was a grappling mêlée.

It is instructive to turn from the theory of battle to the experience of the London merchant William Towerson, caught poaching in Portuguese waters in the company of a French sea-captain from Rouen off the Guinea coast of Africa in January 1557. Towerson, in the armed merchantman *Tiger* of London, 120 tons, was accompanied by the *Hart* of London, 60 tons, and a pinnace. The *Tiger*'s main armament must have been a gun-deck battery, for Towerson tells us that, when attempting to fire from to windward of the Portuguese, 'our ship was so weak in the side that she laid all her ordnance in the sea'. The most interesting aspect, however, of Towerson's narrative is his evident surprise at the Portuguese tactics in what seems to have been for them a policing operation designed to drive foreign intruders away from the coast. In anticipation of a hand-to-hand encounter, he 'gave all our men white scarfs to the end that the Frenchmen might know one the other if we came to boarding'. There was no boarding; no close encounter. After the English and French ships had, perhaps fortuitously, got to windward of them, the Portuguese

> kept about to the shore again and we after them, and when they were so near the shore that they could not well run any further on that board, they kept about again and lay to the seaward. And then we kept about with them and were ahead of them and took in our topsails and tarried for them. And the first that came up was a small bark which sailed so well that she cared not for any of us and carried good ordnance. And as soon as she came up, she shot at us and overshot us and then she shot at the admiral of the Frenchmen and shot him through in two or three places and went forth ahead of us because we were in our fighting sails. Then came up another caravel under our lee in like case which shot at us and at the Frenchman and hurt two of his men and shot him through the main mast. And after them came up the admiral under our lee also, but he was not able to do us so much harm as the small ships because he carried ordnance higher than they. (Hakluyt, *The Principal Navigations*, Vol. VI, p. 262)

Here we have the first known account in English of a broadside artillery duel at sea between ships ranged in primitive line-ahead formations. It was an effective demonstration of the defensive, not the offensive or so-called 'ship-killing', quality of the broadside sailing warship, the Portuguese tactics appearing to anticipate eighteenth-century French defensive tactics of firing from to-leeward on the upward roll with the object of damaging the masts and rigging of the enemy. The care with which Towerson describes the performances of the 'small bark' and the 'caravels' is worth noting. It suggests that this was something new to him, that in this encounter the Portuguese were the masters and the English the pupils. Also worth noting are his dismissive comments on the performance of what must have appeared to onlookers to be the most formidable vessel present, the lofty-built flagship of the Portuguese admiral. Clearly for Towerson the most impressive fact was the superior fighting quality in an artillery duel of low-built, mobile men-of-war.

Another effective demonstration of the defensive power of artillery has come down to us in a narrative of the adventures of the sea-captain George Fenner of Chichester. Fenner sailed in the *Castle of Comfort*, a well-armed vessel of 150 tons or more, from Plymouth in December 1566 in company with the *Mayflower*, the *George* and a pinnace in search of African gold, and probably also of prizes, in Portuguese African and Azorean waters. During 9–11 May 1567, Fenner had to fight off a series of attacks by a Portuguese squadron near the island of Terceira in the Azores. On the morning of 10 May, the three Portuguese warships already in action were reinforced by four caravels of which three

were at least 100 tons apiece, the other not so big, but all well appointed and full of men. All these together came bearing with us being in our admiral, and one of the great caravels came to lay us aboard (as we judged) for they had prepared their false nettings and all things for that purpose, so their galleons came up in our larboard (i.e. port) side and the caravel in our starboard side. Our captain and master perceiving their pretence caused our gunners to make all our ordnance ready with crossbars, chainshot and hailshot. So the ship and caravel came up and, as soon as they were right in our sides, they shot at us with as much ordnance as they could thinking to have laid us presently aboard. Whereupon we gave them such a heat with both our sides that they were both glad to full astern of us and so paused the space of two or three hours, being a very small gale of wind. Then came up the other five and shot all at us and then went to counsel together. (Hakluyt, *The Principal Navigations,* Vol. VI, pp. 281 ff.)

After a further, apparently half-hearted, attempt at boarding the following day, the Portuguese broke off the engagement. In the words of the narrator, Walter Wren, 'they forsook us with shame, as they came to us at the first with pride'.

During the first half of the sixteenth century the regular navy can have obtained little experience of ship-to-ship fighting with the gun. But with the affairs of the navy and of the principal syndicate of Atlantic adventurers in the hands of the same people, there is a great deal to be said for Rear-Admiral A. H. Taylor's view 'Carrack into galleon', *The Mariner's Mirror*, vol. 44, 1950) that much of the experience which inspired advance in the art of fighting with the gun, revealed to the world in the Spanish war, must have come from another quarter, namely the Channel and Atlantic rovers. The range of evidence available in the sixteenth century must have been much greater than what has come down to us in writing, but what we can glean from Towerson and George Fenner is instructive. Apart from the information about tactics and the effectiveness as gun platforms of low-built, manoeuvrable ships, they also reveal something about their armament. Towerson makes a fleeting reference to anchoring within demi-culverin range; Fenner, to his loading his guns, when the enemy closed, with cross-bars, chain shot and hail shot. These references indicate familiarity with the demi-culverin for fighting at range and the perier for close work.

A shift towards the building of smaller warships can be detected in the production by Henry VIII, as early as 1538, of ships variously called galleys, galleasses, galliots or galleons. These names, borrowed from Venetian terminology, suggest vessels of comparatively low freeboard with the beakhead of the *galleazza* replacing the lofty forecastle of Henry's class of great ships. Henry was clearly with this class of vessels in search of greater mobility. It would, however, be premature to see in their introduction a swing away from the heavy man-of-war. They seem to have been designed not as front-line capital ships but as a screening force to protect the flanks of the main battle order against enemy galleys in coastal waters.

In 1559, however, a new policy does seem to have been proposed, the chief advocate thereof being William Winter. Winter was well equipped through experience of war at sea in the regular forces and through close association with privateering syndicates to offer an opinion on the composition of the fleet. He recommended a reduction in the number of heavy ships in a proposed permanent fleet of twenty-four capital ships and an increase in the number of ships of 500 tons or less. His estimate of the national requirements was six ships of 200 tons, six of 300 tons, four of 400 tons, four of 500 tons, two of 600 tons, one of 700 tons and one of 800 tons. The time, however, was not yet ripe for so radical a department from the Henrician concept of the battle fleet. We do not know the source of the opposition to Winter, but it is perhaps significant that a sixteenth-century naval theorist John Montgomery, in *A Treatise concerning the Navy of England written in Anno 1570*, allocated to the main fleet and such 'tall merchant ships' as might join it a defensive role in home waters, supported by coastal block-houses. He visualised a navy of sufficient strength 'to receive the charge and to defend itself, notwithstanding the enemy were two or three ships against one; for in giving the charge is a greater danger than in receiving the charge and especially upon so forceable, worthy and warlike a navy as the navy of England is'.

The mobile gun platforms which Winter seems to have had in mind were not as well cast for a static defensive role as were majestic high-charged ships of the Henrician model. It is legitimate to suppose that Montgomery was reflecting rather than leading prevalent opinion, for additions to the royal fleet in the 1560s made no break with tradition. In the words of Sir Julian Corbett, commenting upon the navy list of 1565:

Through some influence that is not to be traced, the list shows a distinct reaction towards the early ideas of Henry VIII. The energies of the dockyards had been spent upon the construction of two more unwieldy vessels, the *Triumph* of 1,200 tons and the *White Bear* of 1,000, while another large vessel of 800 tons, renamed the *Victory*, had been purchased of some English merchants. Of the proposed tale of twenty-four great ships no more than seventeen existed. Of these, besides the three already named, only two, the *Hope* of 600 tons and the *Aid* of 250 tons, were new, and to make up even the reduced number of seventeen the *Jesus* had to be retained and two other old ships the *Minion* and the *Primrose*, that had been disposed of were brought back into the service. (*Drake and the Tudor Navy*, Vol. I, pp. 141 ff.)

Adherents of the high-charged ship were never wholly lacking throughout the sixteenth century. Montgomery, writing again in 1589 of 'the ships royal as we used to call them' warns that 'as it is not good for them to be high-builded for gathering of much wind, no more is it seemly or sightly to build them too low for disgracing. For such royal ships in my judgement would ever be builded in such form and order as might always carry such gear and countenance as the very sight of them might be a terror to the enemy'. Approval of the moral effect of the old style of great ship was shared by practical seamen. The ideas of the naval theorist chimed in with those of Richard Hawkins (1560–1622), son of John, who favoured 'lofty-built' ships 'for majesty and terror of the enemy', for their superiority when it came to boarding and for the heavier weight of artillery and stronger crews they could carry.

All the arguments therefore were not on the side of low-built, nimble men-of-war, especially when the royal ships were considered to have a primarily defensive role against invaders. And it would be wrong to dismiss the opposition to Winter and later to John Hawkins as simply retrogressive. Despite the opposition, however, the new opinions gained the ascendancy from about 1570 onwards with the launching of the *Foresight* of 300 tons. The *Foresight* was the prototype of a class of warship described as 'race-built' by Richard Hawkins, 'low and snug in the water like a galleass' by Sir William Monson; while William Borough, clerk of the ships, following the death of George Winter in 1582, refers to the reconstruction of older warships by the removal of the upperworks as 'a transforming or reforming them to galleasses'. We call them, as did William Winter, galleons: flush-decked ships of 300 to 500 tons, the ideal proportions thereof, according to sixteenth-century experts, being of length three times to breadth. It is worth noting that this development sharpened the differentiation between the royal warship and the merchantman, the latter needing a wider beam for cargo space. The most famous of the Elizabethan galleons was the *Revenge* of 450 tons, 92 feet in length and 32 in the beam, which was launched in 1575. She achieved fame when chosen by Drake as his flagship in 1588 and immortality when defended to the death by Sir Richard Grenville in 1591.

Why the change of shipbuilding policy should have occurred when it did is something of a mystery. It may well be that John Hawkins, disillusioned by the unseaworthy qualities of the *Jesus of Lubeck* on the second and third slaving voyages, threw his weight behind the reforms through his influence with Gonson, though surely his biographer, J. A. Williamson, goes too far in describing the new ships as 'Hawkins's galleons' and was surely in error when he wrote of William Winter and his colleagues that 'the carrack-built floating castle was their every man-of-war'. The evidence suggests that Hawkins's partiality for the galleon was but one factor in the outcome of a behind-the-scenes conflict over ship design in which Winter played a progressive part and in which accumulated experience rather than the inspiration of any one man tilted the balance of opinion within the naval hierarchy.

There were, it is true, differences between Hawkins and Winter after 1577 and a struggle between them for dominion over the Navy Board. At one level this was a clash of conflicting personal ambitions: leadership of the board was not formally vested in any one office; its acquisition was largely a matter of strength of personality. Winter, Sir William as he was since 1573, had been the dominant personality during Gonson's term of office and had become accustomed to the exercise of leadership. Now he found his position threatened through the appointment as treasurer, with the backing of Burghley, of a younger man convinced that responsibility without power was incompatible with the management of naval finance. At another level, it was a clash of views over control of naval expenditures. The strength of Hawkins's determination to concentrate this control in his own hands led to the conclusion in 1579 of the so-called first bargain which embodied agreements between the Crown and Hawkins and the Crown and the master-shipwrights, Matthew Baker and Peter Pett. By these agreements, £2,200 of the ordinary annual expenditure on the royal ships was placed on contract to Hawkins and the shipwrights without their having to account for it in detail.

In 1585 came the even more comprehensive second bargain between the Crown and Hawkins alone. He undertook the whole of the ordinary work – the repair of ships afloat or grounded, the payment of shipkeepers, clerks, watchmen and the garrisons of dockyard and harbour defences, the provision of moorings, the repair of wharfs and storehouses at Chatham, Deptford, Woolwich and Portsmouth – in return for £4,000 a year. He also undertook the completion of extraordinary work – principally heavy repairs to ships in dry dock – in return for £1,714 a year. The attractiveness of these arrangements from Burghley's point of view is understandable, pressed as he was to find money for the building of new warships in readiness for a Spanish war which he had reluctantly accepted was more probable than not. He could expect the existing establishment to be maintained at less expense than in the 1570s, secure in the knowledge that, if Hawkins fell down on cost, the burden thereof would be his, and that, if he fell down on efficiency, the defects would be exposed by his rivals on the board.

In an age when, as we have already seen, servants of the Crown did not distinguish sharply between public and private interests, and when, too, it was the custom that they should profit personally from the astute disbursement of the public monies allocated to them, it was natural that the quarrel over naval finance should be littered with charges and counter-charges of abuses and covetousness. Hawkins had not hesitated when advocating the new system of control to accuse his colleagues of malpractices, stating that the queen had been monstrously overcharged for both the ordinary and extraordinary maintenance of the ships and that public property had been put to private use. He named names and the name most frequently cited in connection with the abuses which he claimed to have unearthed was that of Sir William Winter. Sir William none the less retained his post and, presumably, Burghley's confidence, though he did withdraw temporarily from public administration in 1580 to command a squadron of warships in operation off the Kerry coast of Ireland during the Munster rebellion.

Nor did Sir William have inhibitions about making counter-charges, detecting, or professing to detect, in the conduct of Hawkins evidence of misdemeanours no different from those of which he had been accused. He attempted through Burghley in April 1585 to prevent the conclusion of the second bargain.

It may please your lordship I have some understanding of the conditions that John Hawkins requireth should pass between the queen's majesty and him touching the bargain that he offereth at this time unto her highness, your lordship and other my good lords of her majesty's privy council for the joining the ordinary and the extraordinary together, which truly doth carry a show of good and acceptable service; but I am sorry to speak it (and I desire comfort at God's hands) there is nothing in it but cunning and craft to maintain his pride and ambition, and for the better filling of his purse, and to keep back from discovering the faults that are left in her majesty's ships at this day which should have been perfected by the bargain made between her majesty and the two shipwrights Pett and Baker. (wherein Hawkins was an invisible partner). What was promised should be performed by that bargain, your lordship I doubt not doth remember, and so do I, Holstocke and Christopher Baker, howsoever their indentures were passed by John Hawkins and such as he pleased to call unto him for the doing thereof. And albeit that the queen's majesty hath disbursed in clouds the sums of £1,500 per estimation over and besides the yearly sum of a thousand pounds allowed them for the ordinary, which the said carpenters should in truth have laid out, yet what faults remaineth in the navy the thing will show itself (if plain dealing be not suppressed); which matter I speak not to flatter you. By the living God, I see your lordship doth as a most faithful servant and councillor to her majesty go about to withstand as near as you can; for were you not another Ulysses that hath tied yourself to the mainmast, this mermaid Hawkins would draw you overboard as he hath done your better [i.e. the queen], your equals and your inferiors. For he careth not to whom he speaketh, nor what he saith; blush he will not. (J. S. Corbett (ed.), *Papers Relating to the Navy during the Spanish War, 1585-1587*, Navy Records Society, Vol. 11, pp. 207 ff.)

There is no need for an inquisition into the comparative honesty of the protagonists. It was a quarrel about the size and distribution of what were recognised by all as legitimate profits, and embedded within it was a quarrel about standards of performance. Burghley behaved as though he neither wished nor expected things to be otherwise; which indeed they could not be as long as the state was dependent in great areas of public life upon the ambitions and interests of private persons instead of upon those of an organised, salaried bureaucracy. Resignations were neither offered nor demanded. During the years of the bargains, Sir William, as surveyor and master of the ordnance, made an immense contribution to the arming of the fleet. In December 1587, when the second bargain, an essentially peacetime improvisation, was about to expire, he and Holstocke certified to Burghley concerning Hawkins that, having used their best circumspection 'to deal indifferently between her majesty and him', they were satisfied with his performance of the bargain and 'thoroughly persuaded in our conscience that he hath, for the time since he took that bargain, expended a far greater sum in carpentry upon her majesty's ships than he hath had any allowance for'.

The 1580s were years of expansion for the fleet of royal men-of-war. During 1585-7, sixteen new ships, built variously at Chatham, Deptford, Limehouse and Woolwich, were added to the list. They included the galleons *Rainbow* (1586), *Vanguard* (1586) and *Ark Royal* (1587). With the nine warships built during 1570–83, the number of new acquisitions since 1570 amounted to twenty-five. In addition, there was rebuilding of ships suitable for remodelling as galleons. This strenuous reinforcement of the regular element, the measures taken to mobilise selected merchantmen and the compulsory recruitment of seafarers provided England with a fleet to meet the Spaniards in 1588. This fleet was in no sense of the term a professional state navy. Ashore its management was largely in the hands of men who had participated in the promotion of the drive for transoceanic trade and plunder; afloat its conduct was largely in the hands of men whose maritime experience had been accumulated in the same movement. The Drakes, the Fenners, the Hawkinses, to mention but three families who, with their associates, were prominent in 1588, were professional fighting seamen. They were not professional naval officers accustomed to the subordination of private interests to those of the state within a disciplined career structure. They brought to the fight great skill and great ardour inspired by patriotism and in many cases religious zeal. Their attitude to formal war, however, was coloured by their corsair experiences. They saw it as the continuation of a familiar process which offered opportunities for individual initiative in quest of individual fortunes. Although glimmerings of a concerted higher strategy can be detected, the navy was hardly as yet a reliable instrument of policy. In the end this was because the Elizabethan state lacked the financial resources to make it so. But there was a great deal of truth in the queen's bitter comment that they went more for profit than for service.

CHAPTER 3

New Worlds and the Old in Foreign Policy and Strategy to 1585

Mid sixteenth-century England was a fallen imperial power, harrowed by prospects of internal disorder and obsessed by fear of France. The old-fashioned imperialism of Henry V – 'no king of England, if not king of France' – had turned out to be the stuff that dreams are made of. Henry VIII's youthful attempts to revive it had faded away in an awakening to the realisation that English power could not compete on the European mainland with that of either of the two great continental dynastic empires headed by the houses of Habsburg and Valois. Moreover, the mounting clash between these rival imperialisms for dominion in Europe threatened to engulf the Western world with incalculable dangers to England's insular independence, the consolidation of which, cemented by the Anglican Reformation, became the keystone of Tudor policy in the mature years of Henry VIII.

Of the two dynasticisms, that of the Valois of France was generally regarded by Englishmen as the more menacing. For a century and more the Valois had been making gains in northern France which could only be considered detrimental to English security. During the last phases of the Hundred Years War they had conquered Normandy and Picardy; they had followed up with the absorption of the Duchy of Brittany in 1491. They had thus gained control of the south coast of the English Channel, with the important exception of the last remaining English foothold in France, the port of Calais. They had thereby succeeded in the almost total elimination of what R. B. Wernham ('Elizabethan War Aims and Strategy', S. T. Bindoff, J. Hurstfield, C. H. Williams (eds.), *Elizabethan Government and Society*, p. 341) calls 'the land buffer of cross-Channel possessions and satellites that had long cushioned England itself against direct attack'. They had also acquired in Brittany and Normandy extensive maritime resources, including a breed of hardy and resourceful seamen, as the basis of naval strength. As we have seen, Henry VIII responded with a programme of modern naval rearmament on a scale unprecedented in English history, and, as an insurance against setbacks at sea, with the building of a chain of coastal forts from east to west along the channel coast.

For much of his reign, and most significantly during the years of dramatic internal change when loyalty to the Tudor dynasty might have been strained beyond its limits in the event of foreign intervention, Henry was spared the agonising decisions in foreign affairs that were to confront his daughters. For these were the years of the Italian wars when the focal area of the Habsburg–Valois conflict was beyond the Alps where the belligerents poured out money and men to an extent which limited their activities elsewhere in Europe. Protected by the naval shield, Henry was able to enjoy the alleged prerogative of an insular state, that of taking as much or as little as it wished of war between neighbouring continental powers.

During the 1540s, however, a shift of the focal area of the conflict from Italy to the Rhineland and Flanders created a new situation. It heightened the international importance of the English Channel as a link between the Spanish and Netherlandish dominions of the head of the house of Habsburg, the Emperor Charles V. The policy of England now became of immediate concern to the rival continental states. An Anglo-Habsburg alliance was calculated to secure communication via the Channel between the two chief bases of Habsburg power and also to make it easier for Charles V to launch an offensive from the Netherlands into north-eastern France. An Anglo-Valois alliance was calculated to endanger those same communications and to put at risk the security of the Netherlands. There was, however, implicit in any policy of foreign alliance a danger that English interests would be subordinated to those of the ally. This danger was highlighted in the 1550s, first by the policy of Northumberland, the most powerful figure in the council of the sickly juvenile, Edward VI, and secondly, perhaps more vividly, by that of Mary Tudor. Both Northumberland and Mary brought themselves into disrepute by jeopardising English interests abroad in the pursuit of domestic aims; Northumberland through rapprochement with Henry II of France, whereby he hoped to consolidate his own position in England by the exclusion of Mary Tudor from the throne and the establishment of a Protestant, necessarily anti-Habsburg, succession; Mary through marriage with Philip, the son and heir of Charles V, whereby she hoped to achieve the permanent reconciliation of England with Rome within the framework of what she hoped would be a fruitful Habsburg alliance. Mary's policy ended in disillusion in 1558, the year of her death, with the loss of Calais, the last vestige of the English empire in France. It can be seen now as an omen that Calais should have been lost in the very decade when English interest, fostered by Northumberland, in oceanic enterprise was manifesting itself more strongly than ever before. It is doubtful, however, whether the new Elizabethans thought of themselves as living in a year of destiny.

The consequences of Mary Tudor's Spanish match discredited the Anglo-Habsburg alliance. There was a reaction against continental entanglements and a swing in favour of independent English action in pursuit of independent English interests. However, the circumstances of the time did not permit a withdrawal into insular isolation. In 1558 there was still a danger that England, as guardian of a strategically important international waterway, might be involuntarily drawn, as Italy had been drawn, into the international conflict with a consequential dilution of her separate identity. Would the English Channel prove to be any more substantial than the Alps as a barrier against foreign intervention? More immediately, would England be exposed to intervention through French activity on her northern border in the kingdom of Scotland? The alarming growth of French influence in Scotland remained a threat even after the great powers made their peace at Cateau-Cambrésis in 1559. Mary Stuart, Queen of Scots, was at the centre of a dynastic web. Her mother, Mary of Guise, belonged to a politically ambitious family which aimed at a dominant position in the French state. Mary Stuart was herself married to the dauphin who became Francis II on the sudden death of his father Henry II in 1559. Thus the queen-regnant of Scotland was queen-consort of France and at the same time a member of a family which was poised to make a bid for supreme power during the minority of Francis II. The dynastic entanglement did not stop at this. As Mary Stuart, direct descendant of Henry VII, possessed a respectable genealogical claim to be heiress-presumptive to Elizabeth I, and as she also possessed, in the eyes of some English Catholics, a legitimate claim to be Queen of England, the Franco-Scottish alliance filled Englishmen with forebodings that its consequences would be not only the establishment of a French province on the northern borders, but an end also to all hopes of domestic security and tranquillity.

The threat of English absorption into a Franco-British union had no sooner posed itself than it began to recede with the outbreak of rebellion in Scotland, led by the lords of the congregation, which was fuelled by aristocratic discontent, nationalistic fervour and Calvinistic zeal. It was the first great manifestation of the power of Calvinism, harnessed to political and social grievances, to deflect the course of history from the track along which it seemed destined to travel. The recession was, however, a slow and uncertain process. The survival, with English aid, of the lords of the congregation, the death of Francis II and the emergence within France of strenuous opposition to the Guise faction eased the pressure. But the threat to England inherent in the

Franco-Scottish alliance finally receded altogether only when Mary Stuart, her position in Scotland made untenable by the success of the lords of the congregation, fled across the border in 1568 into Elizabeth's protective custody, from which she was to be released only by execution at Fotheringhay Castle in 1587.

During this turbulent period a constant factor working in favour of the survival of Elizabethan England was the policy of Mary Tudor's former husband, Philip II of Spain. As ruler both of Spain and the Netherlands, Philip II, like his father before him, had an abiding interest in the existence of a friendly, independent England strong enough to resist the ambitions of France. Under Elizabeth I the Anglo-Habsburg connection was not the same as it had been under Mary Tudor. England's determination not to be dependent upon Habsburg power, Philip II's disapproval of the Elizabethan Anglican Church settlement and his diplomatic support of Portuguese objections to English adventuring in African waters made for changes of emphasis. These changes, however, did not outweigh the mutual advantages which the two parties hoped to derive from the relationship. Evidence of Philip's concern that England should not disintegrate in religious civil war was reflected in his constant opposition at Rome to any papal denunciation of the English queen as a heretic; an action frequently recommended by the representatives to the papal court of France. Philip may have recoiled from the idea of extending toleration to heretic subjects; he also recoiled from the idea of England being governed by a Catholic queen bound to the French interest. Anglo-Habsburg understanding was not in the interests of Philip alone. Spain in the Netherlands, to some extent beholden to England for the security of communications up and down the English Channel, was a desirable barrier against the expansion of France eastwards along the coast beyond the Dover Straits. There were also traditional economic links between England and the Netherlands. By the 1560s, the great boom of the recent past in English cloth exports there was over. But, even in decline, cloth exports remained an important economic asset and the English commercial colony in Antwerp still accounted for something like one quarter to one half of the port's entire trade. The golden age of the Anglo-Burgundian alliance might be no more, but Charles V's belief 'that at all costs England and the Low Countries should be bound together, so that they can provide each other with mutual aid against their enemies' seemed, despite some loss of mutual trust, to reflect an unchanging truth.

As things turned out the destinies of England and the Netherlands were to be bound together in ways unforeseen by Charles V. On his abdication in 1556, the emperor partitioned his sprawling inheritance between his brother Ferdinand, who succeeded as Holy Roman Emperor and ruler of the nucleus of lands around Austria, and his son Philip, who succeeded as King of Spain, Naples and Sicily, Duke of Milan, ruler of Franche-Comté, territories in North Africa and the Spanish possessions in the Caribbean and America, and Overlord of the Netherlands. This last – a portion of the Burgundian inheritance – was a patchwork of seventeen lordships with a feeble central constitution, no common language, a nobility tenaciously determined to retain its traditional liberties and privileges, which were rooted in provincial particularism, and urban patricians as jealous as the nobility of their liberties and privileges. Beneath this surface glitter were turbulent craftsmen and artisans, boisterous seamen and a discontented unskilled labour force. The Netherlands were unique, in an age when uniformity was increasingly regarded as an indispensable condition for social order and stability, in their dedication to the ideal of diversity in a mobile, weakly governed society. To Philip II they were incomprehensible; to Elizabeth I, a mysterious puzzle which refused to go away.

Had Philip II been prepared, as had been Charles V, to accommodate his methods of government in the Netherlands to their deeply rooted tradition of provincial and urban liberties, had he been in sympathy with the prevalent Erasmian Catholicism, then the link between Spain and the Netherlands might have prospered to the benefit of both, particularly of Spain. They offered a protected market for Spanish wool, of which they imported annually 60 per cent of Spain's total output, as raw material for the cloth industry of Artois, Brabant and Flanders, the drapery of the Netherlands. They also absorbed colonial produce, cochineal, hides, spices and sugar, and Mediterranean produce, including oil, salt and wine. The Netherlands was a source of vital goods to Spain since traffic from the Baltic in cereals and shipbuilding materials, imports of which were indispensable, was handled by merchants of the Netherlands who specialised in the purchase and shipment of these commodities. As a focal point of trade and a centre of international finance, Antwerp was the commercial hub of Philip's dominions with a colony of Spaniards, the largest foreign colony, numbering 300 in 1560. Vast numbers of merchantmen belonging to the Netherlands found employment in the two-way trade and vast numbers of merchants likewise, for the Iberian peninsula was a vital outlet for the manufacturers and industries of the Netherlands as well as being the destination of much of the carrying trade.

Philip's education and experience of government were, however, different from those of Charles V. His political formation was almost wholly Castilian and rooted in the principles of absolutism. While it would be false to depict Philip as a doctrinaire absolutist totally insensitive to regional variations within his dominions, he could not accept constitutional restraints, calculated, as were those of the Netherlands, to hinder the raising of taxes and the imposition of religious uniformity. The conflict in the Netherlands between absolute monarchy with its centralising tendencies and provincial constitutionalism with its centrifugal tendencies was legally a domestic matter. But when the opposition hardened into armed resistance, it could no longer remain domestic, partly because neighbouring powers, including England, were bound to develop an interest in the wider repercussions of civil war, partly because the rebels looked outside for aid, even to the Turk, thus internationalising the problem, and partly because in so far as Philip was fighting to exterminate nascent Calvinism in the Netherlands, the war necessarily acquired an international dimension as an aspect of the conflict between Geneva and Rome.

England was bound to be sensitive. As discontent in the early 1560s turned into rioting and then into fighting, the queen and her advisers were haunted by the spectre of a collapse of the fabric of government, rendering the Netherlands vulnerable to France. There were other worrying factors. Disturbance in the Netherlands might have incalculable effects upon English cloth exports and upon the Antwerp money market. These worries were shared by the Merchant Adventurers, for the English cloth industry, mainly as a result of the imported skills of émigré Protestant textile workers from the Netherlands, was now competing actively in the Netherlands market itself with the fine cloths of Artois, Brabant and Flanders. In addition to fears about the damaging effect upon business of political and social instability, the Merchant Adventurers found themselves faced with protective measures initiated by Cardinal Granvelle, chief minister of Philip's council of state. But Granvelle's response went beyond orthodox protective measures. He was irritated by suspicions that English merchants deliberately encouraged minority Protestant groups in the Netherlands. At a higher level, he detected in the encouragement given by Elizabeth to the potentially revolutionary Huguenot movement in France in 1562 evidence that England was aligning herself with International Calvinism. These suspicions were reinforced when English privateers accepted letters of marque issued by the prince of Condé to prey upon French Catholic shipping and proceeded by their indiscriminate conduct in the Channel to threaten Spain's lifeline. Anglo-Spanish relations took a plunge in the autumn of 1563 when Granvelle closed the ports of the Netherlands to English cloth and, following retaliatory action by the Elizabethan government, closed them in December to English ships. Granvelle's response was more rapid and urgent than that of Philip, who delayed until 1564 in taking action against English ships and cargoes in Spanish ports as a protest against channel piracy. Granvelle believed that the English economy was so dependent upon the Netherlands that the stoppage of trade would put an end to the dangerous tendencies exhibited by Elizabeth. The Merchant Adventurers, by shifting the staple with small success to Emden in 1564 and much greater success to Hamburg in 1567, demonstrated his misjudgement. They also weakened one of the bonds of interest which had seemed to make England and the Netherlands mutually dependent in economic terms.

The poison that was to destroy the Anglo-Spanish relationship was then already at work when, to complete his government's suppression of armed rebellion in the Netherlands in 1566–7, Philip decided, against the advice of some of his councillors, upon the total military subjugation of the provinces, a policy which necessarily included the extermination there of Protestantism. His chosen instrument was Spain's greatest military commander, Fernando Álvarez de Toledo, Duke of Alba, who left Spain for Italy at the end of April 1567. After assembling an army at Milan, he marched northwards through the Mont Cenis, past Geneva and over Franche-Comté, Lorraine and Luxemburg, entering Brussels in September. The passage of Alba's army aroused fears throughout Protestant Europe, especially in the areas contiguous to the line of march, of a great Roman-Spanish design to destroy heresy by fire and sword. That its declared aim was to consolidate Philip's sovereignty in one of his own dominions did not allay these fears. England and France may not have trembled as had Geneva and some of the German Protestant princes. None the less the establishment of a Spanish army, which was soon to grow to 25,000 men, in the heart of north-western Europe altered in menacing fashion the balance of military power. It was a change which, whatever the domestic reasons for it, disturbed both states.

On land at least the revolt was apparently broken. Its leaders, William of Orange, Louis of Nassau and Henry of Brederode, Lord of Vianen, had gone abroad, as had countless of their followers. Alba was systematically crushing residual pockets of resistance and eliminating those whose record during the troubles made their loyalty to the regime suspect. Though governed by a Protestant *politique* who detested Calvinism, lived in fear of the unpredictable consequences of revolutionary movements and distrusted aristocratic liberties, England could not stand idly by while a spearhead of Spanish power, hostile to the reformed religion which was identified with English independence, was deployed across the Narrow Seas like a dagger pointed at her heart. Henceforth the end of English policy was its removal; the means to this end, the pacification of the Netherlands on terms which would permit a reduction of the Spanish military establishment.

Although to bring about the desired pacification Elizabeth preferred diplomatic persuasion and sharp reminders that England lacked neither the will nor the means to protect her own interests to military intervention, her policies during 1567–73 took on a distinctly anti-Spanish tinge. Her only direct intervention was the detention at Plymouth in 1568 of four vessels laden with money for the payment of Alba's troops. This produced a rift which lasted, with damaging effects upon Anglo-Netherlands trade, until 1573 when Elizabeth made restitution. The extent to which the survival of Spain's political presence in the Netherlands was dependent upon English goodwill was also illustrated during these years in bloody fashion. English privateers, unrestrained by the government, flocked in greater numbers than ever before to join the Huguenot privateering packs of Normandy and La Rochelle to disrupt communications between Spain and the Netherlands, the proceeds of the captures often being sold in English ports. The havoc was increased by the emergence of the *gueux-de-mer*, the notorious Sea Beggars led by William de la Marck of Liège, Baron of Lumey, who, furnished with letters of marque issued by William of Orange, aimed to continue the revolt of the Netherlands with a reign of terror at sea. Elizabeth, of course, did not create this wave of religious fury and vicious depredation which swept the English Channel. It is doubtful whether, even had she tried to do so, she could have calmed it. But she did acquiesce in the activities of the privateers by taking no immediate steps either to restrain her own subjects or to exclude privateers in general from English ports. The restraint of her own subjects, integrated as they were within a turbulent maritime community, was probably beyond her powers; the exclusion of foreigners was another matter. When Elizabeth did decide upon the expulsion of the beggars in 1572, they departed. Their departure had consequences unforeseen by her. On 1 April 1572, a fateful day in European history, they made a landing on The Brill, went on to seize strategic ports in the provinces of Holland and Zeeland and set the Netherlands ablaze again with revolt. This time it was not to be extinguished.

In so far as it is possible to impose a consistent set of priorities upon Elizabethan foreign policy after 1572, they seem to have been the survival of a Spanish political presence in the Netherlands, the termination of the military presence and the continued exclusion of the French. As long as all three remained seemingly attainable without recourse to the test of war, Elizabeth and the influential Burghley did not believe that England's interests required a commitment to the cause of rebellion in the Netherlands. From 1578 onwards, however, the conditions which made sense of this policy gradually passed away. In the first place, the new Spanish governor, Alexander Farnese, the Duke of Parma, succeeded through the exercise of a high degree of military and political skills in winning back the southern and eastern provinces and appeared to have final victory within his grasp, especially after the assassination of William of Orange in 1585. In the second place, during the 1580s the religious civil wars in France entered a new and dangerous phase with the emergence as heir-presumptive to the French throne of the Huguenot leader Henry of Navarre, an event which drove the Guise faction and its instrument of policy the Catholic League to turn to Spain for assistance. In the third place, Phillip II's annexation of Portugal in 1580 brought with it the necessary resources to make Spain for the first time an Atlantic power. Faced with the prospect of a hostile Catholic front dominated by Spain in Western Europe, Elizabeth and Burghley were forced to revise their interpretation of Charles V's dictum that England and the Netherlands should be bound together to provide each other with mutual aid against their enemies. In 1585 Elizabeth concluded the treaty of Nonsuch, with the rebels pledging military aid in return for the right to garrison The Brill and Flushing with English troops, and sent out a force of 7,000 men led by the Earl of Leicester. In the same year she authorised a strike, led by Francis Drake, against the Spanish Caribbean.

That military intervention in the Netherlands in a conflict intrinsic to the power patterns of Europe should be accompanied by a strike in the Caribbean is a remarkable indication of a global element in English strategic thought. Sir Francis Walsingham, formerly ambassador to France, now the queen's principal secretary and militant advocate within her councils of anti-Spanish Protestant patriotism, wrote to Leicester in April 1586 of the rumoured effect of the strike upon Philip II's credit with his bankers.

> The enterprise of Sir Francis Drake layeth open the present weakness of the king of Spain, for of late he hath solicited the pope and the dukes of Florence and Savoy for a loan of 500,000 ducats but cannot obtain neither the whole nor part of the said sum. The Genoese merchants that were wont to furnish him with money in time of necessity, for that they fear a revolt of the Indians, begin to draw back. (J. A. Bruce (ed.), *Correspondence of Robert Dudley, Earl of Leycester, during his government of the Low Countries in the years 1585 and 1586*, Camden Society, 1844, p. 223)

And again in July 1586, when there were signs that the queen was regretting her military commitments to the rebels, he wrote to Leicester of the undesirability 'for her Majesty to take any resolution in the cause until Sir Francis Drake return, at least until the success of his voyage be seen, whereupon in very truth dependeth the life and death of the cause according to man's judgement'. Whether this was a resumption of the ideas already thrown out in April or whether, as his biographer Conyers Read (*Mr Secretary Walsingham and the Policy of Queen Elizabeth*, Vol.III, p. 160) suggests, it was an allusion to the queen's need for plunder to finance the campaign in the Netherlands, does not alter the fact that American treasure was seen by Walsingham as binding the New World to the Old in a strategic unity.

The story of how European conflicts acquired in the sixteenth century an Atlantic, indeed a global, extension (for enterprise in the Pacific also came gradually within its orbit) is central to our understanding of Elizabethan strategy. It owed more to the efforts of individuals whose objectives were short-term, personal and financial than to any systematic policy of state. The enlarged opportunities for personal aggrandisement and profit arising out of Spanish discovery and exploitation in the Americas were first seized by the French during the Habsburg–Valois wars through an extension into the Atlantic of the traditional privateering war against enemy shipping in European waters. French corsairs may well have crossed the Atlantic in the first decade of the sixteenth century. Privateers from the Norman ports were quickly active in the region of the Azores following the outbreak of war in 1521, and their first great recorded success occurred in 1523 when privateers belonging to Jean Ango of Dieppe captured two homeward-bound Spanish ships richly laden with booty. This striking demonstration of the possibilities of enrichment was followed by the arrival in American and Azorean waters of wave upon wave of French raiders who plundered indiscriminately Spanish and Portuguese shipping without regard to the existence of a state of war or not. In response to the depredations of the French raiders, Charles V instituted in the 1540s and Philip reorganized in the 1560s a system of convoy for Spanish transatlantic trade and its mobilization into annual fleets.

During the 1550s, persistent raids were carried out by squadrons of privateers which pillaged and sacked the more lightly defended Spanish settlements. There are signs here of a co-ordinated and systematic effort to achieve an overall strategic purpose. But for clearer evidence of an assumption that Spain's power in the Old World was linked to its wealth in the New, particularly to the flow of silver from the mines at Potosí, we must await the western design under consideration by Henry II in 1558. This was probably inspired by Gaspard de Coligny, admiral of France and a prominent Huguenot. It was that a squadron of twelve warships and a force of 1,200 troops should sail to the Caribbean in the spring of the year, sack Santo Domingo and Puerto Rico and proceed to Nombre de Dios where the troops should be landed to cross the isthmus and seize Panama, storehouse of the bullion shipped from Peru. The object of the proposed raid was to divert a year's supply of treasure into the coffers of France and to create such lack of confidence in Spain's capacity to police the Caribbean that Philip's revenue from the Indies would be cut off for two years.

Although not attempted because of the treaty of Cateau-Cambrésis, the western design of 1558 contains strong hints of a new strategic departure with its view of the Caribbean not only as a soft target for marauders but also as an area where the power of the Spanish colossus overshadowing Western Europe might be successfully assailed. If this interpretation of the design is valid, then we are witnessing the birth of the 'blue-water strategy', which was to fascinate seamen and statemen throughout the sailing-ship era and give to successive European wars between powers having a stake in the overseas world an extra-European dimension within an overall strategic purpose.

The French Florida venture of 1562–5, sponsored by Coligny, with the acquiescence at least of Charles IX, and led by Jean Ribault and René Goulaine de Laudonnière, shows some element of continuity with the design of 1558 while including other motives. It was in part an aspect of French colonial ambitions in latitudes where the climate favoured both settlement and the production of tropical commodities. This interest was consistent with attempts, backed by Henry II, in the 1550s to obtain a footing in Brazil. Another inspiration was the planting of a transatlantic refuge for French Huguenots should the pressure for uniformity imperil their security in France. A transatlantic plantation of this kind provided for Huguenots an additional attraction of being, if successfully established, a blow against the Spaniards whom they identified as mortal enemies of their religion. The idea of installing themselves in Florida was further reinforced by that of establishing a base or bases from which to attack the annual fleets on their passage through the Florida Strait *en route* to Europe. Coming as it did when Philip II had already under consideration the improvement of the convoy system, the Florida colony was seen as a direct threat to Spain's imperial communications. Its destruction in 1565 demonstrated not only Philip's implacable determination to defend Spain's monopolistic claims, but also his appreciation that the New World could no longer be strategically isolated from the power struggles of the Old.

The existence of new opportunities for trade and pillage in the Atlantic world was also apparent to English merchant adventurers and seamen, as is evidenced by the Africa voyages of the 1550s and 1560s and the three transatlantic slaving voyages of John Hawkins during 1562–8. It would be wrong, however, to equate them with an anti-Spanish vendetta or to assume the existence of some conscious anti-Spanish strategy. The privateering aspects of the African ventures were an extension into tropical waters of the privateering industry which had flowered in England since the 1540s largely as a result of uncertainties in the domestic economy. As for Hawkins, his transatlantic interests reflected a family interest going back to the previous generation, and it is by no means impossible that he had hopes in the early 1560s of obtaining a licence to trade with the Caribbean within the framework of Anglo-Spanish friendship. At the same time, his links with the Huguenot privateers of Normandy and La Rochelle and his personal relations with Jean Ribault gave him some insight into the chances of enrichment which existed in the Spanish Caribbean. And such hopes as he had of winning legal recognition from Spain can hardly have survived much longer than the first voyage, much less the destruction of French Florida.

Privateering – if that be the right term for actions of such dubious legality – at the expense of foreigners, particularly Portuguese, in tropical waters was therefore already the practice of the leading syndicates before Hawkins and his kinsman Francis Drake returned to England in 1569 with news of the Spanish attack upon their ships at San Juan de Ulúa. The news, coming at a time of existing Anglo-Spanish tension, did nothing to improve relations, but it hardly inaugurated an era of 'cold war'. Nor did it create the overseas privateering movement. What it did was to stimulate an embittered anti-Spanish feeling in the privateering hotbeds of the west country and to launch Francis Drake on the spectacular career of depredations at the expense of Spain which was to consume much of the remaining years of his life. Even so, the expeditions to the Indies of 1570–73 which laid the basis of his personal fortune and made him a landowner were hardly part of some grand anti-Spanish strategy, rather a remarkable display of individual opportunism, coloured by hostile sentiments, in pursuit of self-advancement and self-enrichment.

These same years witnessed the flowering in England of that patriotic Protestantism which instinctively recognised Spain as its mortal enemy. Already in 1571 Walsingham was advocating war with Spain from the embassy at Paris.

I think it dangerous to advise a prince to wars for that the issue of wars is doubtful. Notwithstanding, things may so fall out sometimes as nothing can be more dangerous than not to enter into wars. Wars grounded on ambition for increase of dominion are always unjust, but wars grounded on necessity for safety's sake are necessary. I leave to your lordship [Leicester] to judge by consideration of the state of things, as well at home as abroad, whether necessity does not urge us thereto at this present. One supplying my place [ambassador to France], only beholding the state of things abroad and not understanding the inward secrets of home matters, may rather guess than presently know what is meet in so weighty a cause, notwithstanding I am hold privately to discover unto your lordship my folly in setting down mine opinion of a matter, both without the compass of my calling as also my understanding. First, I conclude that we rest on evil terms with Spain, whereof there must grow redress either by composition or by sword. Redress by composition may seem scarce sure, as that which will serve their term but for a while, they can disguise their malice for a time. Redress by the sword, comparing our forces with theirs may appear at the first sight void of all possibility. But, if you consider the opportunity that this present time offereth, that doubt to man's judgement may soon be avoided, though victory (as well as other things else are) is in the hands of God, who many times disposeth the same contrary to man's judgement; but foreseeing and judging of likelihoods as men may foresee and judge, there is great appearance that the pride of Spain may be so presently daunted as we may not fear this malice. The remedy perhaps may seem more dangerous than the disease, for, in seeking to abate the pride of Spain we may advance another [France], whose greatness will contain no less danger. For the answering whereof your lordship shall understand that thus standeth the case. The princes of Germany, who can be content to be parties in the enterprise, do forsee that if the whole Low Country be united to the crown of France, it would grow too great. They mean to capitulate with him to content himself with Flanders and Artois which once pertained to the crown. And as for Brabant and other parts, which once pertained to the empire, they mean to reduce them to their old state, committing the government thereof to some prince of Germany, which in reason cannot be but to the prince of Orange. Holland and Zeeland they wish were united to the crown of England which they desire for two respects, the one to make the enterprise more easy by having her assistance, the other, the better to bridle France if he seek to exceed his portion . . . (Conyers Read, I, p. 153)

Whatever the merits and demerits of the argument (and it is interesting that Walsingham sought to solve the problem by a warlike partition of the Netherlands), there can be no doubt that, in appointing him one of her principal secretaries in 1572, the queen admitted to her councils a highly intelligent exponent of hostility towards Spain.

Walsingham, along with naval officials and courtiers such as the Earl of Leicester and Christopher Hatton, was thereafter associated with the major oceanic enterprises. He was involved as both investor and high-level promoter of Drake's voyage of 1577-80, the voyage of circumnavigation. The voyage of circumnavigation was in some respects the revival of a project put forward in 1574 by Richard Grenville, William Hawkins and other west-country gentry and merchant adventurers to go in search of lands 'southward beyond the equinoctial' not already in the possession of any Christian prince. Their aims seem to have included an attempted settlement on the southern coast of America, possibly in Chile. The project was turned down by the queen, most probably because it was considered likely to damage the improving relations with Spain. In 1577, for reasons that do not seem to make much diplomatic or political sense in the then state of relations with Spain, the queen was more amenable to the promptings of anti-Spanish councillors and, even more remarkably, willing to allow the command to be entrusted to a man whose record hardly suggested that he would confine himself to places 'not under the obedience of any christian prince'.

Walsingham's role emerges in John Cooke's report of the speech made by Drake following the execution of Doughty.

> My lord of Essex wrote in my commendations unto secretary Walsingham more than I was worthy, but belike I had deserved somewhat at his hands, and he thought me in his letters to be a fit man to serve against the Spaniards, for my practice and experience that I had in that trade. Whereupon indeed secretary Walsingham did come to confer with him, and declared unto him that her Majesty had received divers injuries of the king of Spain, for the which she desired to have some revenge; and withal he showed me a plot (quote he), willing me to set my hand and to note down where I thought he might most be annoyed. But I told him some part of my mind, but refused to set my hand to anything, affirming that her Majesty was mortal, and that if it should please God to take her Majesty away, it might be that some prince might reign that might be in league with the king of Spain, and then will mine own hand be a witness against myself. Then was I very shortly after and in an evening sent for unto her Majesty by secretary Walsingham, but came not to her Majesty that night, for that it was late. But the next day coming to her presence, these or the like words [she said]: Drake, so it is that I would gladly be revenged on the king of Spain for divers injuries that I have received; and said further that he was the only man that might do this exploit, and withal craved his advice therein. Who told her Majesty of the small good that was to be done in Spain, but the only way to annoy him was by his Indies. (W. S. W. Vaux (ed.), *The World Encompassed by Sir Francis Drake*, Hakluyt Society, First Series, Vol.16, pp. 215 ff.)

Drake was of course asserting his authority following the quelling of a mutiny, and his stress upon the queen's personal involvement and the confidence she is alleged to have placed in him are all in one with this purpose. With so many interests involved, the aims of the voyage are difficult to elucidate, but the primary objects seem to have been reconnaissance and pillage. It is unlikely that Drake would have been nominated, given his financial triumphs in the Caribbean, had pillage not been high on the list of the investors' priorities. The voyage was therefore in the established freebooting tradition. But it is worth noting, without investing Drake with a high strategic purpose, the reference to his alleged statement that the way to annoy the King of Spain was 'by his Indies'. As the reported conversation was couched in terms of 'revenge' for divers injuries, we should not perhaps make too much of it. Nevertheless the possible existence of the idea that attacks upon Spain in the New World were a valid alternative to attacks upon her in the Old cannot be dismissed out of hand.

Drake's return laden with treasure was the signal for a popular reception in which the queen and her subjects participated. It reflected the widespread anti-Spanish sentiments of all levels of society, Protestant patriotism, and for the queen, who knighted him, and the investors the joy of personal enrichment. It also stimulated ideas of a systematic maritime offensive. Even before Drake's return, Humphrey Gilbert, a Devonshire landowner, had been granted letters patent for a colonising venture in North America in an area sufficiently close to the Caribbean to be employed as a base against Spain. Gilbert is an interesting example of the development within the privateering movement of strategic ideas associated with the dependence of the King of Spain upon American treasure. He was the nephew of Sir Arthur Champernoune, vice-admiral of Devon and a powerful promoter of privateering. Gilbert's ideas were unfolded in his discourses to the queen of November 1577 on how to annoy the King of Spain. Both discourses include an assumption that war is inevitable; both reflect the theory that the power of Spain in Europe depended upon American treasure.

Now these matters considered it is good cause to provide beforehand how and by what means such and so great a prince as the king of Spain is, with all the whole troop of the catholics, may best be withstanded and most endamaged with least charges to the queen's Majesty and most assurance to the realm, if at time he shall move war to the queen's Majesty as by all the reasons before alleged that it is to be doubted he will. Therefore according to my duty and to the best of my poor knowledge I do show hereafter following by what means the king of Spain may be brought to know that any kind of peace shall be better for him than wars with England . . .

The first way by the which this may be done is to send a power of men and ships to the island called Hispaniola, otherwise Santo Domingo and the island of Cuba which be joined both together, and to set the men on land and to take both the islands, which may easily

be done because there is but few people in them both and those that
be there be only in the port towns by the sea side; and within the
land is few people or none at all. This being done the place is such
that hardly any power can remove them, and the places be such as
it may let [obstruct] all the trade of the king of Spain into the
Indies . . .

The second way by which the king of Spain may mightily be
troubled, when need shall require, is by taking of the fleets that come
out of the islands homewards for Spain in which cometh all the king's
treasure and of the subjects also; the which treasure hath been the
principal aid wherewith to do all the great acts that that [sic] the
Emperor Charles did in his time and the pride of the Spaniards to
this day . . .

It is also to be remembered that the least loss that may happen
in any parts of the Indies to the king of Spain will be more grievous
unto him than any loss that can happen to him elsewhere; and this
is also most sure that the queen's Majesty at all times that needs shall
require shall do more by this means with the charges of twenty-
thousand pounds than by any other means with a hundred thousand
pounds. And also it is most certain that the king of Spain being set
a work by these ways, the queen's majesty shall little need to care
for any harm that he can do in these parts. (D. B. Quinn (ed.), *The
Voyages and Colonising Enterprises of Sir Humphrey Gilbert'*
Hakluyt Society, Second Series, Vol.83, i, pp. 176 ff.)

The strategic motive also found a place, along with commercial,
economic and social motives, in the younger Richard Hakluyt's
Discourse of Western Planting (1584). For Hakluyt, as for Gilbert,
'Indian treasure' was the lubricant of Spanish imperial machinery.

But the planting of two of three strong forts upon some good havens
(whereof there is a great store) between Florida and Cape Breton
would be a matter in short space of greater damage as well to his
fleet as to his western Indies, for we should not only often times
endanger his fleet in the return thereof, but also in few years put
him in hazard in losing some part of *Nova Hispania*. Touching the
fleet, no man (that knoweth the course thereof coming out between
Cuba and the Cape of Florida along the gulf or straits of Bahama)
can deny that it is carried by the current north and north-east towards
the coast which we purpose, God willing, to inhabit; which happened
to them not two years past as Mr Jennings and Mr Smith, master
and master's mate of the ship called the *Toby* belonging to Bristol
informed me and many of the chief merchants of that city . . . Besides
the current it is also a thing without controversy that all southern

and south-eastern winds force the Spanish fleet returning home upon the aforesaid coast and consequently will bring them into our danger after we shall be there strongly settled and fortified. (E. G. R. Taylor (ed.), *The Original Writings and Correspondence of the Two Richard Hakluyts*, Hakluyt Society, Second Series, Vol.77, p. 240)

Hakluyt also envisaged a two-edged weapon: the use of English plantations as bases for war against Spain's American territories in alliance with indigenous people and escaped slaves.

Generally speaking, the economic and social aspects of Elizabethan colonising projects in North America were overshadowed by the privateering aspect. The financial and strategic incentives of privateering were stronger and seemed in the circumstances of the time more worthwhile than the patient, often in the short term unrewarding, establishment of economically viable plantations. That western planting should have come to be regarded as an extension of privateering is not surprising, for there was an abundance of plans for major offensive operations in the Atlantic. The first was that of John Hawkins in August 1579. Entitled 'A provision for the Indies fleet, drawn by Mr. Hawkins, Admiralty', it called for a squadron of four medium-sized royal warships, five armed merchantmen and eleven pinnaces, manned in all by 1,130 men. It was to seek the Spanish treasure fleet and, if it missed it, move on to sack the Caribbean. 'There is,' wrote Hawkins, 'to be stricken with this company all the towns upon the coast of the Indies, and there need not be suffered one ship, bark, frigate or galley to survive untaken.' The queen, however, had yet to be convinced that the attempt, which anticipates some features of the 1585 campaign, was worth the risk of open war with Spain.

The flight from Portugal in 1580 of the Portuguese pretender, Dom António, thrust the Azores, the waters around which were the focal area of all Iberian-bound transoceanic trade, into the strategic foreground. Encouraged by reports that the Azorean island of Terceira was loyal to the pretender, the English government entered into negotiations with him for its capture and use as a base for raids upon the Spanish treasure fleet and Portuguese carracks returning from the Orient. Leicester and Walsingham, Drake and Hawkins, even the cautious Burghley, agreed in June 1581 to prepare a combined operation leading to the capture of the island. Besides having a supporting role, the fleet of two great ships and six pinnaces was 'to spend the time about the islands until the end of September waiting the coming of the fleet from the West Indies. If these should be missed then may the whole fleet range all the coast of the West Indies and sack all the towns and spoil wheresoever they find them by sea or land' (E. G. R. Taylor (ed.),

The Troublesome Voyage of Captain Edward Fenton, 1582–83, Hakluyt Society, Second Series, Vol. 113, pp. 7 ff.).

Whether Burghley was committed to the extent that Leicester and Walsingham were is doubtful. Like the queen, Burghley was both attracted by the prospect of participating in a profitable campaign under Dom António's flag and frightened by the prospect of stumbling into war with Spain. While the men of war fretted for permission to sail, the queen and her scribes sought to insure against the risk of becoming involved in war without an ally by obtaining a pledge of French collaboration in the Terceira venture. The English negotiators, however, failed to convince the French court of the value of an alliance which did not take sufficiently into account French ambition and interests. With the failure of the negotiations the queen's interest rapidly cooled. By August it was clear to Dom António that he had nothing to gain from England. He departed for France, where he succeeded next year in obtaining French support in a disastrous campaign for the realisation of his Azorean dreams.

The failure to obtain official, or at least semi-official, backing from the English government did not put an end to Dom António's links with the English maritime community. He issued commissions in the 1580s much as the Prince of Condé and the Prince of Orange had done in the 1560s and 1570s. John Young of Chichester sent his ship the *White Bear* to sea in 1582 under the pretender's flag. Other English privateers known to have been at sea in 1582 with a commission from Dom António are the *Archangel* of London, the *Prosperity* commanded by Clinton Atkinson, the *Greyhound* commanded by Thomas Beavyn, the *Diamond* of Thomas Walton, the *Antonio* of Plymouth which joined his forces off La Rochelle. At least another five English ships, two owned by Drake and one by the Earl of Shrewsbury, also sailed for the pretender in 1582. The Fenners of Chichester obtained a commission in 1584 when Edward Fenner and his nephew William put to sea in the *Galleon Fenner* on a profitable voyage in association with the pirate John Challice.

Continuous negotiations, of which little evidence survives, seem to have gone on between the Hawkins family and the pretender. Dr J. A. Williamson (*Hawkins of Plymouth*, p. 218) has drawn attention to an undated fragment which sheds some light on them.

And further we do licence the said W[illiam] H[awkins] and his company to serve Dom Antony, K. of Port. against his enemies, and do hereby allow anything that shall be done in the service of the said K.Dom Antony; and such pay, reward, wages, or both, either in money or commodities, as shall be taken in and for the said service, the said Wm.H. and deputies may hereby freely and lawfully sail and utter in any place upon the coast of England or anywhere else within our dominions, without anything to be said unto him for the same.

It is likely that this document pre-dates the voyage of 1582–3 led by sixty-three-year-old William Hawkins, the elder brother of John. William Hawkins's aims seem to have been a mixture of illicit trade with Portuguese Atlantic possessions, Cape Verde and Brazil, and plunder. As a commercial venture the voyage was a failure; but William led his squadron into the Caribbean, whence he returned with pearls, treasure, hides and sugar. According to the Spanish ambassador, Bernardino de Mendoza, writing in November 1583, the ships lay at Plymouth laden with great booty.

In July 1584 John Hawkins came forward again with a proposal for a systematic offensive against Spain's oceanic lifelines without charge to the queen. He recommended an agreement with Dom António whereby English gentry, merchants, shipowners and pirates would wage war against Spain under his flag and be joined by raiders from the Netherlands and France. The queen's commitment would be to permit them to victual, refit and sell their booty at a west-country port, presumably Plymouth, where the Hawkinses were dominant, on payment to her of a percentage of the profits. Hawkins's plan, though not adopted, had the merit, in the midst of much confusion of aim and dispersal of effort, of attempting to harness aspirations, including his own, for personal enrichment to a clear-cut strategic design. This was Hawkins's second memorandum, nor was it to be his last, on the subject of an Atlantic offensive. He was already emerging as the most influential advocate of systematic commerce raiding as the infallible prescription for victory. He did not, however, take part in the 1585 transatlantic offensive, in which the leading role was played by Francis Drake.

The English offensive of 1585 was by no means planned, directed or financed by the state. Though blessed with royal approval in that the queen subscribed money and a stiffening of royal warships, it was essentially a private joint-stock venture, or series of ventures, financed by the officers-in-charge, landowning gentry, courtiers and noblemen, merchant adventurers, including the Hawkinses, and businessmen of London. The queen's reliance upon private adventurers no doubt reflected her lingering preference for war by proxy; it also reflected a permanent feature of Elizabethan war finance: the inability of the state to assert control of the maritime war by meeting the cost thereof out of public funds. As it was, the offensive embodied the strategic wisdom of the age that licensed commerce raiding with its fusion of public and private interests was the irresistible weapon of sea warfare.

Francis Drake sailed from Plymouth at the head of a powerful force of twenty-one public and private fighting ships and eight pinnaces in September 1585, sufficiently late in the year to miss the worst of the Caribbean hurricane season. The whole force, including soldiers under Christopher Carleill, Walsingham's stepson, numbered 2,300 men. Vice-admiral to Drake was Martin Frobisher, veteran of the African voyages of the 1550s, an experienced privateer and leader of the searches for the North-west Passage in the 1570s. Thomas Fenner, a close associate of Drake, served as staff-captain. Several survivors of the circumnavigation held individual commands. It was the largest and most ambitious expedition ever to leave England to strike at targets in the New World. The trail of pillage and destruction began in Europe with the replenishment of supplies through the seizure of ships and goods at the Spanish port of Vigo. The second port of call was Santiago in the Cape Verde Islands, where more supplies of food and drink were obtained. We are reminded by events during the next stage of the voyage, the crossing of the Atlantic, that in sixteenth-century conditions of victualling, hygiene and medicine, disease was a constant threat to the oceanic strategy made possible by the improved sea-keeping capacity of the sailing ship. Within two days of setting sail from Santiago 'there fell a great sickness amongst our men, not in one ship but in all the whole fleet, so that in the Admiral there were sick above an hundred men at one time, and there were about sixty men sick in the Vice-admiral at the same time, and so in other ships according to their number. There died divers of this disease both in our ship and others, sometimes one, sometimes two or three in a day' (J. S. Corbett (ed.), *Papers relating to the Navy during the Spanish War, 1585–1587*, Navy Records Society, Vol.11, p. 12).

It was therefore with a force weakened in numbers and fitness that Drake entered the Caribbean at the end of the year. His first target was Santo Domingo on the island of Hispaniola. After the city had been occupied and looted – the quantity of bullion was a disappointment – the Spaniards agreed to pay a ransom of 25,000 ducats. The second target was Cartagena on the Spanish Main, which was similarly occupied, looted and evacuated on payment of a ransom of 107,000 ducats. Evidence from both English and Spanish sources suggests that Drake intended to follow this blow with an onslaught on Panama, which 'standeth upon the sea coast in the South Sea, and doth [receive] all the treasure that cometh by water from the new kingdom of Peru, which may be taken without resistance; this town may be a prey of a million of ducats' (Corbett (ed.), *Papers relating to the Navy*, p.72). But disease continued to take its toll. One hundred men were said to have been lost by sickness at Cartagena. Increasing weakness seems to have sapped ambition. Instead of making for Panama after quitting Cartagena, Drake hovered off Cuba while contemplating an attack upon, and a possible occupation of, Havana. But with a Spanish fleet reported to be on its way to the Indies and with the military officers doubtful that they could do much with their weakened contingent, it was decided to abandon the Caribbean.

Drake did not, however, set course directly for England. During the raids on Santo Domingo and Cartagena he had taken on board the ships many black slaves and Moorish and Turkish galley slaves as well as household equipment. He now determined to deliver the equipment and the slaves to the newly established colony at Roanoke Island. Whether a visit to Roanoke had been discussed by Drake in 1585 with Richard Grenville and the leading colonial promoter, Walter Ralegh, is unknown. There probably was some co-ordination as Ralegh had helped to finance the Drake expedition. And Drake may have been anxious to examine the settlement as a base for future operations against Spanish shipping and trade. The argument for there having been some co-ordination, though not a prearranged plan, is strengthened by Drake's conduct in seeking out and making a devastating raid on San Agustín, Spain's chief base in Florida and hence a danger to the fragile Roanoke plantation. It is clear, too, that, had he been able to find it, he would have assaulted the more northerly Floridan base of Santa Elena in the same way. We do seem to catch a glimpse during this phase of the campaign of a collaborative oceanic strategy. It was, however, only one of the operations which Drake had in mind and may never have come to pass had he been able to get at Panama or Havana.

When Drake arrived off Roanoke in June 1586 he found a dispirited body of men, just over a hundred in number, looking out for reinforcements and supplies from England. As a base for maritime operations Roanoke Island suffered from want of an adequate harbour. The first request of Ralph Lane, the governor left behind by Grenville in 1585, was for a ship to reconnoitre the coast in search for better harbour facilities. Drake furnished a ship, but the intentions of Lane were immediately thwarted by its loss in a sudden gale. More serious, however, than the want of a harbour was the dependence of the colonists on supplies from England. Dependence upon the mother country was perhaps inevitable during the years of foundation; but the late arrival of supplies enkindled desires for repatriation. Lane and his men, their expectations of relief disappointed, were anxious to return home. The proposed coastal reconnaissance was intended to locate a site for a new settlement which would be occupied at a later date after the colonists had returned to England to prepare a new venture. In the event, they embarked with Drake in a little over a fortnight after his arrival for a passage to England. They missed their first reliefs, already in mid-Atlantic, by a narrow margin. That Drake's raid should have ended in the abandonment of the first overseas base for operations against the Spanish empire is an ironical comment on the inadequacy of privateering as the foundation of self-sufficient operational bases in the wilderness.

The Caribbean offensive of 1585–6, though it did not realise either in damage to the enemy or rewards to the investors all the hopes of Drake and his sponsors, convinced Philip II that the security of the imperial communications was at risk. The war may have had its roots in power struggles intrinsic to Europe. But the growth of the belief among the enemies of Spain that conflicts could be resolved in their favour through resolute action in the extra-European world by public and private war fleets created new strategic patterns and new threats to international stability. The idea that a great continental power could be brought to its knees, profitably and inexpensively, through systematic plundering turned out to be an illusion. In the last quarter of the sixteenth century it was not only a persistent and powerful illusion but a potent influence on international affairs. 'The onslaughts in the Atlantic,' observes J. H. Elliott in *The Old World and the New, 1492–1650*,

> may not have been sufficiently co-ordinated to acquire the status of a systematic offensive, but they were at least based on a common assumption that Spain's colonial empire was the source of its economic strength. It was this assumption, too, which helped to dictate Philip's response, for the objective of the Spanish Armada was, in the words of the king's secretary, 'no less the security of the Indies than the recovery of the Netherlands'. (p. 93)

CHAPTER 4

Honour, Safety and Profit, 1585–1604

A first step towards understanding the conduct at sea of the Anglo-Spanish war is to rid ourselves of the insular myth that sixteenth-century Spain, being dominated by priests and soldiers, was necessarily ignorant of most things, above all of sea power. The importance of maritime communications, and hence of sea power, to so scattered a monarchy as that of Philip II was apparent to the king and his advisers. For the first twenty years of the reign, however, assessments of Spanish naval requirements had a predominantly Mediterranean orientation, for they were made not in the light of a hypothetical Protestant menace but of an actual Islamic menace. Supported by raiders from the satellite settlements in North Africa, Ottoman galley fleets periodically ravaged the trade routes and coasts of the western Mediterranean, threatening not only to turn it into a Turkish lake but to establish bridgeheads within Spain itself through collusion with disaffected moriscos of the Iberian peninsula. The morisco rebellion of 1568–71 in Granada underlined the extent to which the initiative in the Mediterranean belonged to Islam. Even after the victory of the Holy League at Lepanto in 1571, Ottoman control of the eastern Mediterranean and their capacity to strike westwards seemed largely undiminished. Only in the late 1570s, when the Ottoman Empire was obliged to disengage in the Mediterranean to deal with urgent problems on other frontiers, was the pressure on Spain relaxed.

Philip II's response to Ottoman aggression was a programme of galley building at Barcelona, Naples and Sicily early in the reign. At the same time, negotiations, successfully concluded in 1562, were conducted with the papacy for the levying of a new tax, the *subsidio*, on ecclesiastical revenues in Spain and Italy to finance the galley fleet. By 1564, seventy-one galleys were in commission, and by 1568, ninety-one. Losses in the campaigns of 1570–71 were rapidly made good. By 1574 Philip's galley fleet numbered 146: 46 in the squadron of Spain, 24 in the squadron of Genoa, 54 in the squadron of Naples and 22 in the squadron of Sicily. At a cost of more than 3,500,000 ducats the Spanish monarchy had become a Mediterranean naval power of the first rank. As long as Spain and the western Mediterranean were threatened by the Ottoman Empire and its North African satellites, as well as by the Iberian moriscos, the building of the Mediterranean galley fleet was a rational priority. Given the financial restrictions upon naval expenditure, the development of a Spanish Atlantic sailing-ship navy was hardly feasible in the circumstances of the 1560s and early 1570s. It is true that during the closing decades of the Habsburg–Valois conflict squadrons made up of armed private ships under contract to the Crown were fitted out as required to defend the sea lanes of the Caribbean and those between Spain and the Netherlands. But there was not as yet a consistent and wholehearted shipbuilding programme.

That the emergence of Spain as an Atlantic naval power was a slow process does not mean that the problem of the Atlantic went unrecognised. Alarm bells began to ring in the 1560s with the Huguenot plantation of Florida and the incursions into the Caribbean of John Hawkins. The destruction of the Florida settlement and the defeat of Hawkins at San Juan de Ulúa, far from breeding complacency, convinced the king and his advisers of the need to improve the continuity and quality of existing protective measures. This led to the creation in 1570 of the *Armada para la Guardia de las Indias* – the Indian guard – a squadron of eight royal sailing ships under the command of Pedro Menéndez de Avilés which was funded by the treasuries of New Spain and Peru. During the same years, concern about the upsurge of maritime terror in north-western waters gave rise to talk of the equipment of a squadron to deal with the Protestant maritime guerrillas. In 1574 a force was fitted out at Santander with the aim of complementing the Spanish military presence in the Netherlands with a naval presence off the coast of Holland and Zeeland. Shattered by disease, it never sailed, though it survived as a flotilla to defend the coasts of northern Spain against piratical attacks.

By the early 1570s therefore the idea of an Atlantic navy – the *Armada del Mar Océano* of the future – was alive. But to translate the idea into reality required more than intellectual assent. The ideal of Philip and his advisers was a fleet of specialised state-owned warships; but the creation almost from scratch of a permanent professional sailing-ship navy was by any standards a formidable undertaking. It required an immense initial outlay and continuous expenditure when Spain's resources were already fully stretched. It meant entering into competition with the shipping industry for materials, skilled workers and seamen. It raised the question whether the proposed warships should be built under contract in private yards or by a royal workforce directed by royal administrators in public yards. The financial and organisational complexities encouraged deferment. An attempt was made in 1576, on the recommendation of Alonso Guttiérez, a far-sighted and persistent advocate of an Atlantic fleet, to negotiate an agreement between the Crown and the city of Seville for a programme of warship construction. It failed, however, for want of conviction on both sides.

The annexation of Portugal in 1580 was a turning point in the history of Spain as an Atlantic power since it brought with it a squadron of Portuguese galleons and a new Atlantic frontier which made the indecisiveness of the 1570s a luxury that could no longer be afforded. As soon as the annexation had been completed, it was decided to replace the worn-out ships of the Indian guard with nine new warships to be laid down immediately at Santander. Contracts were also drawn up in 1582 with private shipbuilders in northern Spain for the construction of 15,000 tons of shipping for war service: a contract which, if it had been completed according to schedule, would have provided the king, taking into account the Portuguese galleons, with the nucleus of a powerful Atlantic navy by 1588. The force available was gradually increased as well through the requisitioning of suitable native and foreign merchantmen in the ports of the Iberian peninsula and through the hiring of ships from Mediterranean and Adriatic shipowners.

The chief focus of anxiety in the early 1580s was the Azores, where support for the anti-Spanish pretender, Dom António, was sufficiently strong to encourage him to believe that, with foreign aid, they might serve as a base for the recovery of Portugal. By soliciting aid from England and France and by encouraging raiders to operate in his name, Dom António thrust the Azores into the front line of a conflict over Spain's oceanic communications in an area where the routes from the East and West Indies converged. Philip II's answer was the subjugation of the islands in the campaigns of 1582–3 led by Alvaro de Bazán, Marquis of Santa Cruz, a veteran of Lepanto and arguably Spain's greatest sixteenth-century sea officer. In both campaigns Santa Cruz met and defeated squadrons of broadside sailing ships which had been fitted out in French ports. The battles for the Azores were indicative of Spain's emergence as an Atlantic power. Their outcome encouraged the belief, not least in the mind of Santa Cruz himself, that the hour had come for a trial of strength with England, upon the result of which would depend the future of both Europe and the Atlantic world.

To the Spanish equivalents of Francis Walsingham and his circle, Philip II's English policy had been a series of ineffective half-measures: a degree of formal support, coupled with ambassadorial intrigues, for English Catholics; connivance with the disastrous landing of papal volunteers in County Kerry during the Munster rebellion of 1579–80; the periodic imposition of short-lived embargoes upon English ships in Spanish ports. Philip II, like Elizabeth I, was an unwilling crusader. But with it becoming increasingly clear that his policy was persuading England neither to acquiesce in the reassertion of Spanish authority in the Netherlands nor to desist from maritime terror, he became more receptive to arguments in favour of all-out war. The idea of the Enterprise of England began to take shape in August 1583 when Santa Cruz, fresh from his victories in the Azores, recommended the launching from Spain in 1584 of an invading armada, led by himself, to conquer England and proceed thereafter to the subjugation of the Netherlands. This solution to the English problem was not unacceptable to the prudent king. 'The situation is such,' he replied, 'that it is not possible to speak with certainty at the moment . . . but I am ordering provisions of biscuits from Italy and expediting the construction of galleons and the hire of ships in Vizcaya, and everything else which is necessary in preparation for a favourable opportunity; and I am also ordering Flanders to be ready for what you suggest' (quoted by J. Lynch, *Spain under the Habsburgs*, Vol. I: *Empire and Absolutism, 1516–1598*, pp. 311 ff.).

Flanders meant, of course, the Duke of Parma. The correspondence between Philip II and the duke in September–November 1583 brings to light an alternative plan for the enterprise. Parma was on balance more interested in the conquest of the Netherlands than the conquest of England. Departing from the increasingly fashionable doctrine that the conquest of England was a necessary condition for that of the Netherlands, he was inclined to think that the latter, if successfully completed, would facilitate the former. He offered with some reserve therefore the advice that, if secrecy were preserved, he could ferry 34,000 troops in barges across the Narrow Seas from Nieuport and Dunkirk in a single night. He hoped to preserve secrecy and achieve surprise by masking the preliminary movements of barges and troops under the guise of operations in the Netherlands. Philip was not convinced that an invasion of England from the Netherlands was feasible without naval cover. Not yet fully committed in principle to the idea of invasion, he made note of the two plans and took no further action until the autumn of 1585 when, besides instructing Santa Cruz and the Duke of Medina Sidonia, governor-general of Andalusia, to equip a fleet for the interception of Drake, he showed a renewed interest in the Enterprise of England. Its first result was the preparation by Santa Cruz of the famous estimate of March 1586 for a seaborne invasion from the Iberian peninsula.

The estimate doomed the project. Santa Cruz called for 150 great ships made up of all the royal galleons and the largest and most heavily armed merchantmen that could be obtained in the ports of the monarchy. He also required 40 heavy transports, 320 auxiliary craft, 40 galleys and 6 galleasses. This fleet was to be manned by 30,000 seamen and to carry an invading army of 64,000 soldiers. He calculated that, with ordnance, powder and shot, ship's tackle, biscuit (373,337 cwt), bacon (22,800 cwt), cheese (21,500 cwt), salt beef (16,040 cwt), wine (46,800 pipes) and all other provisions, the cost of a campaign of eight months would be nearly 4 million ducats. Garret Mattingly in *The Defeat of the Spanish Armada* makes the fair comment that 'in terms of the mission to be undertaken the admiral's estimate was reasonable; in terms of economic realities it was absurd' (p. 81).

The request that Santa Cruz prepare an estimate did not mean that the king had ruled out the employment of the army of the Netherlands and its commander-in-chief. He was in correspondence with Parma, while Santa Cruz was at work, and was sent the substance of a scheme on 20 April. As in 1583, Parma offered to lead a descent upon England to sail from Dunkirk, Gravelines and Nieuport and to land between Dover and Margate. An essential condition for the lightning dash envisaged was the preservation of secrecy. On this score Parma was not at ease.

> Tout le monde parle ici en public de l'enterprise. Soyez certain que ces bruits arrivent aux oreilles d'Elisabeth. Aussi les Anglais se préparent à la défense; ils essaient de conclure des accords avec les Français, les villes maritime de la Baltique, la Suède, le Danemark et les protestants de l'Allemagne. (L. van der Essen, *Alexandre Farnèse: prince de Parme, gouverneur-général des Pays-Bas (1545–1592)*, V, p. 164)

> [Everybody here is talking openly of the enterprise. You may be sure that these rumours reach the ears of Elizabeth. The English are preparing to defend themselves; they are trying to reach understandings with the French, the Baltic maritime cities, Sweden, Denmark and the German Protestants.]

Although he would have preferred a largely unescorted passage with himself in sole command, he had to acknowledge that, if secrecy were lost, it would be necessary to cover the enterprise with a powerful fleet equipped in Spain.

From the ideas of Santa Cruz and Parma, Phillip II created the grand design unfolded in 1587 but not, for reasons soon to be made clear, attempted until 1588. It owed more to the ideas of Parma than to those of Santa Cruz, though it allowed a more substantial role to the forces sailing from Spain than had originally been envisaged by the duke. The design had the great merit of avoiding the gamble of an unescorted crossing by the army of the Netherlands. Thirty thousand men of this army assembled with barges on the Flemish coast were to be the spearhead of the invasion. Santa Cruz was to sail from Lisbon with a fighting fleet and transports, having on board a strong contingent of Spanish infantry. He was to advance up the English Channel, rendezvous with the barges, escort them to a point of disembarkation on the coast of the Thames estuary, reinforce the landing force with Spanish infantry and stand by to secure communications with the Netherlands.

To accomplish this, His Majesty reckons that, if the Marquis should assemble the forces earmarked for him and at hand for his Armada, he would have more than 16,000 regular Spanish infantrymen, many of them veterans; and more than 22,000 soldiers and sailors combined, as appears from the private estimates already sent to His Majesty.

His Majesty also understands that the Duke of Parma is either now, or will shortly be, in the vicinity of Ostend with an army of 30,000 to 40,000; and having learnt of the capture of Esclusa [Sluys], His Majesty sent word to him not to disarm, but to maintain his army intact on the coast, on the pretext that he intended to complete the capture of the Flemish ports. Simultaneously with the sending of this despatch to you, another is going forward to the Duke, advising him of the decision which will be disclosed below, and ordering him to be prepared.

This decision of His Majesty's is that the Marquis should unite the fleet he has brought with him with the fleet from Andalusia, including the galeasses and the food storeships, and all the others he might find at Lisbon, and also the Oquendo fleet, which will either arrive before the Marquis leaves, or which he will encounter before he reaches Cape Finisterre; and that he should take on board the Armada the seamen and soldiers to the number indicated in the estimates or their approximate number; as well as heavy artillery and draught animals. All this should be done with the greatest possible secrecy, which is of the utmost importance; at most allowing it to be thought that the fleet is bound for Ireland, which is the rumour now being spread abroad.

With these forces and fleet the Marquis should set sail in God's name, for the English Channel, proceeding along it until he should anchor off Margate Cape [North Foreland], having first sent word to the Duke of Parma of his approach. The latter, obeying the orders given him, as soon as he should see his crossing made secure by the presence of the Armada at Margate, or in the vicinity of the Thames estuary, if the weather should have freshened, would then proceed to pass across his whole camp in small vessels of which there will be more than enough in those ports, for the crossing only. His Majesty desires Duke and Marquis, cooperating closely with each other, the one on land, and the other on the sea, to carry through, with God's aid, the principal plan of the invasion of England. Until the Duke of Parma should cross safely with his army, the Marquis should fix his attention solely on making secure the Duke's passage, and defeating whatever enemy fleet might attempt to intercept it; although when once the Marquis has gained with his fleet that port, and is thus able to prevent the union of the vessels in the River of London and on the East Coast of the island, with those of the South and West coasts, the enemy will hardly be able to collect a fleet with which he could dare to seek out ours. Once the Duke has landed in England, and the Marquis has given him – as His Majesty desires and has commanded him to do – the 6,000 picked Spanish infantrymen (since the Duke has few Spaniards and without these 6,000 the Marquis will still have some 10,000 soldiers and from 14,000 to 18,000 men aboard the fleet), the two should consult together as to what further use is to be made of the Armada. They should then decide whether the Marquis should continue to secure the crossing for our men and cut off foreign aid for the enemy; whether he should try to capture another port, thus creating a diversion elsewhere, and himself also land; or whether attempt to capture the enemy's ships in the various ports in order to rob him of his maritime forces, which are his chief source of strength. The decision to be taken is left to the Commanders who, being present, are the better able to decide on what would be the most suitable course of action for the Marquis to take. (C. C. Lloyd (ed.), *The Naval Miscellany, Vol. IV*, Navy Records Society, Vol. 92, pp. 9 ff.)

The campaign contemplated for 1587 was postponed because of delays in assembling at Lisbon the necessary forces and because of the diversion caused by 'the departure of Drake and the security of the fleets' (Lloyd (ed.), *The Naval Miscellany*, p. 7) which obliged Santa Cruz to sail on a different mission.

Drake had made his departure from Plymouth Sound on 12 April 1587. The object of the mission, which helped to create his late nineteenth-century reputation as a strategic genius born ahead of his time, was to disrupt the Spanish preparations for invasion. He had sailed at the head of a composite force of royal and private ships under orders from the queen and council which left considerable scope for opportunistic improvisation. 'Sir Francis Drake,' wrote Walsingham to Edward Stafford, the English ambassador in Paris,

as I doubt not but you have heard, is gone forth to the seas with four of her Majesty's ships and two pinnaces and between twenty and thirty merchantships. His commission is to impeach the joining together of the king of Spain's fleet out of their several ports, to keep victuals from them, to follow them in case they should come forward towards England or Ireland, and to cut off as many of them as he could, and impeach their landing, as also to set upon such as should come out of the West or East Indies into Spain, or go out of Spain thither; but now upon knowledge received that the king did dissolve his preparations, having already discharged the Easterlings, there is new order sent unto Sir Francis Drake to take a milder course, for that he was before particularly directed to distress the ships within the havens themselves. (J. S. Corbett (ed.), *The Spanish War, 1585–87*, Navy Records Society, Vol. 11, p. 104)

There are several features of the operation which shed a revealing light upon both the Elizabethan way of warfare and the Elizabethan sea forces. The first is the characteristic attempt to preserve the distinction between a punitive strike and an act of open war by countermanding that part of Drake's original orders which permitted him to enter the harbours of the enemy. There is an element of mystery about the apparent wavering. The new orders, though this does not emerge from Walsingham's letter to Stafford, failed to reach Plymouth in time to inform Drake before he sailed of the government's revised thinking. We cannot tell whether the restriction was intended to leave the door for negotiations as wide open as possible or to serve as a device to enable the government to claim, should Drake meet with disaster, that he had exceeded his instructions.

The composition of the force is also of interest. It consisted of twenty-three ships, of which four galleons, the flagship *Elizabeth Bonaventure* (550 tons), the *Golden Lion* (550 tons), the *Rainbow* (500 tons), the *Dreadnought* (400 tons) and two pinnaces, the *Cygnet* and the *Spy*, were royal warships. Of the remainder, two vessels were the private property of the lord admiral and ten were 'London ships' owned by London merchant syndicates including the Levant Company. The Londoners had equipped their ships for war at their own expense and they expected rewards. Upon their arrival at Plymouth a legal agreement was concluded between them and Drake for the equitable distribution of 'whatsoever commodity in goods, money, treasure, merchandise, or other benefit whatsoever shall happen to be taken by all or any of the foresaid ships or their company, either by sea or land . . .' (Corbett (ed.), *The Spanish War*, p. 105). Pillage therefore was high on the list of objectives. This entrepreneurial attitude to maritime war was not necessarily incompatible with the pursuit of strategic objectives of the sort outlined in Walsingham's letter; but it could cause conflicts of interest within the fleet and lack of constancy of purpose. The Londoners were said by the contemporary seaman and naval commentator Sir William Monson to have 'adventured only in hope of profit, for their condition is to prefer gain to themselves before any respect of service or security to the kingdom' (M. Oppenheim (ed.), *The Naval Tracts of Sir William Monson*, Vol. I, Navy Records Society, Vol. 22, p. 137).

Nor was the conduct of Drake himself a model of strategic consistency. He began with the famous Cádiz raid, a brilliant piece of opportunism inspired by intelligence obtained at sea that merchantmen packed with provisions were preparing there to join Santa Cruz at Lisbon. In less than twenty-four hours he destroyed or captured between twenty and thirty ships and acquired a useful quantity of supplies. His next move, following a parade of strength off the Iberian coast, was to occupy a station off Cape St Vincent, a commanding position astride the routes between the Mediterranean and Atlantic ports of Philip II. He put landing parties ashore to disarm the castle and other near-by fortifications at Sagres, thus securing the fleet anchorage as if in anticipation of a long stay. Having already reduced the number of ships available for service through the Cádiz raid, he now scoured the waters off the cape and captured many ships, including some bound for Lisbon with barrel-staves for the manufacture of casks and water butts. Then just as suddenly as he had descended on the station, he abandoned it on 1 June and made sail for the Azores, where in contemporary opinion he crowned the campaign with the seizure of the wealthy carrack *San Felipe* which was bound for Lisbon with a cargo of Asiatic produce.

The sudden abandonment of a position, described by Drake's staff-captain Thomas Fenner as 'so greatly to our benefit and so much to their disadvantage', provoked neither criticism nor dissension. As long as naval expeditions had, because of government penury, to be largely self-financing, there could in truth be no service without profit. The dissension which did break out during the voyage had nothing to do with a clash between service and profit. It centred on Drake's style of leadership. Neither Drake nor Thomas Fenner was in any sense of the term a modern, even a late seventeenth- or eighteenth-century, naval officer. Nearest to being a professional officer of the Crown was the second-in-command, William Borough, the clerk of the ships on the navy board, who sailed as 'vice-admiral at the sea unto the now lord admiral of England'. But his appointment was, like those of Drake and Fenner, *ad hoc* and quite unrelated to the conventions of a professional officer corps. Drake as 'general' was the chief. What this entailed, however, in the sixteenth century was undefined. For Drake, who owed his rise to gifted individual endeavour unrestricted by formal restraints, being chief meant that sole responsibility and sole command were vested in him. For Borough, an experienced seaman in the queen's service, member of the Navy Board and, for the occasion, vice-admiral to the lord admiral, the chief was rather the president of a council of officers. The quarrel between them, though it contained differences over the conduct of affairs and included accusations of cowardice and treachery against Borough and of disobedience to royal orders against Drake, was about the nature of command.

Borough's protest to Drake brings out the differences:

> For that hitherto, in all this voyage since our coming forth (albeit there have been often assemblies of the captains of this fleet aboard of you, called by a flag of council, which I have judged had been chiefly for such purpose), I could never perceive any matter of council or advice touching the action and service for her Majesty with the fleet now under your charge to be effectually propounded or debated, as in reason I judge there ought to have been, as well for the better ordering of affairs, .business, and attempts, as also for your own security. (For when you shall deal by advice and counsel of such as are appointed for your assistance, and such other of experience as may be worthy to be called thereunto, howsoever the success fall out, it shall be the better for your discharge.) But at all and every such assembly you have either showed briefly your purpose what you would do as a matter resolved in yourself (and of yourself for ought that I know, unless you have called unto you such as haply will soothe you in anything you shall say, and so concluded the matter with his or their consents beforehand) in such sort, as no reason made by any other not fully agreeing with your own resolution could be accepted to take any place. Wherein we, I speak chiefly for my own part, have served but as witnesses to the words you have delivered; or else you have used us well by entertaining us with your good cheer, and so most times after our stay with you most part of the day we have departed as wise as we came, without any consultation or council holden.' (Corbett, (ed.), *The Spanish War*, pp. 123 ff.)

Sentenced to death *in absentia* by Drake after his ship the *Golden Lion* had parted company during the voyage to the Azores, Borough emerged unscathed for an inquiry into his conduct and remained an officer of the Navy Board. It is evident that Drake's concept of command and responsibility was at variance with the then customs of the service, though it must be said also that, stripped of his personal extravagances, it was to become a foundation of future naval discipline.

The Cádiz raid and the operations off Cape St Vincent slowed down the preparations at Lisbon for the invasion of England. Drake's abandonment by the departure from off the cape of the strategic advantage brought them to a halt. It had the decisive effect, quite unforeseen by Drake, of forcing Santa Cruz to sea towards the end of June with a squadron of Portuguese galleons on an Atlantic cruise of almost three months' duration in vain pursuit of the raiders. This put an end to Philip II's hopes of an autumnal invasion in 1587. The postponement deprived Spain of the services in the enterprise of Santa Cruz, who died in February 1588.

More serious than the death of Santa Cruz, the last frantic preparations of this mammoth logistical undertaking were overshadowed by a shortage of artillery and powder. Handicapped by lack of money, organisational inadequacies and technical deficiencies, especially in the casting of iron guns, the Spanish armaments industry was unequal to the demands of the new sea power. The legend that the Spaniards underrated the importance of artillery has long been exploded; but the effort to transform Spain from a Mediterranean galley power into an Atlantic sailing-ship power in less than a decade imposed intolerable strains upon her financial and technical resources. Fresh evidence coming to light from the Spanish archives (I. A. A. Thompson, 'Spanish Armada Guns', *The Mariner's Mirror*, vol.61, 1975, pp. 355 ff.), which seems to chime in with evidence brought to the surface by nautical archaeologists, points to the conclusion that the Spanish Armada fought at a disadvantage in 1588 in both long-range and, to a lesser extent, in heavy short-range artillery.

None the less the Armada, though it failed to match up to the ideal of the regular naval force originally envisaged by Philip and his advisers, was a formidable instrument of war. In the front line of battle were eight new galleons of the recently refurbished Indian guard, eleven somewhat older royal Portuguese galleons, a powerful Florentine galleon appropriated from the Grand Duke of Tuscany, four heavy Castilian armed merchantmen and four Neapolitan galleasses, vessels designed to combine oar-power and sail-power. They were supported by 40 armed merchantmen drawn from Iberian, Italian and Adriatic ports, of which many were heavier, though less manoeuvrable, than their English counterparts. With 25 bulky transports and a collection of smaller vessels, the whole amounted to about 130 sail.

As the time of confrontation grew nearer it is difficult to detect on the English side any clear-cut anti-invasion strategy. While neglecting no opportunity still of reaching a settlement by negotiation, the queen and council kept the sea forces ready for action, wavering all the time between defensive and offensive action. The most powerful advocate of offensive action was Drake. Impressed by his advocacy of the importance in naval war of offensive action in enemy waters, influential historians, including Sir Julian Corbett (*Drake and the Tudor Navy*, II, pp. 139 ff.), have credited him with the invention of a new strategic doctrine. Drake's ideas in 1588 certainly departed from the largely defensive concepts found in the writings of John Montgomery, but they had been anticipated by those of Sir Edward Howard in Henry VIII's French war of 1512–13. Howard's policy had been that the great ships should 'lay before the haven of Brest and so for still to abide before the haven of Brest th[at the] army of France should not come out, while the small ships s[hould run] upon the galleys' (A. Spont (ed.), *Letters and Papers relating to the War with France, 1512–13*, Navy Records Society, Vol. 10, p. 146). Moreover, whereas Howard was already formulating in 1513 something recognisable as the strategy of naval blockade, Drake was nowhere near so precise. According to his mouthpiece, the Florentine writer and historian Petruccio Ubaldini, Drake had no set plan. Perhaps he did not need one. He mentioned blockade; he talked of raids on Spanish towns; he hinted that his reputation was such that the very report of his presence off the Iberian coast would deter the enemy. He was certain only of success.

He was no more specific in his address to the council of 9 April nor in that to the queen of 23 April.

I have received from Mr Secretary some particular notes, and withal a commandment to answer them unto your Majesty.

The first is that your Majesty would willingly be satisfied from me how the forces now in Lisbon might best be distressed.

Truly this point is hardly to be answered as yet, for two special causes: the first for that our intelligences are as yet uncertain; the second is, the resolution of our people, which I shall better understand when I have them at sea. The last insample of Cadiz is not of divers yet forgotten; for one such flying now, as Borough did then, will put the whole in peril, for that the enemy's strength is now so great gathered together and ready to invade.

But if your Majesty will give present order for our proceeding to the sea . . . then shall your Majesty stand assured with God's assistance, that if the fleet come out of Lisbon, as long as we have victual to live withal upon that coast, they shall be fought with, and I hope, through the goodness of our merciful God, in such sort as shall hinder his quiet passage into England; for I assure your Majesty, I have not in my lifetime known better men, and possessed with gallanter minds, than your Majesty's people are for the most part, which are here gathered together, voluntarily to put their hands and hearts to the finishing of this great piece of work; . . .

The advantage of time and place in all martial actions is half a victory; which being lost is irrecoverable. Wherefore, if your Majesty will command me away with those ships that are here [Plymouth] already, and the rest to follow with all possible expedition, I hold it in my poor opinion the surest and best course; and that they bring with them victuals sufficient for themselves and us, to the intent the service be not utterly lost for want thereof; whereof I most humbly beseech your most excellent Majesty to have such consideration as the weightiness of the cause requireth; for an Englishman being far from his country, and seeing a present want of victuals to ensue, and perceiving no benefit to be looked for, but only blows, will hardly be brought to stay . . . (J. K. Laughton (ed.), *State Papers relating to the Defeat of the Spanish Armada, Anno 1588*, Vol. I, Navy Records Society, Vol. 1, pp. 149 ff.)

The waverings of queen and council in the face of so many imponderables and uncertainties are understandable. Intelligence from the Continent was in the nature of things almost invariably out of date. There were 700 miles of open sea between Plymouth Sound and the Rock of Lisbon. It was within the bounds of possibility that the Spaniards would escape interception by English men-of-war on course for the Iberian coast by making a broad north-westerly sweep into the ocean, and that having reached the latitude of 50° N. they would make a dash for the exposed mouth of the English Channel. Not that the court had much to offer as an alternative strategy to that of Drake. One piece of vague advice to the lord admiral, Charles, Lord Howard of Effingham, was that the fleet should 'ply up and down in some indifferent place between the coast of Spain and this realm, so as you may be able to answer any attempt that the said fleet shall make either against this realm, Ireland or Scotland' (Laughton (ed.), *State Papers*, p. 192). Perhaps the general uncertainty owed as much to a looming crisis over supplies of food and drink, upon which Drake laid so much stress in his letter to the queen, as it did to conflicting theories of maritime strategy. There are sure indications that the inadequacies, which were to bring about the virtual collapse of the English navy as a fighting force in late August, were apparent earlier in the year. The truth seems to be that, despite the noble work of Edward Baeshe during his long tenure of office as surveyor of victuals, the procedures and facilities of the victualling service were not geared to cope with the unprecedented demands of the sea forces in 1588. Both divisions of the fleet, the Narrow Seas squadron under Lord Henry Seymour in the Downs and the larger western squadron at Plymouth, where Howard took command early in June with Drake as vice-admiral, were worried by want of victuals.

The plight of the western squadron was the more serious of the two. Plymouth was remote from the central government distributive agencies and the counties of Devon and Cornwall did not afford an abundance of supplies from their own resources. There are reasons for believing that the problem played a part in determining the recommendations of the first council of officers over which Howard presided. Although we have no account of its deliberations, we have his word that Thomas Fenner, Martin Frobisher and John Hawkins took the lead in backing Drake's view, which was generally supported by all present, that the surest way to meet the Spaniards was upon their own coast. We cannot, however, assume that the unanimity of seamen 'of greatest judgement and experience' was an uncomplicated declaration of faith in the value of an offensive strategy, for there are dark hints in Charles Howard's report of anxiety, lest the fleet disintegrate in port for want of sustenance. 'I am verily persuaded,' he wrote, 'that they [the Spaniards] mean [nothing] else but to linger it out upon their own coast, until they understand [that] we have spent our victuals here; and therefore we must be busy [with] them before we suffer ourselves to be brought to that extremity' (Laughton (ed.), *State Papers*, p. 200). Queen and council finally accepted the advice of the seamen, authorising Howard at the end of June to act as he and his advisers thought fit. Armed with this authority he led the western squadron out of Plymouth in an attempt to settle the issue in Iberian waters. Thwarted by southerly winds, he was back in port on 22 July with several armed merchantmen in want of repair, many sick in need of treatment ashore and a lack of provisions and fresh water. The wind, which had been foul for Howard, was fair for the Duke of Medina Sidonia, commander of the Spanish Armada.

Medina Sidonia had been appointed to the chief command following the death of Santa Cruz. His administrative experience as governor-general of Andalusia included collaboration with Santa Cruz in the fitting-out of the Spanish sailing-ship fleet. Largely because of his inexperience at sea, of which, as his famous disclaimer to Philip II indicates, he was well aware, English historians have in the past tended to regard his appointment with amazement, bordering at times upon ridicule. But was his appointment any more bizarre than that of Charles Howard, who was equally inexperienced at sea? And were not both men fulfilling the aristocracy's historic function of military leadership in assuming command of non-specialised, non-professionalised sea forces at a time of crisis for their respective countries?

As far as officers are concerned, the social composition of the two fleets was not strikingly dissimilar. The English had an advantage in range and depth of fighting experience at sea through being able to call upon the services of the Drakes, the Hawkinses, the Fenners, the Winters and their followers, as well as individuals like Martin Frobisher. But the English by no means enjoyed a monopoly of experienced fighting seamen among the officers. The Spaniards, on the other hand, though many members of the nobility flocked to serve under Medina Sidonia, had no monopoly of noble blood. The ramifications within the English fleet of the Howard family serve to make this point. Charles

Howard proved, as did Medina Sidonia, a capable leader ready to profit from experienced advice; he was also a dedicated nepotist. Among the relatives holding posts of responsibility in 1588 were Lord Henry Seymour, commander in the Narrow Seas, Lord Thomas Howard, son of the fourth Duke of Norfolk, commander of the royal galleon *Golden Lion*, Lord Edmund Sheffield, commander of the *White Bear*, and Sir Robert Southwell, son-in-law to Howard, commander of the *Elizabeth Jonas*. Another son-in-law, Richard Leveson, a future vice-admiral of England, served as a volunteer on Howard's flagship the *Ark Royal*. If the sixteenth-century state still looked to the nobility to provide natural leaders of the armed services, the nobility looked to the armed services to provide it with posts of honour and profit.

The historic sighting of the Spaniards off the Lizard took place in the morning of 29 July. Two months had passed since Medina Sidonia had led them out of the Tagus, one of which had been spent at Corunna refitting ships and replacing stocks of rotting food and foul water. Medina Sidonia had now to force his way up the English Channel through enemy coastal waters – a passage along the French coast was prohibited by navigational hazards – towards the rendezvous with Parma upon which hinged the outcome of the campaign. During the next ten days, while the Armada covered the 240 nautical miles to Calais at an average speed of two knots, the protagonists remained in almost continuous contact without ever coming to really close grips.

This tentative fencing reflects the reluctance of both sides to commit themselves to a decisive battle except on terms of their own choosing. Charles Howard and the English seamen had a preference for battle at culverin range, keeping at a distance the lofty and less manoeuvrable Spanish ships and relying upon the penetrability of the culverin to achieve victory. The Spaniards proposed, should battle be forced upon them, to deny the English the advantage to be derived from manoeuvring at a comfortable distance by closing the range and getting to close quarters. 'You should,' wrote Philip II before the Armada sailed, 'take special note, however, that the enemy's aim will be to fight from a distance, since he has the advantage of superior artillery and of the large number of fireworks with which he will come provided; while ours must be to attack and come to grips with the enemy at close quarters; and to succeed in this you will need to exert every effort' (Lloyd, *The Naval Miscellany*, p. 16). But Medina Sidonia was only to fight a battle if he could not otherwise protect the passage to England of the Duke of Parma. The doctrine of A. T. Mahan that the pursuit of 'ulterior objects', such as the invasion of England, should always be subordinated to winning 'control of the sea' through the destruction of the enemy had not been heard of by anybody in 1588. When the Spaniards deployed off Plymouth on 30 July, they deployed not into an order of battle but into an order of convoy, a crescent formation in the horns of which were stationed the most powerful men-of-war. It baffled and frustrated the English throughout the Armada's progress up channel.

The channel fighting calls into question the stereotype of the sixteenth-century naval revolution as a transition from 'man-killing' to 'ship-killing' weapons. Although both sides expended more than they could afford of powder and shot in the cannonades off the Eddystone, Portland Bill and the Isle of Wight, the sound and fury signified very little. The English lost no ships; the Spaniards, two. Neither was the victim of gunfire. The *San Salvador* was irretrievably damaged by an internal explosion and captured; the *Nuestra Señora del Rosario*, flagship of the Andalusian squadron, was crippled in a collision, fell out of the formation and was later made prize by Drake. Far from providing the world with its first massed display of the destructiveness of broadside artillery fire, events in the Channel demonstrated two permanent facts of life in the sailing-ship era: the survivability of a well-handled convoy and the defensive capacity of a disciplined force of broadside sailing ships.

If battered for long enough at close quarters, ships could of course be sunk by gunfire. To this extent use of the term 'ship-killing' is valid. However, the more one studies fighting at sea in the days of sail, whether between single ships, squadrons or grand fleets, the more one is struck by the inconclusiveness of much of it and by the fact that defeated ships were less often sunk than rendered incapable of further resistance because of structural damage and heavy casualties. The English sea forces in 1588 were hardly equipped for destruction in the Mahanian sense. They had no system of fleet tactics on which to base an accurate and concentrated cannonade of the enemy. The experience of their fighting seamen with the culverin and demi-culverin, neither of which was remotely effective at a range of more than 500 yards, was considerable. It had, however, largely been gained in encounters fought either to keep would-be boarders at bay or to incapacitate often weakly defended potential prizes. The untidy cannonades failed to arrest the Armada's progress to its rendezvous with Parma. On 6 August it anchored in unbroken formation off Calais. Parma's successes in the Netherlands had not, however, extended to the capture of Flushing, which meant that there was no harbour under Spanish control capable of accommodating the Armada. This was a decisive factor in the events of the next few days.

Inherent in the dualism of the invasion plan was the risk that one arm of the two services would fail to co-ordinate its movements with those of the other. In the event, Parma was unable to bring out his barges because the invasion ports were blockaded by shallow-draught

Dutch armed boats patrolling the Flemish banks. Medina Sidonia could not lift the blockade since the banks were too shallow for his warships. Having no harbour in which to shelter, he was marooned in an open roadstead with the Flemish banks to leeward and the united squadrons of Howard and Seymour to windward. The English were thus provided with an opportunity of dislodging the formation through one of the oldest tactics of naval warfare, attack by fireships. By throwing the Spaniards into confusion, the fireships created conditions favourable for the English to close the range in the running fight off Gravelines during which Medina Sidonia gradually restored order and edged his battered force out into the North Sea in the face of fierce attacks. He paid a heavy price in casualties and structural damage and lost three front-line warships, one of them, the Biscayan *María Juan*, being sent to the bottom by gunfire.

Gravelines marked the end of the fighting. Both sides had reached, and the Spaniards had probably passed, their effective endurance as fighting machines. Avoiding the Zeeland banks with the aid of a fortuitous shift of wind, the restored crescent formation drifted away to the north. With their powder and shot almost exhausted and with stocks of food and drink running low, Medina Sidonia and his officers reconciled themselves to returning to Spain via the north-about route around Scotland and Ireland. The English, worried by similar shortages, though their ships were structurally in better shape, kept the enemy under observation from a respectful distance as far as the Firth of Forth. Having no prospect of bringing him to battle and with sick lists increasing alarmingly they then turned away.

The Spaniards were left alone to discover the price of defeat. During the long haul home a mixture of unfavourable winds, bad weather, structural damage, navigational errors and sickness caused the heaviest losses of the campaign through shipwrecks off the Scottish and Irish coasts. When it was all over, Medina Sidonia brought home two-thirds at most of the ships which had sailed with him. Some of the wrecks have in recent years become known to a wide public thanks to the nautical archaeologists. Work off Fair Isle on the Rostock freighter *El Gran Grifón*, off Lacada Point, County Antrim, on the Neapolitan galleas *La Girona*, in Kinnagoe Bay, County Donegal, on the 1,000-ton Venetian-built *La Trinidad Valencera* and in Blasket Sound, County Kerry, on the Venetian-built *Santa María de la Rosa* has yielded valuable information about the design of the ships, the casting of the guns and the sub-standard quality of the round shot. We may be sure that the sea has more secrets to yield. And such work may influence increasingly our understanding of the failure of the Armada, particularly its failure to inflict anything more than trivial casualties and damage on the English when they closed the range at Gravelines.

The general reaction in England to the departure of the Armada was relief rather than elation. There was some feeling that it was only a matter of time before the Spaniards came again. The entrepreneurs of maritime war, who tended on the whole to underrate the power of Spain, did not see things in this light. Led by Drake and Sir John Norris, who had acquired a high military reputation in Ireland and Netherlands, and backed within court circles by Robert Devereux, Second Earl of Essex, the son of Drake's patron in the 1570s, they came forward with a scheme of separating Portugal from Spain with the aid of Dom António, of seizing the Azores and of destroying shipping at Seville. The campaign was to be largely financed by private adventurers, including London merchants interested in entering the eastern seas who looked forward to winning commercial concessions in the Portuguese empire after the establishment of António in Lisbon.

The promoters aimed to raise £40,000 and twenty well-armed merchantmen. For so ambitious an amphibious campaign, however, they needed government financial backing as well as troops, artillery and a stiffening of royal warships. The queen and council, while taking a less complacent view than Drake and the promoters of Spanish weakness, agreed to participate. It might indeed be argued that, given their incapacity to launch an offensive out of their own resources because of heavy public expenditure in 1588 and the continued financial commitment to war in the Netherlands, they had no choice but to reach an agreement as the sole means of retaining some semblance of control over the maritime war. The agreement revealed a significant shift in the balance of power within the sea forces of the realm. The private adventurers were undertaking to do with state aid what the state could not yet do for itself. When the expedition, a veritable counter-armada having as one of its aims the invasion of the King of Spain's dominions, eventually sailed, it was their leader Drake, not as in 1588 the queen's lord admiral, who put to sea at the head of a vast force of six royal warships, armed merchantmen and transports with 19,000 troops on board.

The contribution made by the state was by no means negligible. In addition to six warships, the queen agreed to supply 10,000 troops, £20,000, later increased to nearly £50,000 as a result of victualling problems caused by the unauthorised recruitment of volunteers by Drake and Norris to swell the army, and a siege train which was not in the end forthcoming. State participation combined with foul winds to delay the sailing of the expedition from February to April. It would be misleading to attribute the delay, as it was once fashionable to do, to royal timidity. The contingent of 10,000 troops and transports could not be furnished without drawing upon those serving in the Netherlands. To achieve this, Dutch assistance and co-operation were indispensable.

Negotiations with the Dutch, who were suspicious about any weakening of the land forces facing Parma, were always difficult, periodically acrimonious and inevitably protracted.

The most serious consequence of the delay was that it provided time for the maturing of differences between the Crown and the adventurers over the aims and conduct of the expedition. Elizabeth and her councillors questioned the wisdom of Drake and his fellow promoters in investing so much hope in the strength of Portuguese support for Dom António. They suspected that a Portuguese uprising in his favour would be conditional upon the success of the army after it had landed in Portugal and that the successes of the army would be conditional upon a Portuguese uprising. Having a sufficiently sizeable stake in the venture to press their views upon the promoters, they proposed that priority be given to a target apparently more attainable and certainly more in accord with the interests of government than the attempted realisation in Portugal of Dom António's flights of fancy. This was the destruction of Spanish warships which had staggered into the Biscay ports of Santander and San Sebastián in the autumn of 1588 and now lay there immobilised.

A situation had thus arisen in which the public and private sectors of English seapower were at odds over the aims and conduct of the expedition. Each was, because of its inner weakness, dependent upon the other and thus unable to seize unfettered control of the operation. Since Drake was the promoters' rather than the queen's admiral, the balance of power was probably tilted in favour of the private sector, but not so far that the queen's wishes could be dismissed out of hand. Drake, always quick to spot a catch, realised that a raid on the Biscay ports with its attendant risk of being embayed by westerly winds was incompatible with a drive upon Lisbon. Being unable to disregard the queen's intentions, he resolved the dilemma by substituting Corunna for Santander and San Sebastián on the not implausible grounds that a fleet of Baltic merchantmen laden with war material essential for the recovery of Spanish seapower had put in there. He reinforced this argument with a claim, not unequivocally supported by the evidence, that the winds were unfavourable for a passage to the Biscay ports.

Had Corunna been packed as expected with Baltic ships stuffed with naval stores, the attack there, though hardly tending to improve the chances of success in Portugal, would have made strategic and financial sense. In the event only one galleon and a handful of small ships were found in the harbour. Notwithstanding this, Drake and Norris having dealt with the vessels and seized a quantity of provisions and stores, proceeded to a vain attempt to capture the town. The explanation that they were detained by contrary winds and had no choice but to attempt something cannot in the light of the available evidence be totally rejected; but given the way in which the expedition had been financed, the leaders' decision may well have been influenced by the prospects of pillage and a ransom. Whatever the truth, the fortnight spent at Corunna had disastrous consequences. Already depleted by desertions, the expedition was gripped at Corunna by a deadly sickness which was probably rooted in victualling deficiencies, though attributed by Monson to 'the immoderate drinking of the soldiers'.

After Corunna, despite the arrival of welcome reinforcements with the Earl of Essex on board, the heart seems to have gone out of things. For the Lisbon operation the army was put ashore at Peniche, forty-five miles north of the capital. It marched through apathetic countryside, continuously losing men through desertion and disease, to reach the gates of Lisbon, the defences of which were effectively manned, six days later. Drake meanwhile was out of communication at this critical stage, having sailed to the mouth of the Tagus and anchored in Cascaes road. The plan was that he should advance up the Tagus and support Norris's attack upon the capital from the river. Drake's career hitherto was crowded with examples of rapid and decisive action. Now he became curiously indecisive. Having learnt of Norris's arrival before Lisbon, he promised more than once to come up river to his aid and stayed where he was. He explained his immobility on the grounds that 'the sickness and weakness of the mariners and soldiers was so extreme as they were not able to handle the tackle of the ships' (quoted by K. R. Andrews, *Drake's Voyages: A Re-assessment of their Place in Elizabethan Maritime Expansion*, 1967, p. 143). At the same time it does appear that Drake's star was on the wane, that his confidence was sapped by the magnitude of the undertaking. After the retreat and re-embarkation of the army the process of physical and moral disintegration had gone too far to salvage anything from the wreckage of the expedition. There was talk of an Azorean operation; but *sauve-qui-peut* was the order of the day as the survivors made for England independently of each other and the leaders.

The collapse through internal stresses of the English counter-armada before it had seriously tested the defensive capacity of the enemy reflected chronic financial and organisational inadequacies. The same lack of finishing power can be detected in the failure to put into effect the idea of a 'silver blockade'. This strategy was the logical outcome of the growing belief in the 1570s and 1580s in the dependence of the King of Spain upon a steady flow of bullion from the Indies for the sustenance of his power in Europe. Its advocate was John Hawkins, who in February 1588 and at intervals thereafter gave a new twist to the commonplace belief that commerce raiding was the key to victory by proposing that systematic blockade by regular warships was the key to successful commerce raiding.

In the continuance of this war I wish it to be ordered in this sort, that first, we have as little to do in foreign countries as may be but of mere necessity, for that breedeth great charge and no profit at all.

Next, that there be always six principal good ships of her Majesty's upon the coast of Spain, victualled for four months and accompanied with some six small vessels, which shall haunt the coast of Spain and the Islands, and be a sufficient company to distress anything that goeth through the seas. And when these must return, there would be other six good ships, likewise accompanied to keep the place. So should that seas be never unfurnished; but as one company at the four months end doth return, the other company should always be in the place.

The charge of these companies would not be above 1,800 men in one fleet, which may be £2,700 a month for wages and victuals. And it will be a very bad and unlucky month that will not bring in treble that charge, for they can see nothing but it is presently their own.

If this may be done with so easy a charge, and recompensed double and treble, why should we stick at it? Some will say, the king will always make a fleet to beat us from the coast. There is no doubt but, with an infinite charge, he may make an army. But it shall be sufficient that this small company shall live daily in their sight and weary them, and gain daily upon them. For an army, as he provideth, cannot continue any long time. His fleet from the Indies and all places can have hard escaping; which if we might once strike, our peace were made with honour, safety and profit (Laughton (ed.), *State Papers*, pp. 60 ff.).

Whether Hawkins was right in his assessment of Philip II's dependence upon 'his fleet from the Indies' we do not know because it was never tested. Whether he was right in believing that systematic blockade of the western approaches to the Iberian peninsula could be enforced even by squadrons of regular warships whose nearest base was distant Plymouth is open to question.

The Earl of Essex, leader of a spectacular raid upon Cádiz in 1596, underlined this point in a paper on strategy written shortly after his return to England from the operation. Like Hawkins, Essex regarded systematic blockade as the infallible recipe for victory. Taking a somewhat wider view than many of his contemporaries, he believed that Spain's capacity to continue the war was dependent upon the security of two maritime lifelines: that from the silver mines of Peru and that from the plains and forests of Northern Europe, the source of indispensable supplies of corn and naval stores. He urged that both could be cut simultaneously by the proper application of force in Iberian waters. Unlike Hawkins he associated the success of a blockade with the establishment of a bridgehead on the enemy coast in a port to which the blockading squadron could resort 'for harbour and succour'. He described naval operations attempted without such as 'idle wanderings upon the sea' and recommended the seizure of such place or places by an élite striking force 'that shall be able to conquer and dwell' (L. W. Henry, 'The Earl of Essex as Strategist and Military Organizer (1596–7)', *English Historical Review*, vol. 48, 1953, pp. 363 ff.).

Essex's dismissive reference to 'idle wanderings upon the sea' reflect his disillusionment with a blockade through which the bulk of Spanish trade and the king's consignments of bullion, though sometimes delayed, had passed with disconcerting ease and regularity. As a comment upon events, it is fair. Between 1589 and 1591 squadrons commanded by Hawkins himself, Martin Frobisher, Lord Thomas Howard and Richard Grenville, and, if we may include a force with a high proportion of private ships, George Clifford, Earl of Cumberland, had cruised in Azorean and Iberian waters without achieving the promised results. The curtain came down in 1591 after Howard and Grenville were overtaken off Flores in the Azores by a superior enemy squadron under Alonso de Bazán. Howard successfully retreated with the majority of the ships; but his vice-admiral Grenville on board the queen's galleon *Revenge* was cut off. After a prolonged resistance, Grenville was killed and the *Revenge* forced to surrender.

This defeat was followed by the virtual withdrawal of regular warships from the enterprise and its abandonment to uncoordinated flocks of privateers. The support of the crown had in any case never been more than fitful. Instead of continuous blockade by regular squadrons operating in rotation there had been intermittent cruises in the focal areas of the transatlantic trade on the expiration of which the seas were left open for considerable intervals. Whatever one's doubts about the possibility of enforcing a blockade in waters remote from base, it must be said of Hawkins's 'blue-water' strategy that it failed because it was never tried. Responsibility for this belonged to the queen and council, who more than once broke the pattern by diverting warships to other operations. During the winter of 1589–90, for example, Hawkins fitted out six warships with which to institute the blockade in early spring. In February 1590, however, he was forbidden to sail because of reports of a Spanish squadron being equipped at Corunna. In June 1590 a squadron of six warships under Martin Frobisher was sent to the Azores and Hawkins was sent out to watch Corunna. Victualled for six months, Hawkins planned to relieve Frobisher in October when the latter, who was supplied for four months, came to the end of his tour of duty. He was still off Corunna when he was recalled to home waters because of Spanish activity in Brittany.

The explanation of the government's failure to back consistently a strategy which was certainly cheap and potentially profitable is that its freedom of action was restricted by uncomfortable facts and disturbing uncertainties. Hawkins's call for oceanic warfare as an alternative to continental warfare was overtaken by the danger that the war might be lost on the Continent before it was won on the ocean. The defeat of the Spanish Armada had not diminished Parma's prospects in the Netherlands, which meant that an already straitened treasury had to find the means of making a major military and financial contribution to the Dutch cause. Then the murder in Paris in August 1589 of Henry III, the last king of the house of Valois, led to the creation of a new war zone in northern France as Spain combined with the French Catholic League, whose centres of power were chiefly in Paris and the country north of the Loire, to block the succession of the legitimate claimant Henry of Navarre, the leader of the Huguenots. Elizabeth had no option but to go to the aid of Navarre, for the crisis which followed the death of Henry III threatened to turn northern France into a base of Spanish power.

Spanish military interventions were two-pronged. Three thousand five hundred troops were sent from Spain to Brittany in September 1590. Detachments from Flanders led by Parma himself crossed the frontier to the relief of the garrison of Paris in August 1590, and that of Rouen, where Parma received the wound from which he died later in the year, in April 1592. A Spanish force was stationed in Paris from February 1591 until the fall of the capital to Navarre in March 1594. After Navarre had won recognition as Henry IV and declared war on Spain in 1595, a campaign in Picardy led to the Spanish capture of Calais in April 1596 and to a briefer occupation of Amiens in 1597. Although in retrospect Philip II's attempt to subvert the legitimate succession to the French throne may seem to have been a colossal miscalculation, the Spanish presence in Brittany and Normandy was a threat to English interests. It revived fears, commonplace in the youth of the queen and her generation, of hostile concentrations across the Channel; fears which were exacerbated in the 1590s by an uneasy feeling that the outcome might have been different in 1588 had the Spaniards had access to a port in northern France. Until the mid-1590s therefore, when the French monarchy and the northern provinces of the Netherlands appeared to be reasonably secure, the struggle for survival required a continuous financial and military contribution to the campaigns in Brittany, Normandy and the Netherlands. The collapse in north-western Europe of the anti-Spanish cause would have tilted the balance of maritime power against England not only by making the Channel the first as well as the last line of defence but by providing Spain with advanced bases for a drive for mastery in the northern seas. The ragged, ill-paid English armies in France and the Netherlands manned the barricades of English seapower. The alternative to a continental commitment was the prospect of being outdone at sea.

Even from Iberian bases Spanish squadrons harassed and inhibited the English throughout the 1590s. Far from being a time when the English were free to impose upon history their own version of the influence of seapower, the last nine years of Philip II's reign were relatively prosperous for the Spanish navy. The first sign that the Spaniards were preparing for a renewal of the maritime war was the movement from Santander to Corunna for refit in July 1589 of some sixty warships including galleons. This fleet in being caused the postponement of Hawkins's 'silver blockade' in February 1590. More disturbing again from the English point of view was the renaissance of the Spanish sea forces through an energetic shipbuilding programme. Beginning in 1589, Philip II built a fighting navy, spearheaded by more than twenty galleons, of which twelve 1,000-ton ships − the so-called Twelve Apostles − were completed by 1591. Altogether some seventy warships of all rates, including the *galizabras* employed with such success on the treasure routes, were built between 1589 and 1598, the majority under the direction and supervision of royal officials. The ideal of a navy composed exclusively of royal warships continued to elude Philip because of the incapacity of the Spanish shipbuilding industry to meet his demands. He made good the deficit through the systematic commandeering and hiring of merchantmen in Iberian, Mediterranean and Adriatic ports.

The defeat of Howard and Grenville off Flores in 1591 was a sign of the times. It made clear that there could be no 'silver blockade' without a reinforcement of the squadrons on overseas service. In other words the cheap and profitable victory envisaged by Hawkins was already out of reach. With a Spanish army in Brittany threatening the occupation of Brest, there could be no reduction in the number of ships available for service in waters around the British Isles. The security of England, not to mention that of Ireland, was complicated by the prevailing south-westerly winds which made it easier for the Spaniards to sail for the British Isles at times of their own choice than for the English to intercept them. 'Command of the sea,' as Cyril Falls reminds us in *Elizabeth's Irish Wars*, 'becomes a relative phrase when applied to a situation in which the fleets of one belligerent and their accompanying transports may evade those of its foe and plant an army on its soil' (p. 8). This hit-or-miss element in sixteenth-century naval warfare kept the English on tenterhooks, for they could not predict the time or the place of a second coming by the Spaniards.

These inhibiting factors, reinforced by a Spanish hit-and-run raid mounted from Brittany against the Cornish coast, influenced the attitude of the queen to plans of Drake and Hawkins for a raid on the

Caribbean in August 1595, when the eased situation in north-western Europe made possible a renewed search for a naval offensive. The original plan, with which Drake and Hawkins had been associated since 1593, was for an operation against the isthmus of Panama. The expedition, like that of 1589, was jointly financed by the queen, who also furnished six warships, and private adventurers clustered around Drake and Hawkins who were appointed to a joint command overall. It was sponsored at court by the rising star of English offensive strategy, the Earl of Essex, through whose influence Sir Thomas Baskerville was appointed to command the army of about 1,000 men. However, as the time for sailing drew near, the queen's anxieties for the security of the realm produced a clash, comparable to that of 1589, between the interests of government and those of the adventurers.

> Besides this it is certain that these preparations made in Spain are so great as the like were not in the year 1588 and it is not to be doubted but that the intention is in the next summer with the same great armies to invade our realms of England and Ireland also. Whereupon we found it very dangerous to yield to your departure at this present, especially before the present attempt for Ireland might be discovered. But most of all dangerous if you should not the next summer in convenient time be returned to help to do some service according to the strength of your ships against the Spanish army that should attempt the invasion of this realm, which is to be thought would be attempted about June or July if not sooner. But forasmuch as we are sufficiently informed both by men of good experience here as also by that assurance which yourselves upon your departure gave us that you shall not need for any action of importance to tarry out longer than six months at the furthest, unless you should spend time in other unnecessary or vain attempts wherein we little doubt of *your* discretion seeing you can well consider that as *our* affairs do stand, time to us is a thing most precious: we have thought good to let you know that both in regard that your own delays hath made your journey and purposes now so notorious (yea in particular to the Spaniard) as they have sufficient warning to provide for your descent, and seeing that by one of his fleets already being safe came home his means are so increased as if the other be not some way intercepted or diminished he shall be in better case than ever he was, and we by your absence worse furnished than ever. (K. R. Andrews (ed.), *The Last Voyage of Drake and Hawkins*, Hakluyt Society, 2nd series, Vol. 142, p. 23)

The differences were resolved by a substitute scheme, to which the queen gave assent at the end of August, that the expedition should make first for San Juan de Puerto Rico where, according to fresh intelligence, a disabled ship laden with bullion was to be found, strike next at Panama and return by mid-May 1596. Panama, a major blow at which would have damaged Spain's financial and political standing, was now a secondary target in what had become a state-backed treasure hunt.

Differences between the adventurers themselves turned the treasure hunt into a misadventure. The appointment of Drake and Hawkins to a joint command has always been something of a mystery, since their incompatibility in personality and methods of work was well known. The one documented contemporary explanation is that the queen imposed Hawkins on Drake to bridle him. It seems more likely, since both were involved in the preliminary planning, that the arrangement was the result of a temporary alliance between competing factors in the world of privateering, each of which expected through its figurehead to be represented in the leadership. This explanation receives some support from the list of private ships and commanders which gives the impression of a force made up of two divisions: one packed with followers of Drake, the other with those of Hawkins. It is strengthened by Thomas Maynarde, a young kinsman and follower of Drake, to whom we owe the observation that 'this fleet was divided into 2 squadrons not that it was so appointed by her Majesty for from her was granted a powerful authority unto either of them over the whole, as any part' (Andrews (ed.), *The Last Voyage*, p. 87) and that the two squadrons were separately victualled. Maynarde also commented in his narrative upon tension between the two commanders during the preparations at Plymouth, noting that 'whom the one loved the other smally esteemed'.

On the sixth day at sea there was a quarrel between Drake and Hawkins over victualling and a week later an even more bitter quarrel over Drake's proposal for an attack upon either Madeira or Grand Canary. This proposal, motivated by anxiety over profit and provisions, was at variance not only with their instructions but with all previous understandings. John Hawkins, slave trader and professional maritime predator, is not a particularly sympathetic figure, but he has some claim to be more highly regarded than Francis Drake as a founding father of English naval strategy and considerable entitlement to sympathetic consideration during the public row with Drake on the newly built queen's warship *Defiance*. Strategically, Drake's proposal, which had the support of Baskerville, made little sense. As the queen had already pointed out the Spaniards had probably discovered during the long period of preparation that a strike against the Caribbean was intended and that any further loss of time might be fatal to its chances of success. Now the man, who had written in 1588 that the advantage of time and place was half a victory, showed little appreciation of either. The strength of his following and the support of Baskerville enabled him to win the argument and to lose the campaign.

Not only was the attack on the Grand Canary a failure, the time lost proved to be irrecoverable. Time was of the essence. The idea that the Spaniards undertook systematic counter-measures throughout 1595 in response to accurate and up-to-date intelligence of English intentions does not stand up to close examination. Although there was a general alert in the Caribbean, both San Juan de Puerto Rico and Panama were vulnerable at the time of the expedition's departure from Plymouth at the beginning of September. The sailing from Sanlúcar to San Juan, two days after Drake and Hawkins had put to sea, of five frigates under Pedro Tello de Guzman to collect the bullion was no more than a tardy, routine precaution. Pedro Tello did not know that the English were at sea; much less that San Juan was their target. Had it not been for the delay at the Grand Canary, Drake and Hawkins would have almost certainly got off Puerto Rico before the arrival of the frigates and taken the defenders unaware. As it happened, Pedro Tello arrived before them with the urgent information collected from the crew of an English straggler, the bark *Francis*, that the enemy had entered the Caribbean and was on his way. This fortuitous incident made all the difference, for the Spaniards, apart from unloading the treasure and bringing it ashore, rapidly completed their defensive preparations by both land and sea in such fashion as to be able successfully to resist the English attack. The capture of the *Francis* was a piece of bad luck for the English; but it can be fairly said that they had made their own bad luck.

John Hawkins died of illness off Puerto Rico, leaving Drake in command. Drake was under strain, talking vaingloriously as they sailed away of leading the expedition to even richer places. As the news of the happenings at Puerto Rico spread rapidly across the Caribbean to distant Panama, one catches glimpses of the pressures under which Francis Drake was labouring during what proved to be the closing weeks of his life. This was his attempted come-back six years after the Lisbon fiasco and subsequent eclipse from favour. It would be judged in the brutally competitive Elizabethan maritime community by its success as a treasure hunt. 'We must,' he remarked to Maynarde, 'have gold before we return to England.' He believed, or affected to believe, that the answer to his problems lay in Panama. But since the abortive attempt upon Puerto Rico, the military authorities on the isthmus had accepted reinforcements from Peru. Baskerville's attempted march across the mountains from Nombre de Dios was repulsed with considerable losses from enemy action and disease. Drake now seems gradually to have come to terms with the painful truth that 'he never thought any place could be so changed, as it were from a delicious and pleasant arbour, into a waste and desert wilderness, besides the variableness of the wind and weather so strong and boisterous as he never saw it before, but he most wondered that since his coming out of England he never saw sail worthy the giving chase unto' (Andrews (ed.), *The Last Voyage*, p. 101). Drake died wretchedly, as did so many of his companions on the voyage, of dysentery. If Maynarde is to be believed, his last days were overshadowed by a mood of disenchantment in the fleet. 'Like as upon the coming of the sun, dews and mists begin to vanish, so our blinded eyes began now to open and we found that the glorious speeches of a hundred places that they knew in the Indies to make us rich was but a bait to draw her Majesty to give them honourable employments and us to adventure our lives for their glory' (Andrews (ed.), *The Last Voyage*, p. 99).

Had Drake come home with the defeated expedition, he would have found himself eclipsed. He would have also found preparations afoot, in spite of, and to some extent because of, the recent Spanish occupation of Calais and the threat therein to the security of the realm, for an operation against the Spanish mainland. Various targets seem to have come under consideration, including Ferrol, which was increasingly a principal base of the Spanish navy. In an age when close and continuous observation of distant enemy bases was ruled out by organisational and technical deficiencies, an eliminatory raid upon a fleet in being offered a solution to the other otherwise insoluble problem of masking its movements. Ferrol, however, was rejected in favour of Cádiz because of its prestige and the wealth of merchantmen having resort there. War against enemy property as a means of serving one's country and making one's fortune was always likely to win an Elizabethan strategic argument.

Despite the treasure-hunting element the Cádiz expedition showed some signs of a shift away from the view that offensive war could be safely entrusted to private entrepreneurs. When it sailed at the beginning of June the expedition numbered over a hundred ships including a Dutch contingent of eighteen ships-of-war and six victuallers. The army, stiffened with 2,000 veterans from the Netherlands campaign, numbered perhaps some 8,000 men. The English sea forces were divided into four squadrons, each one of which had under its convoy a group of victuallers and transports. At the head of the first squadron was the lord admiral, Charles Howard, who flew his flag as in 1588 on board the *Ark Royal*. Howard's vice-admiral was his son-in-law Sir Robert Southwell who was on board the *Lion*. The second squadron was commanded by the joint leader of the operation, the Earl of Essex, who had as his captain on board the *Repulse* William Monson, author of the famous *Naval Tracts*, an important, if sometimes misleading, source for the study of the Elizabethan navy. Lord Thomas Howard led the third squadron, having as vice-admiral Robert Dudley of the house of Leicester. Walter Ralegh, in the new royal galleon *Warspite*, the first ship to bear this famous name, led the fourth squadron with Robert Crosse, who had been closely linked with Drake, as vice-admiral.

Not since the general mobilisation of 1588 had government equipped so large a fleet. With the lord admiral again at sea in command of a force which included seventeen royal galleons, this was something like a navy of England hurling defiance at the king of Spain by laying waste one of his harbours and the traders and men-of-war discovered there. Even so, the Crown's capacity to control its armed services at a distance from England and its officers' capacity to control either themselves or the forces under them remained limited. Though a demonstration of Spain's vulnerability to the long arm of English sea power and hence a humiliation to her, the expedition did not fulfil all the expectations of its members. Damage to Spanish warships included the destruction of two galleons of the Twelve Apostles class and the capture of two others. Many richly laden merchantmen were burnt by the Spaniards themselves as an alternative to their being made prize by the enemy. But the raid developed into an orgy of pillage with Essex's arguments in favour of permanent occupation being submerged in a general desire among all ranks for personal enrichment and a rapid return home with the loot, most of which found its way into private pockets rather than into the treasury.

It was this aspect of things which prompted Essex, who was convinced that the place could have been held, to advocate a systematic blockade of Spain enforced through the occupation of a suitable harbour on Iberian soil for the use of a blockading squadron. His strategic ideas made sense to the council, which was receptive to the argument that such a blockade would not only threaten the silver fleets but also the flow of naval stores and corn from the forests and granaries of Northern Europe. Recognition of the importance of the Baltic trade to Spain's capacity to make war is one of the maturer aspects of Elizabethan strategic thought. The government had been trying with small success since 1589 to impede the carrying trade between the Baltic and the Iberian peninsula by restricting the passage through the Dover Straits of northern merchantmen laden on Spanish account. It was quite unable, however, to attempt the closure of the north-about route around Scotland and Ireland and was attracted by Essex's claim that the trade could be effectively blocked by the consistent application of force at the receiving end. England's attitude to the Baltic trade incurred the opposition of neutral states in Northern Europe and, remarkably enough, that of the Dutch, who regarded participation in a lucrative trade with the common enemy as a means of raising essential revenues to meet the expense of continued war. These sixteenth-century quarrels foreshadow later conflicts over belligerent and neutral rights and English rejection, sometimes in the teeth of armed opposition, of the doctrine of 'the freedom of the seas'. Although unable to impose them upon foreigners with interests of their own, the Elizabethan government attempted to apply these principles throughout the war.

The government also saw other advantages in the employment against the enemy mainland of a select force of crack troops in collaboration with the fleet. In October 1596, Philip II, partly as a reprisal for the Cádiz raid and partly as a response to overtures from the Irish chieftain Hugh O'Neill, Earl of Tyrone, had launched an armada from Ferrol. Though scattered by autumnal gales, it was evidence of the threat to the British Isles posed by the Ferrol squadron. Its destruction was therefore made the primary target of a combined operation, spearheaded by seventeen royal galleons, which was fitted out for the summer campaign of 1597 under the command of Essex with Thomas Howard and Walter Ralegh serving as squadron leaders.

If all had gone well, 1597 might have been a memorable year for the development of offensive strategy from both the naval and commercial points of view. It proved impossible, however, to hold things together in the face of bad weather and unfavourable winds which forced the expedition to turn back and then detained it in Plymouth where the consumption of victuals at a rate higher than their replenishment and the appearance of sickness rattled Essex to the extent of causing him to disband most of the military force. He led the fleet instead, though an attack on Ferrol was still the ostensible objective, on the so-called Islands Voyage to the Azores where it achieved no more than the earlier forays recently criticised by Essex himself as idle wanderings upon the sea. Essex was to an extent the victim of circumstances over which he had little or no control; but his failure was also one of personality. Despite the fertility of his ideas, he was insufficiently stable to carry them through when faced with practical problems and found release in adventuring. Nor was the experiment with courtly leadership as opposed to that of professional seamen a success. The campaign in Azorean waters was flawed by the inexperience as sea commanders of Essex and Ralegh and disturbed by the quarrels between them. The substitution of quarrelsome self-interested courtiers for quarrelsome self-interested seamen could not transform even a formidable fleet of royal warships into a professional navy.

Fifteen ninety-seven was also the year of the third Spanish armada. It sailed from Ferrol in early October, narrowly missing Essex on his return as the tracks of the two fleets converged in the south-western approaches to the English Channel. Made up of 136 ships carrying 4,000 seamen and 9,000 soldiers, the third armada was Philip II's last throw against England. Led by Martin de Padilla y Manrique, it was to pick up a squadron of galleys and a detachment of infantry in Brittany and proceed to the occupation of Falmouth as a bridgehead for the conquest of England. It encountered no opposition from the English, but was driven away, when almost in sight of the Lizard, by a fierce north-easterly gale, thus meeting the same fate as its predecessor in 1596. Not only was this campaign Philip II's last enterprise of England; it was also Spain's. Financially and physically exhausted by the continental and maritime wars, Spain began to seek accommodations, the first to be completed being the treaty of Vervins with France in 1598, the year of Philip II's death. By the treaty Spain withdrew from Calais and Brittany, thus abandoning her pretensions to a forward base on the English Channel. The only threat thereafter to English interests in the Channel was the dashing galley campaign in the Narrow Seas against Dutch and English shipping led by Frederigo Spinola from Sluys which ended with his death in May 1603 in an engagement with Dutch men-of-war.

The year of the last enterprise of England was also the year of the last great Elizabethan naval offensive. After the Islands Voyage the government, harassed by financial difficulties, the growing reluctance of shipowners in both London and the outports to contribute to the fitting out of fleets, the unwillingness of seamen to enter the service of the Crown and the drain of war in Ireland, surrendered the initiative to privateers outside the waters of north-western Europe. The only cruise of note thereafter by a regular squadron was that led by Richard Leveson, Howard's son-in-law, whom we last encountered as a volunteer on board the *Ark Royal* in 1588, and Sir William Monson in 1602. The squadron, however, was not equipped on the scale of those of 1596–7. Although it made prize of a wealthy carrack, cut out from Cezimbra Bay, it found the elusive treasure fleet, which was actually sighted between the Azores and Spain, too strongly protected.

The impact of privateering was considerable. The queen and her court, landowning gentry, permanent officials of the navy, the great London companies, individual merchants and shipowners, all participated as promoters or active adventurers or both. Privateering gave expression to residual feudal aspirations, to contemporary entrepreneurial aptitudes and to a spirit of individualism untamed by Tudor despotism. It did not fit into the attritional patterns of formal sixteenth-century sea warfare in which, generally speaking, defence had the upper hand and could not therefore be subordinated to a strategy of sea power. It can be seen to have flourished because of restraints upon the Crown's capacity to raise taxes and to mobilise ships and seamen. At the same time, by financing war out of its own resources it eased the financial burdens of the Crown. In so far as much of its effect was uncoordinated and unprofitable, privateering was an unreliable foundation of naval strength.

Its contribution to the war effort should not, however, be underrated, if only because it included some spectacular achievements. The richest single prize of the war, the Portuguese carrack *Madre de Dios*, valued at £150,000, was taken off the Azores in 1592 by ships of a syndicate headed by the brothers Walter and Carew Ralegh. In 1598 the Earl of Cumberland made a loud noise, though not an outstanding profit, by succeeding where Drake had failed, in capturing and sacking San Juan de Puerto Rico. William Parker of Plymouth, who is known to have made six sorties into the Caribbean, crowned his career in 1601 by making a surprise attack on Porto Bello which he seized and held for one day, packing his vessels with bullion valued at 10,000 ducats.

The great official raid of 1595–6 was a failure, but English infiltrations of the Caribbean were a commonplace of war. We have evidence that 235 raiders visited this sea between 1585 and 1603. The peak of the effort was in the 1590s when 56 expeditions, which included 137 individual voyages, were fitted out for the West Indies. Even in the last three years of the war, after the peak was passed, ten expeditions sailed there. This continual though haphazard harassment cost Spain no colonies and little treasure; but it created a state of chronic insecurity in the Caribbean, helped to open its ports to contraband trade, Dutch as well as English, and forced up the expense of defence. Financial strains and the crippling of the Spanish mercantile marine, through losses in European as well as overseas waters, combined with inflationary pressures to increase the cost of shipbuilding and repairs in Spain. One of its victims was the Spanish navy. During the 1590s Philip II had succeeded in maintaining a fleet of forty to sixty-nine ships; between 1601 and 1607 his successor Philip III did not succeed in maintaining more than thirty-two.

After the treaty of Vervins there were financial and political arguments in favour of a negotiated peace between England and Spain. Neither had the striking power to inflict a decisive defeat on the other; both had an interest in bringing to an end an attritional war of financial exhaustion which could be of benefit only to France. At this late hour, however, Philip III and his advisers were tempted by the prospect of creating a 'Netherlands' within the British Isles. In the second half of the 1590s, Tyrone's rebellion from his power base in Ulster had gained support far beyond the confines of the northern province. It had assumed the aspect of an Irish struggle for political independence from England and turned Ireland into a major theatre of war which absorbed the energies and resources of the Elizabethan government and opened up a major chink in its defences. From the Spanish point of view, here was an opportunity not to liberate Ireland from English rule but to use the situation there as a political lever with the aim of negotiating peace on favourable terms. After much debate it was decided in 1601 to send help to Tyrone.

The expedition sailed from Lisbon in September 1601. Commanded by Don Juan del Águila, who had made his reputation under Parma and had since served in Brittany, its composition reflected the increasing enfeeblement of Spain's military and naval potential. Though not necessarily too late, it was almost certainly too little: about 4,500 effective troops and a fleet of thirty-three sail, twenty being ships of the Crown, which was under orders to return after the landing had been made. The army was thus to be abandoned as a hostage to fortune. It was too small to break out of any bridgehead that might be established on the Irish Coast and fight an independent campaign. For this reason Águila favoured a landing at Killybegs, County Donegal, with the aim of quickly joining forces with the northern rebels. He was overruled by a majority which believed that intervention in the south would set the whole of Ireland ablaze by bringing the lords and towns of Munster out in rebellion against the Crown. A landing was therefore made at Kinsale, supplemented later by detachments thrown along the coast of West Cork into Castlehaven, Baltimore and Berehaven.

The Spaniards in Kinsale were as remote as they could possibly be from the army of Tyrone and his ally Hugh O'Donnel and too weak to prevent the English general Mountjoy from blocking them up within the town. Their situation was made worse in November by the unopposed entry into Kinsale harbour of an English fleet under Richard Leveson. Apart from some movement among the lords of the south-west of the province, Munster did not stir. Águila, who had come to give support to Tyrone, was now dependent upon Tyrone for rescue. The attempted rescue failed dismally with the rout of the Irish army outside Kinsale. The rout was a greater disaster for Ireland than for Spain since it led to the virtual collapse of serious resistance to English rule. For Spain the capitulation and withdrawal of Águila and his men was no more than a strategic setback, the result of inexpert advice, failing resources and lack of confidence in the navy's ability to avoid defeat if confronted by the English.

If we take stock of things as the war neared its end, the question of confidence can be seen to have been a matter of importance. Since the 1580s the Spaniards had built a sailing-ship navy which enjoyed considerable defensive success as keeper of the King of Spain's imperial communications, denying to the English the rewards anticipated by them in the sixteenth-century battle of the Atlantic. Its offensive activity, on the other hand, was furtive. The second and third armadas failed because they sailed for the British Isles at an unseasonable time of the year when autumnal gales were probable and the nights were getting longer. The role of the navy in the Irish expedition was that of a quick dash to and from the theatre of operations. A contributory factor here may have been the attritional defensive concepts of Mediterranean galley warfare in which the majority of Spanish sea officers had been reared. More fundamental was the Crown's failure to remedy the ills of the Spanish armaments industry. The Spanish Armada of 1588 had set sail with a warning from Philip II about the English superiority in artillery. We catch echoes of this thirteen years later in the reminder to Diego de Brochero y Añaya, naval leader of the Irish expedition, that the enemy trusted in artillery and would not attempt to board. The strain of trying to achieve great-power status by both land and sea in an age of inflation exacerbated not only the problems of shipbuilding and arms manufacture but the problem of manning as well. This was by no means peculiar to Spain where the Crown's inability to compete with private rates of pay to seamen forced it into increasingly desperate methods of compulsion which were bitterly resented by seamen and frequently evaded. Brochero sailed in September 1601, full of complaints about the number of foreigners, including English prisoners, who had been pressed into service to man the king's ships.

The English, however, did not win the Spanish war. They did not break 'that great empire in pieces' as Walter Ralegh believed they would have done had the queen listened more attentively to her men of war than to her scribes. The Anglo-Spanish peace of 1604 registered a cessation of hostilities based upon a mutual recognition of what seemed to be the facts. It was clear that the Spaniards could neither be dislodged from the southern Netherlands nor compelled to make the sort of concessions in government that would make possible a peaceful reunification of the whole of the Netherlands under Spanish rule. It was also clear that the Seven United Provinces, already becoming known as the Dutch Republic, could preserve their independent status without foreign military aid. As for the New World and Asia, Spain successfully resisted any formal acknowledgement that the English had a legal right of access. If in this sense the Iberian monopoly remained juridicially intact, the English were not compelled as a condition of peace to formally acknowledge the monopoly and were thus left free, in their own opinion at least, to apply the doctrine of effective occupation.

Ralegh's criticism, besides giving the false impression that the queen's men of war spoke with a united voice, reflected the tendency of fighting seamen and occasional fighting seamen, like Ralegh himself, to underrate the durability of Spain. With the advantage of hindsight, it might appear possible to argue that the Spanish empire could at least have been badly dented had the queen mounted a sustained and coherent maritime offensive spearheaded by the regular forces of the Crown and supported by the acquisition of an overseas base or bases. But against this must be set the fact that, in the poltical and social climate of Elizabethan England, no government, however bellicose, could have created a professional navy or found the means and the supporting organisation to conquer and hold an overseas base.

Within the shadow of strategic stalemate the war of plunder boomed, mainly in the eastern Atlantic and the Caribbean. The most successful ventures were those financed by partnerships of merchants, including city magnates, and professional seamen, with frequent involvement of members of the court, nobility and gentry. Such partnerships brought into being a powerful body of men interested in the promotion of oceanic commercial ventures and equipped with the appropriate navigational and managerial abilities to carry them through. Another result of privateering in the 1580s and, more especially, the 1590s was the encouragement of the English shipbuilding industry and the construction of greater numbers of ships of more than 200 tons than England had ever seen. The expenditure of so much energy and so many resources in the war of plunder probably helped in the short term by enlarging the area of private involvement to retard the professionalisation and specialisation of the English navy. In the long term, however, it fostered the skills and aptitudes which made possible England's oceanic advance in the seventeenth century and the foundation of the first overseas plantations.

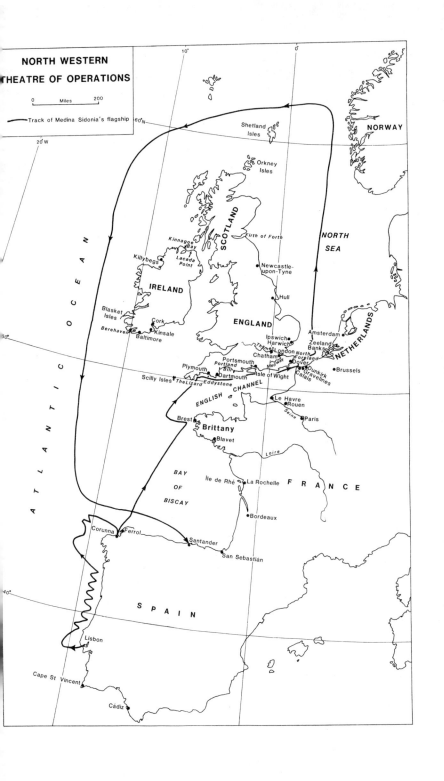

NORTH WESTERN
THEATRE OF OPERATIONS

0   Miles   200

Track of Medina Sidonia's flagship

20° W

10°

0°

NORWAY

60° N

Shetland
Isles

Orkney
Isles

SCOTLAND

Firth of Forth

NORTH
SEA

Kinnagoe
Bay
Lacada
Point

Killybegs

Newcastle-
upon-Tyne

IRELAND

Hull

Blasket
Isles

Cork

ENGLAND

Berehaven
Baltimore

Kinsale

Amsterdam

NETHERLANDS

Ipswich
Harwich
London
Chatham
Medway
Portsmouth
Portland
Bill
Isle of Wight

Zeeland
Banks
North
Foreland
Dover
Dunkirk
Gravelines
Calais

Brussels

Plymouth
Dartmouth
Scilly Isles
The Lizard
Eddystone

A T L A N T I C   O C E A N

ENGLISH   CHANNEL

Le Havre
Rouen

Brest

Paris
Seine

Brittany

Blavet

Loire

BAY

OF

BISCAY

Île de Rhé

La Rochelle

F R A N C E

Bordeaux

Corunna
Ferrol

Santander

San Sebastian

40°

S P A I N

Lisbon

Cape St Vincent

Cádiz

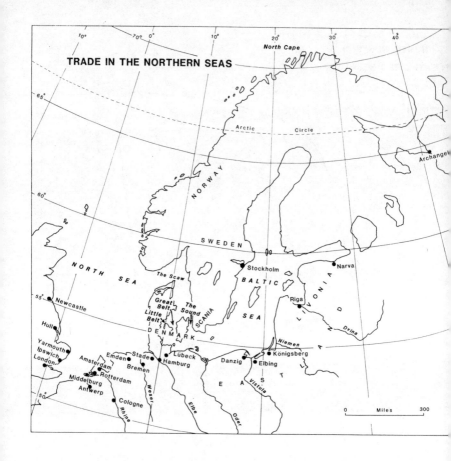

TRADE IN THE NORTHERN SEAS

North Cape

Arctic Circle

NORWAY

SWEDEN

NORTH SEA

The Scaw

Newcastle

Hull

Yarmouth
Ipswich
London

Amsterdam
Middelburg
Antwerp
Rotterdam

Emden
Bremen
Stade

Cologne

Rhine

Weser

Elbe

DENMARK

Great
Belt
Little
Belt

The Sound

SCANIA

Lübeck

Hamburg

Oder

Stockholm

BALTIC

SEA

Riga

LIVONIA

Narva

Dvina

Niemen

Danzig

Elbing

Königsberg

Vistula

Archangel

Miles 300

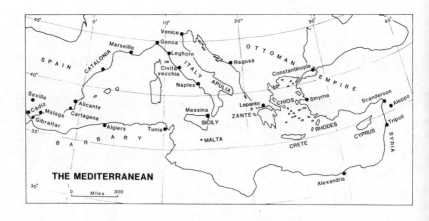

THE MEDITERRANEAN

SPAIN

CATALONIA

Marseille

Venice
Genoa
Leghorn

Civita
vecchia

Naples

ITALY

APULIA

OTTOMAN

EMPIRE

Ragusa

Constantinople

Seville
Cádiz
Málaga
Gibraltar

Alicante
Cartagena

Algiers

Tunis

Messina

SICILY

MALTA

BARBARY

ZANTE

Lepanto

CHIOS

Smyrna

RHODES

CRETE

CYPRUS

Scanderoon

Aleppo

Tripoli

SYRIA

Alexandria

0   Miles   300

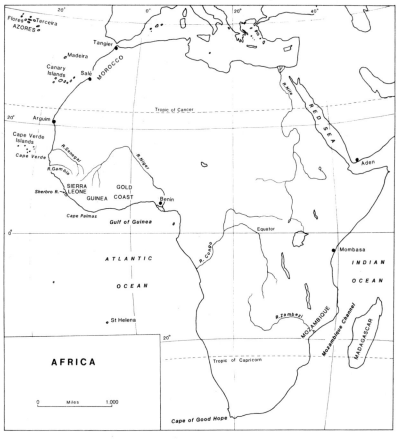

AFRICA

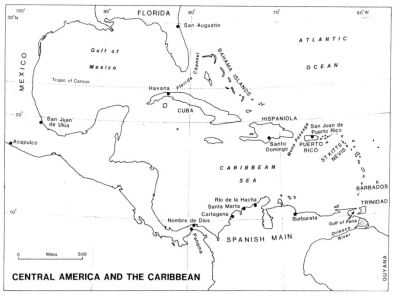

CENTRAL AMERICA AND THE CARIBBEAN

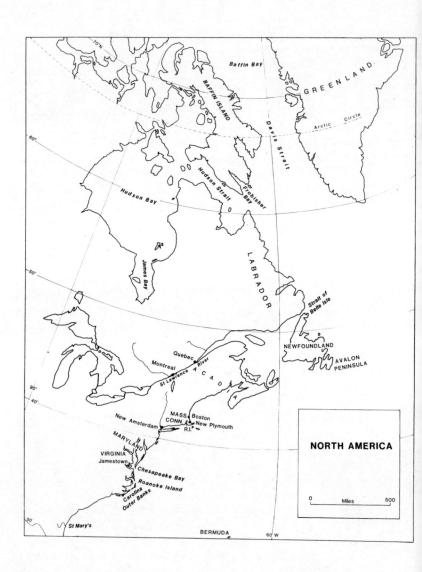

Baffin Bay

GREENLAND

BAFFIN ISLAND

Arctic   Circle

Davis Strait

Hudson Bay

Hudson Strait

Frobisher Bay

James Bay

LABRADOR

Strait of Belle Isle

NEWFOUNDLAND

AVALON PENINSULA

Quebec
Montreal

ACADIA

St Lawrence River

New Amsterdam

MASS. Boston
CONN. New Plymouth
R.I.

MARYLAND

VIRGINIA
Jamestown

Chesapeake Bay

Roanoke Island

Carolina Outer Banks

St Mary's

BERMUDA

60 W

NORTH AMERICA

0   Miles   500

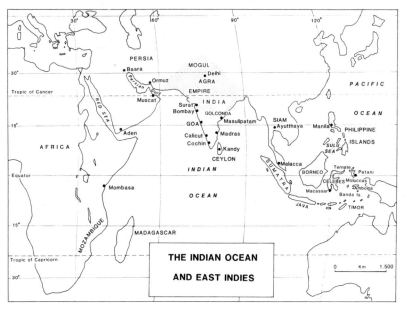

PERSIA
MOGUL
Basra
Ormuz •Delhi
AGRA
Muscat EMPIRE
RED SEA
Surat INDIA
Bombay GOLCONDA
GOA Masulipatam
Aden SIAM
Calicut Madras Ayutthaya Manila
Cochin PHILIPPINE
Kandy SULU ISLANDS
CEYLON SEA
AFRICA
INDIAN
SUMATRA Malacca
Ternate Patani
BORNEO CELEBES Moluccas
Amboina
Mombasa Macassar Banda Is.
OCEAN JAVA TIMOR
PACIFIC
OCEAN
Tropic of Cancer
Equator
MOZAMBIQUE
MADAGASCAR

THE INDIAN OCEAN

AND EAST INDIES

Tropic of Capricorn

0   Km   1.500

Peking
SEA OF
KOREA
JAPAN JAPAN
CHINA Nanking
Hirado
Nagasaki
Canton FORMOSA Tropic of Cancer
Macao
INDIA Manila
PHILIPPINES
SOUTH PACIFIC OCEAN
CHINA
SEA
Malacca
SUMATRA BORNEO Ternate
Tidore
MOLUCCAS Equator
INDIAN Batavia CELEBES NEW SOLOMON
GUINEA ISLANDS
OCEAN Sunda Strait JAVA TIMOR

AUSTRALIA
Tropic of Capricorn

THE FAR EAST

0   Miles   1.250

NEW
ZEALAND

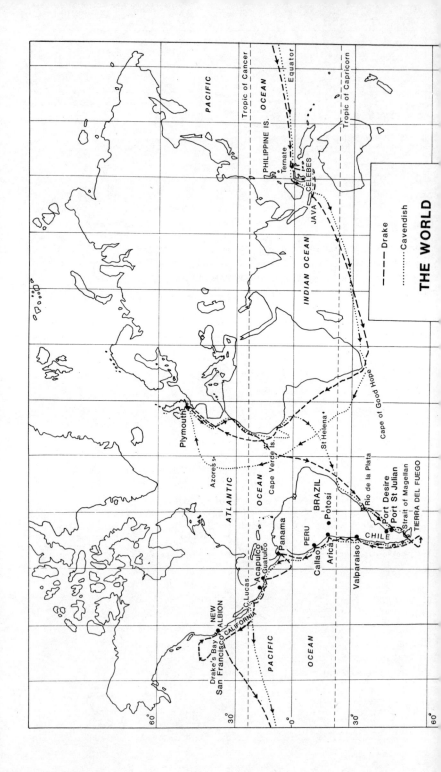

THE WORLD

---- Drake

········· Cavendish

CHAPTER 5

Plunder and Exploration in Time of War, 1585–1604

The tentative probings in the extra-European world which had marked the years before 1585 were significant of a new willingness to experiment in discovery, exploration and commerce, but they had not, except in the case of the Muscovy, Eastland and Levant Companies, which, after all, operated in spheres not wholly novel to English enterprise, yet given any clear leads on what were likely to be the principal directions of further English commercial activity. Was she going to limit her sights to the fringes of Europe and to the British Isles themselves, especially to concentrate on Ireland and the problems of the Scottish succession, limiting herself to something like a siege economy as threats of a Spanish sea invasion loomed up as early as 1582 and were intensified in 1584 after the expulsion of the Spanish ambassador, Bernardino de Mendoza, and perhaps stretching out to do something in the Netherlands where 1584 had seen the rapid extension of Spanish power, culminating in the taking of Antwerp and placing the United Provinces in the gravest jeopardy? Or was she to take up the challenge which the junction of the Spanish and Portuguese empires in 1580 presented in an attempt to drive some wedges into their overseas monopoly so as to weaken her enemy and bring gains for her own subjects and her government?

The outbreak of war in 1585, though it was undeclared war until 1587, showed that she could attempt to move forward on all these fronts. Ireland was to be a major preoccupation in these years, first as the scene of the Munster plantation in the late 1580s, and later of a war of attrition in which ten years were spent in the completion of the English reconquest of the island. The Netherlands were to absorb English money, men and armaments in large quantities throughout the period. At the same time assaults were delivered periodically against Spain, Portugal and their colonies, which played a part in preventing the great Armada of 1588 and its successors from gaining any major successes. By concentrating on attacks on Spanish commerce in the Caribbean and on Portuguese trade with Brazil, and to some extent with the East, the English were able to exploit their maritime resources and their geographical position in relation to Atlantic sea traffic to an extent which would have seemed impossible in earlier years. Yet the war had unfortunate effects on other and more positive aspects of English overseas activity. The attempt to establish colonies in North America was run down and eventually abandoned; and though there was some further limited penetration into the vast area between South America and the Cape of Good Hope, no regular English trade with Asia by sea was established. War thus brought out unexpected aggressive resources in the maritime campaigns, and distorted lines of imperialist development overseas of a more positive character.

The war with Spain began with an economic struggle and was to end with one, leaving the military and naval aspects somewhat undecided. As far back as February 1580, the astute Spanish ambassador in England, Bernardino de Mendoza, had urged Philip II to put a check on Anglo-Spanish trade as the best way to control her aggressive interest in the Netherlands and the Caribbean alike. The English, he said, 'had the carrying trade of Spanish goods in their hands for some years'. The Spanish trade had been so profitable, bringing in 'vast amounts of specie which they can get no other place' (though Drake was very soon to prove him wrong). They were supreme in the carrying trade to and from Spain with other parts of Europe and were going on building ships very rapidly in order to keep up with this. The precise extent to which this is true is difficult to define in real terms – the Dutch after all were already competing in the north – but that the Spanish trade was substantial in the late 1570s and early 1580s is undoubted. Consequently, when a ship, which had had to run a blockade, reported in May 1585 that Spain had embargoed all the English shipping in north Spanish ports, there was a sharp reaction, as this meant the probable seizure of an appreciable section of the English trading fleet. The speeding up of intervention in the Netherlands (not as it proved a very successful venture), the issue of letters of reprisal, in favour of anyone who had been wronged by the embargo or by any other Spanish action, meant that every vessel suitable for the purpose, and some which were not, went off to attack Spanish, Low Countries and neutral shipping if any excuse could be found that the ships were acting as cover for Spanish goods. This did not improve English popularity with neighbouring sea-going powers, but it had a considerable effect.

In one field alone it may be noted that it greatly altered Iberian relations with North America. Portugal had been treated as a quasi-enemy since 1580, but her merchants had some recourse to the English courts. Now, in June 1585, Bernard Drake descended on the Iberian fishing vessels in the inshore fishery in Newfoundland, took or destroyed some twenty of them and brought their crews home as criminals to be tried in English courts. Drake's ostensible function was to warn the by now considerable English Newfoundland fishing fleet not to bring any cargoes to Spain, where they had begun to develop a triangular trade in dried cod, brought from Newfoundland and exchanged for Spanish (or West Indian) goods which were then imported into England. Though the main Spanish codfishery in Placentia Bay and the more important whale fishery in the Strait of Belle Isle were not attacked, privateers, with their new licences to seize Iberian goods, endeavoured to capture as many as possible of the Basque and Portuguese vessels going westward to fish or coming homewards with fish or oil, and they were to carry on this war of attrition successfully for many years, at a time when Spanish fleets needed fish and oil in increasing quantities. On the other side, the English share of the inshore fishery rapidly increased. But Elizabeth throughout the sea war kept her fishing fleet alive and growing for the benefits it could bring to her navy and her armies (as well as by resale to other northern countries), while Spain tended to drain off too many of the fishermen, and above all the whale fishermen and their fine ships, for her navies. One ironic result was to benefit the French Basques: the English courted them for their whale oil and issued them with passports (which English privateers often did not respect), while Spain for her part encouraged the French Basque whalers to step into the places of the Spanish Basque ships and men she was taking for her own maritime needs.

The English riposts to the Spanish embargo – Francis Drake's raid upon the Caribbean in 1585–6 – though not so complete a triumph, either financially or strategically as had been expected, turned Spain away from any serious attempt at conciliation and towards the completion of the great fleet designed to sweep away English resistance. The plunder included hides, sugar, dyestuffs and a number of valuable cannon to feed the war against Spain. At the same time privateers were enriching the south-western ports, opening and providing new revenues for the Crown. The seizures of Portuguese sugarmen from Brazil, in particular, brought a glut of a hitherto scarce commodity.

Many of the products of the East and West Indies, which were formerly brought by legitimate trade to northern Europe in English, Hanseatic and Netherlands ships were now available in England in quantity (even if supplies were necessarily very uneven indeed) and could be re-exported to Germany, the Baltic and even in small quantities to the Levant, since direct external trade with Spain was becoming so much more difficult for neutral ships. This made good to some extent the loss of Spanish commodities, though olive oil was sorely missed. Captured whale oil could replace it to some extent. Train oil (fish oils of various sorts) was indeed available but did not make good soap for the cleansing processes of the cloth trade. The most bulky and frequent captures from Spanish Indiamen were hides, largely the produce of

Hispaniola and the other major Caribbean Islands. These had many uses in England, not least in ships, but there was a surplus for export also.

The privateers therefore created, within a year of the Spanish embargo, a counter-trade, which to some extent neutralised the very considerable effects of the loss of legitimate Spanish commerce, and led to some new types of re-exports. In the meantime the Levant trade, though increasingly under threat from Spanish interception, remained active, wines from the eastern Mediterranean being substituted for Iberian sweet wines and a wide range of Levant and oriental luxuries brought home. The Guinea trade was apparently flourishing, though the ships had to be willing to fight their way out and back (and might pick up prizes on the way). The Muscovy Company commerce was not in very good shape, having settled into a barely profitable exchange of stereotyped commodities. The Baltic trade, on the other hand, flourished, with naval stores being paid for with cloth as usual but also with the proceeds of the economic war against Spain. At home shipbuilding and gun-founding expanded rapidly. The new merchantmen were larger, stronger, more capable of being heavily armed, so that apart from the inevitably large number of small coastal craft, the mercantile marine was becoming increasingly a more formidable auxiliary to the queen's navy.

Though the release of the privateers — several hundred licences to recover losses from Spain by aggressive action being issued during the months from June 1585 onwards — soon began to bring in substantial dividends in the way of plunder from Iberian Atlantic commerce and, a little later, from Caribbean captures, the outbreak of the sea war caused considerable dislocation to established trades, the cutting off of the Spanish trade especially resulting in heavy losses of ships and capital as well as of commerce, and it was by no means certain for some time how far new aggression would balance out losses. The Spaniards were especially hopeful that they would not, and considered that English commerce had faltered and would die and so Spain would achieve a major victory. by a negative economic policy alone. A hopefully pessimistic analysis of English trade, stressing the chances of this occurring, was sent from London by a Spanish agent on 10 November 1586. Englishmen, he said,

were much troubled with this war which they have entered into against Spain, as the whole country is without trade, and knows not how to recover it; the shipping and commerce here having mainly depended upon the communication with Spain and Portugal. They feel the deprivation all the more now, with the loss of the cloth trade with Germany, which they formerly carried on through Holland and up the Rhine, but have now been deprived of by the capture of Nutz on that river. If Berck be taken also, which please God it will be, now that the neighbouring places have fallen, they will not be able to send any cloth at all, and this is causing much dissatisfaction all over the country. The rest of their trade with the other German ports and Muscovy is a mere trifle, as all they brought from these places was sent by them to Spain, and their Spanish trade being now gone, the other is of no use to them, as they do not know what to do with the merchandise they bring hither. All that is left to them is the Levant trade which is with Turkey and Italy, and that with Barbary. If these two are taken from them, which can easily be done, they will be driven into a corner, without any commerce or navigation at all. Their French trade is very insignificant, and is carried on by a few small vessels only. Great importance should be attached to stopping their Levant trade, which may be done by carefully guarding the Straits of Gibraltar against ships from here, whose sailing I will report and give particulars of their number, in order that a sufficient force of galleys and galleons may be placed in the Straits to stop their passage, I will also report the sailing of the ships for Barbary, in order that an effort may be made to impede that trade also; and I can assure your Lordship [Mendoza, by now ambassador in France] if this were done for a single year it would bring them perforce to surrender on any terms which His Majesty might please to dictate, both with regard to the fortresses they have seized [in the Netherlands], and the restitution of their plunder, and above all would prevent them from preying on the seas in future.

He went on to prescribe methods of better protecting the Brazilmen, the Santo Domingo merchantmen, the East India galleons and even the *flota* and *galeones*, as well as the Atlantic islands which the English threatened to seize, and ended, 'Believe me, your Lordship, when I assure you that if this be stopped the country cannot live or maintain itself.'

This forecast was not wholly an unlikely one, but in fact it was not borne out to any great extent. The cloth trade, still England's greatest export market, proved surprisingly resilient both inside Germany, those parts of the Low Countries to which the English had access and Italy, even though it had its difficulties. The Baltic trade was diverted from Spanish to English uses in building up her maritime resources for war purposes and the feeding of the armed forces. The French trade was, in fact, larger and more profitable than the Spanish agent realised, especially with Normandy, and was enlarged by co-operation between English and Rochellais privateers in pillaging Spanish and Portuguese commerce. Strangely enough, the Spanish government was not effective in stopping either the Barbary or the Levant trade, though they made some captures. They began the fortification of key points in the West Indies after Drake's attack in 1585-6 and increased the protection given to the silver fleet, but they did nothing to protect the Portuguese sugarmen coming from Brazil or even the enormous rich carracks from the East Indies from attacks which were increasingly successful. They did little even to safeguard the inter-island commerce in the Caribbean, the ships engaged in which were easy targets for the English as they had long been for the French.

Much of this neglect in the early years of the war was owed to the scale of priorities which Spain adopted. Once the silver fleet was safe – and each year the yield of silver from the New World was rising – the Spanish Crown devoted most of its energies that were not involved in the Netherlands war to the planning and construction of a major ocean-going fleet which must be safeguarded at almost any cost until it was strong enough to attack England and help to beat both Elizabeth and the Dutch into complete submission. One of England's strengths was that she was not vitally dependent on external commerce for her livelihood; one of her weaknesses was that the profits from privateering which were supposed to provide compensation primarily for those who had suffered from loss of the Spanish trade were dissipated by the crews and promoters and did not necessarily accrue to those who had lost by the breach. This was rectified as time went on by the shifting of the privateering business, for such it rapidly became, into the hands of merchant syndicates, composed to a considerable extent of the old-established London firms, who by this means simply shifted their commercial activity into other spheres, even though a considerable number of new men, sailors, gentlemen and small investors, especially in the outports, got opportunities for financial advancement that otherwise would not have come to them.

The Spanish War was far from absorbing all English overseas energies. The search for the North-west Passage was taken up by the London merchant, William Sanderson, and his associates, in co-operation with the merchants of Exeter. John Davis, in three voyages between 1585 and 1587, defined and charted the greater part of the west Greenland coast, much of the eastern part of Baffin Island and part of north Labrador, and so left an enduring name for himself in the annals of Arctic exploration. He failed to find the passage, but claimed on return that the North Water to the north-west of Greenland, which he was the first to enter, presaged a route over the Pole (which Baffin was to find fruitless in the years before 1620). His only economic return was news of fine cod fisheries and whaling opportunities far to the north of where they had hitherto been thought possible and to bring back enough fish to establish his point. Otherwise the expenditure was quite without return.

Drake had been keen to return to the Pacific after 1580 but had never managed to go. Fenton's expedition of 1582 was planned to follow up his contacts with the Moluccas and to open up trade with China (or perhaps the Philippines if Manila could be taken). But it was divided in its aims. Its leaders could not bring themselves to attempt the hardships of the Straits of Magellan or to try the alternative Cape route. Instead they compromised (as Doughty would have done in 1578) by turning back to rob ports in Brazil. Though damage was done to Portuguese settlements and some sugar and other spoil taken, this was an example of a badly run enterprise from which, however, most of the participants returned. Much more effective was that launched by the young Thomas Cavendish in 1586. With three ships he aspired to follow Drake. He did so with great ease and much good luck, choosing the best time to make the passage of the Straits. He found the Spaniards much better organised on the Pacific coast and failed to capture any of their silver ships, but from the fifteen or so vessels he destroyed (so disrupting coastwise traffic) he picked up some bullion and a miscellany of spoil. His voyage was made by the capture of the Manila galleon, the *Santa Ana*, off Cape Lucas at the tip of the California peninsula, in June 1587. From her he took a good deal of gold and jewels, and as much silk and porcelain as he could conveniently carry, putting the ship's company on shore and burning the vessel down to the waterline (she was afterwards salved), thus depriving Spain of its annual oriental cargo on which much store was set, since it supplemented Portuguese imports from the Far East.

Aided by men who had sailed with Drake, Cavendish's own ship, the *Desire*, made a good Pacific crossing, but his consort, the *Content*, was lost in the ocean. Originally he had apparently planned an attack on Manila, but, as it was, he was fortunate not to be attacked from there though he was able to reconnoitre the Sula Sea. After exploring many islands in the Philippines and other groups, he worked his way to the south of Java and there repeated Drake's feat of trading directly for pepper with one of the local rajas. The return voyage was also without serious incident and he arrived back in September 1588 to hear the news of the defeat of the Armada and to bring another instalment of spoil for his own, his backers' and the queen's benefit. The third circumnavigation was another prestige blow to Iberian monopoly of the Pacific and the East Indies as well as a useful temporary addition to English economic resources. But unless it could be followed up it had in itself little long-term significance.

The crisis with Spain had involved neglect of the fledgling colony on Roanoke Island. By late spring in 1586, Thomas Harriot and John

White had almost completed their remarkable survey of the human and physical resources of the area and their map of its islands and waterways, of which the most striking survivals are White's drawings of people, fauna and flora and Harriot's brief published tract. Ralph Lane as governor had antagonised many of the Indian groups on whom his colonists were largely dependent for food. Sir Richard Grenville was expected to arrive at Easter with supplies and reinforcements, but was unable to get away in time, probably owing to the competing demands of privateers for ships and men and supplies. A crisis in Indian relations occurred in early June which Lane resolved by an inroad into the Indians' village and the killing of the chieftain, Wingina, or Pemisapan as he had come to call himself, who had installed the colony on Roanoke Island but had come to fear and hate the Englishmen. When Drake appeared in mid-June, Lane was ready to make a change: he would reconnoitre the Chesapeake Bay, about which some knowledge had been gained, and if it offered a deep-water harbour, suitable as a long-range base for privateers operating against Spain, he would bring his men home and get Ralegh and Drake to start again in a more promising environment. A storm put an end to these plans, and after it was over Drake's diminished fleet brought the colonists willingly home in July, just about the time that Grenville, arriving too late, had given up hope of finding the colonists and had left only a token force to hold the island, he hoped, until 1587. They soon met the brunt of Indian hostility and escaped in their pinnace, never to be seen again.

The news the colonists brought back was very mixed. Some, notably White and Harriot, were optimistic, especially the latter. Harriot in his *A briefe and true reporte of the New Found Land of Virginia*, published in 1588, told how some had behaved badly to the Indians, been punished and 'slandered the country itself': others thought the prospects were no good because they had never moved far from the colony's base and knew nothing of the country, and, he went on:

> Some also were of a nice bringing up, only in cities or towns, or such as never . . . had seen the world before. Because there were not to be found any English cities, nor such fair houses, nor at their own wish any of their old accustomed dainty food, nor any soft beds of down or feathers, the country was to them miserable, and their reports thereof according.

Harriot believed the country was indeed worth settling and that it was possible to live on friendly terms with the Indians. The interior promised to be richer and more fertile than the coastal areas, but even there it would be possible to grow exotic commodities such as were now only to be found in China and other parts of Asia and in the Mediterranean area. His principal recommendation was that if settlers would work with English types of crop and animal they could establish a basic, self-sufficient economy to which exotic additions – perhaps even precious metals – could be made in due course. Lane, in reports to Ralegh, stressed the advantages of the area south of Chesapeake Bay, where Harriot, White and others had lived over the winter, close to the local Indians, and regarded this as the right place to settle.

Ralegh had by now too many commitments to spend much more on the colony, but he encouraged John White, who wanted to try out a colony of workers, not drones, to find some backing in the City of London and to prepare, in spite of the war, a new colonising expedition. This was undertaken, but in 1587 only something more than a hundred, not the several hundred he hoped for, made the journey. However, the party included women and children who could form the basis for a living, continuing community. Disputes with the Portuguese captain, Simon Fernandez, who was also an associate in the colonising syndicate, meant that, instead of touching at Roanoke Island only to pick up the fifteen men left by Grenville (who had long gone) and then going on to the Chesapeake, White and his colonists were left on the island to make the best of the site of the former colony. This he was prepared to do, but his companions insisted that it should be he, who had a daughter and granddaughter among the settlers, who must go home to England to assure them of supplies. It was arranged that some should await his return, but the rest of the colony should go on to settle at their intended destination near the Chesapeake. After White left they are not known to have been seen again by any European. Ralegh and Grenville, now that the war against the Spanish Caribbean was being stepped up, were prepared in 1588 to send out another military holding party such as Lane's so that Chesapeake Bay could be used as a privateering base. These men could also help to protect White's colonists if they were settled near by. But the squadron was countermanded in the year of England's greatest need and incorporated in the great maritime force which was to await and defeat the Armada.

White, with a handful of colonists, got two small pinnaces to sea, but less than halfway across the ocean had his vessels attacked and stripped. He was forced to turn back. Only after the Spaniards had been defeated did a group of city merchants promise to put up money to help him to get back to the colony which he felt must now be under much stress. He was unable to return until 1590 when he set out as a passenger on a privateering vessel, accompanied by a ship supplied by his London backers, to relieve the colony. After taking part in a series of attacks on Spanish vessels and taking one valuable prize, the

Hopewell sailed with the supply ship, *Moonlight*, to the Carolina Outer Banks. White went ashore on Roanoke Island to find no members of the party which was to await him on the island but with indications that they had moved some seventy miles south to remain with some friendly Indians. White was not able to induce the *Hopewell*'s commander to take him there, while the *Moonlight* was shorthanded after an accident to one of her boats, so White was forced to return to England. He found no support for a further return voyage and in 1593 wrote: 'Wanting my wishes, I leave off from prosecuting that whereunto I would to good my wealth were answerable to my will.' The scale on which colonisation was attempted was too small for it to have much chance of success, but the war was decisive in bringing it to an end. The 1587 colony's continued existence in America remained an act of faith which enabled Ralegh to retain his monopoly control of voyages to the North American coast until 1603. It is ironical that, within a very short time of his being committed to the Tower on charges of treason in 1603, news of their survival with the Chesapeake tribe, even though contact was not made with them, apparently reached London and helped to lead to a revival of the attempted colonisation of North America after peace has been achieved. Spain's own plans to destroy the English settlements they believed must exist in the region of Chesapeake Bay, and to establish strong Spanish posts there, were also frustrated by the war, and proposals for reviving them at the opening of the new century came to nothing.

The Armada was of course a great watershed in all aspects of English activity. The mobilisation of manpower, ships and other resources greatly interfered with established commerce with both Europe and overseas. Embargoes on outward shipping in 1588 and 1589 almost brought merchant shipping to a halt, though a few licences were given to vessels to sail and a few slipped away without being checked. The result was, in the period following the naval victory, that internal dislocation and the need to pick up commercial threads once again held back almost every aspect of trade and exploration. How much plunder the Armada brought to Englishmen (Drake and the Plymouth men did well out of his prize) has not been investigated, though much was taken piecemeal by the inhabitants of the Irish and Scottish coasts. Not unnaturally, the privateersmen were the first to return to their trade since the follow-up of the Armada's defeat offered them, it was thought, additional pickings. In the Armada year itself almost any small vessel, unworthy of inclusion in the fleets, took to the seas to engage in robbery of any and every vessel it could overpower: Dutch and French ships competed in a chaotic attempt to steal from Spain and Portugal, as well as from each other, as much as they could. But the restoration of order and discipline in the Spanish forces, which was rapid and effective, soon cooled the ardour of the less well-equipped robbers.

Privateers were active in the Caribbean in 1589; they descended on it in great numbers in 1590. Though a number of important individual prizes were taken, including some with gold and with silver, the major silver ships evaded them. At the Azores too there was a great concentration of privateers in 1589 and 1590 who picked off many small prizes but not major ones. The naval efforts in 1591 to capture the treasure fleet were frustrated as much by Spanish ingenuity in sending the treasure through in fast new vessels (*galizabras*) as by the powerful squadron sent to the Azores to protect the rest of the *flota* and, incidentally, to destroy the *Revenge* though losing several important vessels in the process. It was ironical that, despite the tally of prizes taken by English vessels from Spain and Portugal (notably the great carrack, *Madre de Dios*, in 1592) the vessels carrying the official silver cargoes were never intercepted, and during the decade 1590–1600 Spain in fact received more silver from America than ever before. The attrition of Spanish trade in less valuable colonial products, notably hides, dyewoods, sarsaparilla, guiacum, cochineal and sugar was very considerable, while Portugal lost much in the way of sugar and dyewoods coming from Brazil. The islands vessels, coming to Santo Domingo, before making their way to Havana, suffered most, and the general effect was a great weakening of the already depleted Spanish wealth in the Caribbean islands.

The robbery of towns along the Wild Coast (modern Venezuela and Colombia) continued also. These depredations were gradually reduced by the construction of great new fortifications at Cartagena, San Juan de Ulúa, Havana and San Juan de Puerto Rico, but these were slow to be built and put into operation. In time they became an effective check on English raids, even after the Dutch had joined English and French privateers from 1593 onwards, and enabled the silver to flow freely to Europe. The captures did help the English revenues through such prize goods as were declared for customs purposes, but a great deal was concealed and contributed rather to the private fortunes of merchants and gentlemen from London westwards to Plymouth and Bristol. But K. R. Andrews has shown how these captures led to the creation of a sugar-refining industry in London, while the stolen Spanish goods can be traced as re-exports in cargoes to the Levant, to Russia, and probably also to many other areas of English commerce such as the Baltic.

Theoretically, it ought to have been possible for the English to pick off each year the one or two great carracks which brought spices and oriental goods of all sorts from Goa to Lisbon since the Spanish government did not offer them any convoy protection. Drake had taken the *São Felipe* in 1587 and the capture of the *Madre de Dios* produced a net return (after widespread plunder by her captors) of some £160,000, half of which went to the queen, though she found it hard to dispose of the glut of pepper which was included in her share. But more carracks got through than were captured and it was not until 1601 that another fell into English hands, though four were destroyed. Even the loss of seven carracks was a considerable blow to the fortunes of the Portuguese empire, which began to decline rapidly in the era of Spanish rule and proved wholly unable to stand up to the Dutch assaults and competition which began in 1595 and mounted steadily thereafter. The English were very anxious indeed to take a lead in attacking the Portuguese or at least taking over part of their oriental trade. But Benjamin Woods's expedition in 1591 was a total disaster, and involved a heavy loss in ships, money and men. James Lancaster, starting a little later, lost all his ships but one. She got to Penang, where she attacked indiscriminately Portuguese and native shipping to some effect. But the valuable cargo of Lancaster *Edward Bonaventure* never got to England. Her crew mutinied and the vessel was lost. Her captain, marooned with a few men in a West Indian island, Mona, was eventually rescued by privateers and returned penniless to England.

The way round the Cape of Good Hope was still too difficult, it seemed, for English ships, though the Dutch were to make it successfully from 1595 onwards. Their ships were more carefully chosen: their briefings more thorough. Then, too, all attempts to follow up the western route to the Far East failed. Thomas Cavendish's strong squadron in 1591 was intended to pursue his contacts of 1587 in the East Indies and perhaps make a voyage to China, but he chose the wrong time of year to attempt the Straits and was driven back, eventually being forced to make half-hearted and ineffective attacks on Brazilian ports and to die at sea in 1592, though most of his ships got home. John Davis, in the *Desire*, made a second attempt to pass the Straits but for a different purpose. He believed Drake had not gone far enough to the north in 1579 to find the Strait of Anian and so access to the Northwest Passage, but, though he entered the Pacific, he was driven back by murderous westerlies and barely managed to get his ship home in 1593 with very few of her men alive. Meantime, Richard Hawkins had set out on what was intended to be a third attempt to rob the Spanish coasts of Peru in 1593, but this time he found the Spaniards had built up an effective naval force to resist such attempts and he was overwhelmed and forced to surrender at the Bay of Atacames. He was eventually brought to Spain and ultimately released. But this brought to an end the English attempts to enter the Pacific by the west and indeed the Spaniards won in this area a final victory. Their supremacy there was not to be challenged by the English for nearly a century.

Official English expeditions from 1589 onwards, to carry the war into the Iberian peninsula and into the heart of the Caribbean, can be fairly described as expensive failures. They illustrate how much of the potential and actual profits of the sea war and the privateering campaign were dissipated in the larger ventures in which the queen was a major shareholder, but where the losers were men, in the main, who had gained from privateering, even though some of them lost much more than they had ever gained from robbery at sea. Even if Cumberland did take San Juan de Puerto Rico in 1598, he captured no silver there, though the continued attrition of the summer privateering campaign went some way to counter Spain's attempt at recovery at sea and compensated to some extent for English losses in the earlier campaigns. War at sea, on a small scale, and with prize-taking its purpose, proved in the end more profitable than large-scale operations with strategic or political objectives.

The Northern European cloth trade of the Merchant Adventurers continued through the war years with a substantial measure of success. Exports fell off to some extent, but they picked up again surprisingly well at the turn of the century. Hamburg, briefly, Emden, for some years, and Stade, from 1587, were used as staples for the trade with Germany, and through Germany to northern Italy, but increasingly Middelburg became the principal staple. The United Provinces drew in many of the old cloth-finishing processors from the Spanish-occupied area and provided a growing market for the traditional export, unfinished woollen cloth. In 1587–8 the bulk of London's export trade was still in the hands of the Merchant Adventurers. They did not go entirely unchallenged. The Hanseatic League had in the early sixteenth century handled much cloth and wool exports in exchange for German and Baltic products, but their privileges had been curbed in mid-century and they suffered losses in the Baltic and German markets thereafter, though they kept their privileged 'factory', the Steelyard, in London. In a desperate attempt to check the growing German trade in English cloth, the Hansards in 1597 induced the emperor, Rudolf II, to ban the import of English cloth into the empire: in response the Steelyard was closed and the Hanseatic merchants expelled from England while the imperial decree was largely disregarded.

The Merchant Adventurers had their critics in England too. Their organisation was decried as monopolistic and their trading methods archaic. In 1601, their secretary, John Wheeler published *A treatise of commerce*, in which he defended them. They were not, he said, a London monopoly: fellowships joined together in cities and towns like York, Norwich, Exeter, Ipswich, Newcastle, Hull and elsewhere were partners of the Londoners and had a monopoly of the export of wool and cloth from the River Somme in France to the Skaw in Denmark, and maintained staple marts at one or two places only to concentrate the trade and to draw buyers and sellers to what were in effect great trade fairs. This was, he claimed, mutually beneficial to all the partners, even if the fleets sailed to and from the staple ports through the port of London. Their corporate power enabled them to deal with continental authorities and to make their staple towns an attractive economic asset to whatever city or state accommodated them. He made the interesting claim that monopoly trading companies were in general beneficial to the state:

> Since the erection of the company of Merchants Adventurers, and of other companies trading [to] Russia, Eastland, Spain, Turkey, etc., the navigation of the realm is marvellously increased in number of good shipping, and of able and skilful masters and mariners, insomuch that whereas within these threescore years there were not above four ships, besides those in her majesty's navy royal, above the burden of one hundred and twenty tons within the river of Thames, there are now at this day to be found pertaining to London and other places lying upon the said river, a great number of very large and serviceable merchant ships, fit as well for the defence of the realm (if need be) as for traffic, whereof a good part are set to work by the said company of Merchant Adventurers.

There was no gainsaying this, or his point that merchant ships in convoy going to the marts were less vulnerable to attack than single trading vessels. But in practice privateering had increased the number and size of the vessels owned in the outports, had given their backers ideas for trade in new areas with new commodities, and made the Merchant Adventurers appear conservative and backward-looking, and, especially, favouring London as against the other ports.

In the Baltic in the latter years of the century there was growing competition for timber and naval stores. The English and Dutch were both expanding their shipping very rapidly, but the Dutch much more rapidly than the English. The Dutch flutes, broad-bottomed large-capacity vessels, with smaller crews, carried more timber and so competed favourably with the narrower, if faster and more seaworthy, English vessels. At the same time, the Eastland Company remained active and exported as many Suffolk dyed cloths as it could assemble. But even in the Baltic Dutch-finished broadcloth, sent unfinished from England and finished in the United Provinces, was beginning to compete favourably with the English product. Moreover, much of the increased Baltic trade with England was being carried in Dutch bottoms as the London entries of vessels show. The Eastland Company did reasonably well through their base at Elbing, but was hampered by shortages of shipping as well as by Dutch competition. However, the English hold on the Eastland trade as a whole was slipping very much in the favour of the Dutch.

The Muscovy Company was prosperous enough in the 1580s. In 1587 ten ships brought tallow, wax, hides and flax as their main imports. English heavy cloths continued to be too expensive for the Russians and did not sell in great quantities. Apart from metals, the Muscovy Company exports to Russia were mainly re-exports and so perhaps not as profitable as direct exports of English goods might have been. In the best year, 1587, the official value of goods brought from Russia was some £25,000, but this represented a real value of perhaps £75,000. During the 1590s the trade declined somewhat; Russia was less stable internally and Dutch competition was beginning to be felt. By the year 1601–2 the number of Muscovy Company ships entering London was only five, and one ship from Russia was Dutch. The hopes of an increasing trade in the north-east were fading fast by 1603 and the company was in financial straits.

The Levant trade on the other hand was flourishing. John Sanderson claimed that his ship *Hercules* in 1588 brought £70,000-worth of goods from Alexandria, and it appears that this was so, since the official values for a number of the commodities are known and support his claim. For the year ending Michaelmas 1587, the official value of goods brought from the Levant was some £55,000, suggesting a real value of some £150,000. The goods brought home covered a very wide range – wine, raisins, silks, cottons – a comparably wide variety of spices and medicinal drugs from the East Indies and even a box of porcelain from China. Outward cargoes were less varied, but included some re-exports of prize goods. The company, however, slowly established a market for the heavier finished English cloths. These were saleable in Asia Minor and Persia where the climate required such heavy coverings and these were to be the basis for the company's prosperity in the future. In the shorter run, the attempt to sell the lighter coloured cloths was made but found no great response. Kerseys, shortcloths and a small quantity of the light Devonshire dozens made up some 6·4 per cent of London cloth exports in 1598. The re-expansion in cloth exports as a whole was, however, well under way by 1604. Tin and lead, traditional raw-material exports, were also important. There were fifteen Levant Company ships by 1595 and twenty by 1599 (some of them going to Italian ports rather than farther east). These were large well-armed vessels which, when sailing together, were more than a match for the Algerian and other corsairs. There were frequent attacks but the ships got through. The Spaniards made no systematic attempt to seal the Straits, though they did capture one or two vessels. Leghorn in Italy, Marseilles in France, Smyrna and Aleppo as well as Alexandria were the chief ports. Factors were kept where they could usefully assemble goods. The company (joined with the Venice Company in 1589) was a regulated one, but with high entry fees, and was run very much by Robert Osborne and Richard Staper and, later on, by Thomas Smith the younger, in the interests of a small closed group of rich London merchant houses. This was a successful company whose profits were high and the capital accumulated through it had much to do with the launching of the East India Company.

There was some attempt to organise and develop the Guinea trade also in 1589, but the results for the remainder of the century appear to have been meagre enough, though a little pepper, gold and ivory were brought back. The route along the African coast, however, was a dangerous one and traders found privateering in Iberian waters more profitable than risky voyages to the Gold Coast and Gulf of Benin. Theoretically, the Barbary Company ought to have done better. It received its charter as a regulated company in 1585. The trade carried on had varied fortunes: some merchants did moderately well; a large partnership under its auspices, headed by the Earl of Leicester, in the end proved unprofitable. Much of the original capital of its members was swallowed up in presents to the King of Morocco and it proved difficult to get the Jewish merchants who handled the trade to pay for what they received. Sugar profits were low, probably from competition with Brazil sugar taken by privateers, though saltpetre, not a major export in the early years, was much appreciated in England. The company did not attempt to have its charter renewed in 1597, but the trade continued much as before. Official values of imports in 1587–8 had been as high as £36,572 (about £100,000 at market rates), but only seven vessels entered the port of London from Morocco in 1601–2, so that there was some decline.

There is a genuine question mark over the eventual profitability of the privateering war, but its balance sheet must not blind us to the fact that it gave English sailors an intimate knowledge of the Atlantic Ocean in all its parts and enabled the years of peace which followed to be utilised by expert seamen to convey English traders, pirates and colonists to any place to which they wished to go, while English ships fully proved their capacity for long voyages. But even during the war the English were expanding the range of their operations in the Americas. As early as 1580, Richard Hakluyt the elder had pointed out to explorers that the north-eastern coastline of South America was almost unoccupied by Spaniards, while repeated raids by privateers greatly weakened such towns as the Spaniards had planted to the east of the Gulf of Paria. Moreover, when English ships could demonstrate peaceful intentions, they might be able to buy pearls and other goods from the colonists or from Indians along these shores. Among the novel goods sought by the English was tobacco. Tobacco was increasingly used in England in the 1590s: the demand for it could not be satisfied by consignments captured on the way to Spain. So English traders (often heavily armed for privateering as well) went to look for it. They found it in Guyana, in the Wiapoco and other river valleys not occupied by Spain, but especially they found that the centre of Spanish production was Trinidad. The Spanish governor there, Antonio de Berrio, had made his post for himself by an adventurous voyage down the Orinoco from western South America, but he was not averse to trade, and some cargoes of Trinidad tobacco changed hands to English venturers. Berrio was, however, prepared to resist any English attack on his position: trade must be on his terms. But it was from him that tales of a gold-rich people, under a leader whom the Spaniards called El Dorado, the gilded one, gradually filtered back to England.

We know that Sir Walter Ralegh had been interested in South America as far back as 1587 and had been collecting information about it, some of it through tobacco traders, some through privateering ventures. Like Drake, though for different reasons, he suffered a period of exclusion from court. In order to break out of his rural retreat at Sherborne, he gradually developed a plan to investigate the Orinoco and find the source of the gold supplies of which he had heard. He also genuinely believed that the river might be a back door into the Spanish-held territories of New Granada and Peru. He convinced enough of his friends and some courtiers also that his idea was not wholly chimerical. In 1595 he set out with a moderately strong force to make the attempt. At Trinidad, after a rather nominal Spanish resistance, he made Berrio prisoner and gained from him much of his facts and fancies about the great inland sea round which this gold-rich people was said to live. He made a difficult voyage through the delta and upstream in the Orinoco, getting Lawrence Keymis and others whom he trusted to collect specimens of possible gold-bearing mud and rocks. He went overland to the Caroni River, where native guides directed him, and saw the famous falls. His contacts with the Arawak Indians were friendly as they regarded the English as possible allies against Carib raiders, and he obtained from them a few golden ornaments, one or two of which were of some size. His men failed to discover a mine, but several locations were marked as favouring the existence of gold, and indeed there is a certain amount of alluvial gold to be found along the river, though the richer lodes were some distance away, and there were no gold-rich people to be found. El Dorado remained as mysterious as ever.

Eventually, fever among his men and shortage of supplies forced him to come back to Trinidad. He released Berrio after, no doubt, receiving a ransom in tobacco, and sailed along the mainland coast to the west, doing a little indiscriminate and not very successful raiding but eventually returning to England, defeated but not despondent. Along with his associates, Thomas Harriot and Lawrence Keymis, he worked out a plan for an English protectorate over the Orinoco valley, but he never obtained sanction or finance to attempt to establish it, though Keymis made further voyages for him, picking up information, and tobacco, over the years following, and convincing himself and eventually Ralegh that he knew where the gold could be found. His fine propaganda pamphlet in 1596 extolled the opportunities which the 'Bewtiful empyre of Guiana' offered, but that was all. After the Cádiz expedition, in which he took part, his colonial ambitions were brushed aside but he did not forget them. He then was sent to the Channel Islands to secure them against Spanish intervention. But well before 1604 English ships were going freely to the Guyana rivers to get tobacco and dyewoods and were from time to time discreetly acquiring cargoes from Berrio. A back door was being slowly opened into the Spanish empire, and in 1604 Captain Charles Leigh took out the first English colonists to Guyana before peace was signed with Spain.

In the northern Atlantic, too, the English were active. The queen did as little as she could to hinder the Newfoundlandmen in their summer voyages to catch cod and bring back train oil, since these were badly needed for victualling ships of her navy and privateering fleets. The result was that the size of the ships and the number of the vessels increased during the war years. They drove away the Portuguese and discouraged the Spanish Basques and, with the French, monopolised the fishery. When Henry IV was fighting for his throne, the English Newfoundlanders made common cause with the French loyalists against the ships from ports of the Catholic League, principally those from Brittany. The result was that by 1600 England was sharing the catch almost equally with France. Bringing back more than the domestic market needed, she was selling fish to the Dutch, to the French and even sending a few ships to dispose of it at Leghorn and Marseille. Thus one branch of English commerce developed and flourished during the war, though we must remember that the fishermen were regarded as in a real sense a naval reserve which might be diverted at any time that seemed necessary to defend English shores against Spanish attack or to assist in offensive measures. Whale oil, however, the English could not easily obtain. In 1591 they heard that Bretons and Basques were getting walrus oil from islands in the Gulf of St Lawrence, and in 1593 George Drake of Ashe seized a certain amount in a rather poorly conducted raid on the Magdalen Islands. A Basque Protestant was engaged to teach the English whaling in the gulf in 1593, but did not find them apt pupils. Then, in 1597, Charles Leigh went out on a strange mission to the Magdalen Islands, where George Drake had been in 1593. He was to carry representatives of a radical nonconformist sect,

Brownists who had been imprisoned for some years, to see whether a colony of these obstinate separatists could not be established there to kill walrus and catch cod. However, they were confronted at the islands by sufficient numbers of Basques, Bretons and Micmac Indians to scare them away. The four Brownists went home frightened of America, to lead their little congregation, the first would-be Pilgrims, to safety in Amsterdam. Leigh, however, remained optimistic of English prospects in this region; but the French were very soon to move in in strength to protect their summer fur trade on the River St Lawrence.

Most of the whale oil obtained came from captures of Spanish Basque whalers operating from the Strait of Belle Isle, into which the English did not penetrate, the majority of them being taken as they approached their home ports: more oil came from trading indirectly with Spain by way of the French Basque port of St-Jean-de-Luz. With olive oil cut off, whale and walrus oil were especially valuable for soap-making and hence for cloth-making. The growth of English shipping in the Newfoundland area did not lead, as Edward Hayes, for example, had hoped, to English colonisation of Newfoundland. Instead, plans began to emerge in the 1590s for English colonies in Norumbega and Acadia (New England and the Maritimes). In 1602 Bartholomew Gosnold brought out an expedition to explore the Maine and Massachusetts coasts and built a fur-trading post on the Elizabeth Islands off the southern Massachusetts coast, but his little garrison of twelve men refused to stay there and came home with him. This led, however, to the appearance of a propaganda pamphlet which went into two editions in 1602. It encouraged Bristol supporters of expansion to send out Martin Pring to trade with Indians on Cape Cod in 1603, which he did satisfactorily, bringing back sassafras roots and other products after an easy voyage. This may have led to other small North American trading ventures of which we have no record. If nothing had yet been done about settling North America, the idea was very much in the air before peace was signed in 1604.

One major development sprang from the Levant Company's success. The Osborn-Staper partnership in the latter had brought a group of major city merchants together to make the attempt, with adequate capital, to break into the direct sea traffic with Asia by way of the Cape of Good Hope. A leading spirit in this was Thomas Smith, whose father had made a fortune as customs farmer at London. The incentive sprang not only from the Levant Company's profits but from the remarkable success of the Dutch between 1595 and 1598 in reaping a rich harvest of spices and super-profits from direct voyages. The translation of Linschoten's *Discours* in 1598 provided a guide to what could be done. Consequently, in 1599 merchants got together an unprecedented capital of £60,000 to launch an East India Company. There were unexpected delays in getting a charter, which was granted only at the end of 1603, but Thomas Middleton was sent out with three ships in 1601 in the first successful voyage. While he was away, George Waymouth was sent, in 1602, to look once again for the North-west Passage, though, once more, he failed to find it. Middleton lost two of three ships and arrived back in 1603, but his single vessel produced a major profit for the company. It was just in time. James I dared not now guarantee to Spain in the treaty that English ships would not invade the Portuguese monopoly and the way was opened for expansion.

A good impression of the character of English trade at the opening of the new century is given in the shipping list of the port of London from October 1601 to June 1602: 714 ships (many of them repeaters) entered the port. Of these no less than 360 were Dutch owned, an indication of how the carrying trade was falling into their hands at a time when the Crown was making so many demands on English merchant shipping, though many were very small, while London ships were being diverted to privateering war or to longer voyages; English-owned ships numbered 207; 90 were German, French or Scandinavian. The English ships were larger (average 75·36 tons) than any except the eight Scandinavian vessels, but even the six Levanters in this period averaged only 125 tons. What is interesting is that no less than twelve ships came from the war zone, Spain and Portugal (an occasional English ship putting in and getting out, but mostly foreign bottoms), the Canaries, the Azores (including one English ship) and the West Indies (two English privateers turned traders). It is clear that London trade was very active, but that her mercantile marine was at a disadvantage compared with foreigners. The domination of London in the official market was almost complete. Import duties in 1604 suggested the value of London imports to be in the region of £330,000 compared with a mere £51,000 for the outports. Against this must be set the fact that the privateers, though mainly financed by London capital, normally discharged their prize goods, clandestinely as well as officially, at southern or south-western ports, and that these reached London, when they did so, from Portsmouth, Southampton, Poole, Exeter and even Bristol by road or by coastal transport.

If we try to generalise on the later period of Elizabethan trade we can see that it greatly broadened its scope, but that there was little if any enlargement in total quantities or real value: there was indeed a certain decline, though this is difficult to measure. When we consider that war was continuous throughout the period, however, the record is not a bad one. The basic cloth trade continued to hold up well, even if much of the profits of finishing cloth went to the Dutch; the English mercantile marine was enlarged and strengthened (though its vessels were better as men-of-war than as bulk carriers); much accumulation of capital, mainly in the hands of a small group of London capitalists, had taken place so that they were able to finance considerable expansion once peace came. Capital accumulation in merchant, gentry and aristocratic hands had also been appreciable. But the share of overseas trade in total English economic activity was still small. There had been no breakthrough overseas except in the Levant, though many promising routes and projects had been investigated and were to prove possible to exploit profitably once peace came. The chartered companies had provided some corporate defence for particular branches of trade in time of war. In peace they might well prove obstacles to entrepreneurial development. But it was time to call a halt to the sea war. If James's peace initiatives and the making of peace in 1604 were not universally popular, from the point of view of English commercial and colonial expansion they were timely and even necessary.

At the end of Elizabeth's reign there was a feeling of satisfaction, even complacency, about the condition of the country after a long struggle, and a sense of optimism about the future prospects of the English polity. These are well expressed in a work dedicated to James I in 1604 by the Reverend Matthew Sutcliffe, even if they cast a blind eye on the realities of a long war:

> By means of long peace, this land is altogether grown to great wealth. The country is better cultivated, trade is much increased all arts and occupations grown to greater perfection than in time past. Noblemen and gentlemen have doubled their revenues. Yeomen and merchants aspire to the degree of gentlemen, and divers men of occupation do exceed men of their sort in former times. Whosoever compareth the common people of England with men of their quality in Spain, Portugal, and Italy must needs confess that in wealth and means our countrymen do far exceed them. Finally, never was England so populous and strong in men as in our late Queen's days. Spain and most places in Italy seem desolate by comparison. (*A ful and round answer to N. D. alias Robert Parsons*, 1604, p. 85)

Granted that this was propaganda, but it was written by a man who had been prepared to advocate English expansion in Ireland under Elizabeth and was to play an active part in sponsoring expansionist enterprises overseas under James. It does not coincide with the opinions of many present-day historians, but it does represent a mood, a feeling of national complacency perhaps, but also a sense of potential for action overseas which was to be well displayed in the years following the peace with Spain. The Elizabethan overseas adventurers had played a large part in creating this optimism and it now remained to see whether positive gains could be made in overseas commerce and colonisation which had hitherto been more significant in potential than in results.

CHAPTER 6

Beginnings of Imperial Expansion, 1604–1624

With the change of dynasty new men came into office (even if the ubiquitous Robert Cecil lasted until 1612), and new policies were gradually formulated and put into effect, but the major change was that twenty years of peace followed nearly twenty years of war. There were thus new opportunities for long-range planning in the fields of commerce and colonisation which had not previously existed. It now became possible to carry out large-scale enterprises which had been considered long before, even attempted with inadequate means, but which could not be developed systematically while war was going on. The period was not to be an easy one, the economy was unstable and cycles of expansion and depression can be discerned: such trade crises, plagues and famines still interrupted domestic production and overseas commerce and colonisation alike, yet the atmosphere was very different from that of the Elizabethan period. There was less incautious optimism about new ventures, and more systematic planning (not all of it successful), but, most of all, there was a new willingness to risk capital in novel projects which had at least a moderate chance of success. The precise origins of the capital which was made available is not always clear. The bulk of it came throughout this period and its succeeding one from a relatively small group of very rich London merchants. They were growing richer from legitimate, long-established enterprises, and they were prepared to sink a substantial part of their accumulated wealth into new ventures which retained an appreciable speculative element. Courtiers, encouraged by royal favour and the monopoly grants through which they battened on private industry, gentlemen and provincial merchants who had accumulated fortunes in privateering and war-contracting, along with a vigorous class of small investors, were all prepared to venture sums, small or large, in new ventures. Consequently, in this period, there are very many new initiatives to record, though not all of them by any means proved profitable, and very many speculators lost their investments entirely, notably, for example, in the establishment of Virginia. But even if the initial capital for the founding of a new colony was lost, the end result, if re-capitalisation was possible or if enterprising settlers took matters into their own hands, could still be productive and even successful. Newfoundland, the Maritimes, Maine, southern New England, Virginia, Bermuda, St Kitts Nevis, Guyana and the Amazon were in the west, alone, places where experiments in commerce or settlement were tried and where there were at least some short-term successes, and a few solid roots for later developments, as well as many failures. In the Far East the picture of far-ranging enterprise was comparable. Java, Sumatra, Celebes, the Moluccas and Amboina, Japan, Siam, India and Persia were all the scene of shorter- or longer-term English commercial experiments and commercial contracts. Moreover, the habit of overseas colonisation was established during these years in Virginia, in southern New England, in Bermuda and on the fringes of the Caribbean, even though the settlements were small in scale and far from deep-rooted in the end. Not all of them, by any means, were to prove viable in the long run.

It is not easy in this field to maintain a balanced perspective. Almost every venture into new areas for new objectives had its own interest and significance, but most of them were on such a small scale, and so many left little in the way of results after their failure, that they can easily bulk too large when we consider the whole range of English overseas commerce and colonisation. So far as investment went, the East India Company, the Levant Company, the Newfoundland fisheries and the Virginia colony were relatively highly capitalised ventures, but even they added up only to a comparatively small part of the total of English external commerce and enterprise in this period. The cloth trade was still by far the biggest source of industrial and commercial activity in the English economy. The export of unfinished woollen cloths remained the single most important branch of external trade and its checkered fortunes usually form the main theme of the economic histories of the period. But the cloth trade was slowly changing from unfinished to finished products. Dyed and finished cloths of the heavier types formed a larger part of total exports; the so-called 'new draperies', employing new techniques, and often foreign wool, were becoming a significant element in cloth exports. They were lighter and so could serve a more extended climatic market; they were colourful and so could offer more varied attractions to purchasers over a much wider area. Both in the cloth and metal industries the putting-out system was enlarging in scale, the merchant entrepreneurs supplying domestic or workshop producers with raw materials, semi-finished goods and small doses of loan capital, on a basis of credit, and demonstrating their capacity to market the products of the system on an enlarged scale. Under such a system, market conditions, notably in overseas sales, could rapidly spread their effects through the community.

There was also, as Joan Thirsk has shown in her *Economic Policy and Projects: The Development of a Consumer Society in Early Modern England* (1978), a further very large development of consumer products which demanded little capital in their early stages at least and were in their beginning supplemental to basic employment mainly in agriculture, though they gradually produced full-time family employment. Among the items she mentions for the late sixteenth and early seventeenth century were 'stocking knitting, button making, pin and nail making, salt making, starch making, tobacco-pipe making, pot and oven making, alum mining, ribbon and lace making, linen weaving' (pp. 6–7), together with brewing and distilling, and the garden culture of cash crops like rope, flax, hemp, woad, madder, tobacco (in spite of prohibitions), flowers and vegetables (near large towns), along with viticulture and mulberry growing (the last two failing to thrive). There has been much written about an early industrial revolution in England which began to come to fruition in the early seventeenth century, but orthodoxy among economic historians (e.g. D. C. Coleman, *Industry in Tudor and Stuart England*, 1975, p. 36) is that it is nonsense to talk in general terms about large-scale industrial enterprises in this period, though certain new industries resorted to centralised and relatively large-scale production for technical reasons. At the same time the character of these few industries influenced the effectiveness of English external commerce. The water-driven blast furnaces and tilt-hammers produced increasing quantities of bar iron (though imports from Sweden continued) and provided raw materials for the fabrication of many articles of commerce, both domestic and overseas, which multiplied in the period. The shipyards, some of them very large, produced not only larger but better ships, and the expansion of England's mercantile marine was basic both for her carrying trade as well as for the expansion of her overseas commerce. The new consumer goods, originally developed solely for the home market and continuing to be mainly sold there, soon found their way also to the Americas, Africa and Asia. It is not surprising that the most detailed studies of English-made tobacco pipes and of west-country pottery have been done from sites dating from 1607 onwards in Virginia. Many of the new consumer goods had, in the sixteenth century, come from Europe, and were regarded by some as unnecessary luxuries. In the early seventeenth century they supplied the home market, and the imported luxuries and trinkets which found an expanding market in England were brought direct by English ships from the eastern Mediterranean, from India and from Indonesia as well as from North America and the Caribbean, the most notable for the latter areas being tobacco. Thus, if the relative values of goods imported and exported outside the traditional routes of commerce remained small, they played an important part in the diversification of English trade and in its transition from the export of raw materials and semi-finished manufactures to completely fabricated home-produced goods, though Spanish wool and Indian cotton were beginning to make an appearance among the raw materials they employed. Then, too, re-exports from the Americas, the eastern Mediterranean and, especially, from Asia were beginning to add a new element to English exports, though during the reign of James I they were still not very numerous or valuable.

There were serious trade crises in the seventeenth century – England had two in the years between 1614 and 1625 – working up to what many have called a general crisis, both in the economic and political spheres, towards the middle of the century. But in the mercantile sphere crisis was selective. Over the first quarter of the seventeenth century there was some permanent decline in the prosperity of certain ports and areas but a noticeable advance in others. This favoured zone has been defined by Geoffrey Parker (*Europe in Crisis 1598–1648*, 1979, p. 38) as the ports and hinterlands roughly bounded by Hamburg–Norwich–London–Paris–Southampton, and including the Spanish Netherlands to some extent as well as the phenomenally progressing United Provinces and the English south-east focusing on London. If the United Provinces did best, though at war for all but nine years, much of Normandy did well also. London went on expanding and its trade spreading more widely, even with several slumps, though it had to resist serious competition from the Dutch. The English fought back more successfully than used to be thought and their share of overseas trade and expansion was a significant element in the success which was achieved. This is compatible with crisis and depression in parts of the domestic economy.

The two major successful commercial-imperialistic ventures in the early seventeenth century were the East India Company and the Levant Company. Both had problems to face. The Levant Company – already significant before 1604 – was confronted with major piratical obstruction in the Mediterranean and with phases of political instability in the Levant. The East India Company, apart from having to adjust to the complexities of Asian politics and commerce, had to steer its way between a series of obstacles, notably the existing Portuguese domination of major sections of the East India trade (though it was being weakened by the Dutch), and the more active Dutch intruders, who veered between co-operation and enmity in different areas at different times, sometimes from year to year. In both cases the English showed – more so in the East Indies than in the Levant – a capacity for pragmatic adjustment to changing circumstances which gradually brought them a significant share, if still small as compared with the Dutch, of the trade of Asia, and especially that of India. The Levant Company, too, showed considerable capacity in adjusting its offerings to the changing market conditions of the Levant. Both were organised and directed by a small overlapping group of increasingly rich and powerful merchants. Both companies also sought to keep out interlopers and were in the main successful in doing so. Both found enemies from those who resented the engrossing of super-profits in the hands of privileged trading companies, mainly London-based, and, it was felt, depriving the outports of increasing prosperity, and the 'free traders', as the interlopers saw themselves, of profitable opportunities. The Crown, too, came to feel that the privileged companies were not paying enough for their privileges and did its best to rake off part of their profits by alterations in the customs system and by other means. These attacks were resented by the chartered companies, in turn, since, among other things, they hampered their capacity for further expansion. This issue flared up in Parliament from time to time, with royal impositions on imports, which mainly affected the companies, being attacked, at the same time as the Merchant Adventurers, with the Levant and East India Companies, were being sniped at by the 'free traders'. By and large the Londoners won. There is no doubt, however, that the very success of the old chartered companies, such as the Merchant Adventurers and to some extent the Eastland Company, led to attempts to establish new closed companies in other fields of commerce. The Virginia Company had such a closed field from 1606 to 1624 in much of North America, as did the North-west Passage Company (1612), the Greenland Company (1616), the Spanish Company (which had only a short uneasy life), a French company (which never got off the ground), and various African companies (none of which lasted long) were others. All of these showed the same tendency towards monopoly in external trading, encouraged by the Crown in spite of the attacks and criticisms inside and outside Parliament. The East India Company proved – in spite of periodic disasters – to be a highly profitable concern. By 1613 their annual imports were worth about £300,000, but some of their exports had to be paid for in bullion, which was considered reprehensible in the economics of the time. There is no doubt too that the profitability of the company continued and grew still further in the years from 1617 to 1624, in spite of Dutch hostility and partial success in driving the company from many of its earlier footholds.

The Levant Company and the East India Company had an overlapping directorship, but the former continued to bring from the eastern Mediterranean articles of oriental origin as well as indigenous products. Its main success was in selling finished English cloth of the heavier qualities to Asia Minor and Persia and so helping greatly the fortunes of the troubled textile industry. English tin and lead continued to play a part. Trade to Italy was important (the company had a monopoly of the Adriatic trade but not for that of western Italy); the lighter new draperies found a good market in Italy and products like alum were important in return. Profit figures do not seem to be available, but it was generally felt that the Levant Company was at least as prosperous, if less capital was involved in it, as the East India Company. Its fleets of some fifteen to twenty vessels often went out together. Strongly armed, they were usually a match for the strong pirate fleets of Algiers (mostly English ships led by ex-privateers who played havoc with Venetian shipping). Even in western Italy the company competed with some success with non-company vessels. But these developed their important trade with Leghorn and Marseilles, partly in cloth and to a more substantial degree than before, in dried cod brought directly from Newfoundland.

The Asiatic and Mediterranean trade was supplemented by a growing Spanish trade. Spain's own production was falling off and her Indies were requiring more and more non-Spanish, European goods. English merchants had difficulties in re-establishing themselves in both Spain and Portugal and there was recurrent friction, especially in the years 1604–10, but gradually the trade grew, with England importing light, long-staple Spanish wool and in return exporting growing quantities of light-weight woollen cloth, only in small part made from Spanish wool. Many of the products of the Spanish Indies too reached England in this legitimate way, even though Spanish taxes made prices high, and eventually Spanish tobacco was prohibited in the interests of that produced in English colonies. Some merchants considered the Spanish trade the most elastic of all. It was especially important to the outports, and to their hostility the short life of the privileged Spanish Company centred in London was largely owed.

The success, then, of this period (the African trade did not produce any major returns, though such bullion as it brought was highly regarded) came from development of the older trades and the addition of well-conducted and cautious new commerce with Asia. In these areas there was no depression but almost continuous expansion.

Robert Keale (in *Trades increase*) and Sir Dudley Digges (*The defence of trade*) fought a paper battle respectively against and for the East India Company in 1615. Keale accused the East India Company of having lost too many ships and built too many large ones to the detriment of builders of medium-sized ships, while they were also said to have raised the cost of spices to the Levant Company, which bought them from Arab sources. The main charge was that the company exported bullion and so depleted the nation's resources in precious metal, a vital factor in the balance of trade. He was in favour of expanding the English-based fisheries and the carrying trade, as well as maintaining traditional channels of trade with the Low Countries, Germany, the Baltic, Spain and the Mediterranean, which he claimed were genuinely profitable while the company squandered bullion, ships and men to little real profit. Digges, armed with statistics from the company, was able to show that Keale had exaggerated the losses in ships and men, which, he said, had occurred almost wholly in the early days of the company's life, defended the range of produce which had been brought back as far greater and much cheaper than had previously been available, and was able to point to a substantial, if recent, re-export of a valuable part of the cargoes brought into England. As for bullion, this was, he claimed, Spanish coin bought in the Netherlands, and paid for by English-made commodities, and so represented a net gain, not a loss, in the balance of trade, while he also detailed the English-made commodities which the company had brought out to sell in the East. It was something of a drawn battle, for if Keale had undoubtedly exaggerated the detriment to the country the company's losses had caused, Digges was not wholly frank either: some of the bullion needed had been raised under royal licence in England, and the re-export trade was very new and was to undergo a good many fluctuations before it became a substantial part of the company's routine. Certainly there were ups and downs in the company's fortunes, but from 1617 onwards, for many years after the end of this period, expansion of trade and its judicious promotion at not too great a cost characterised the company's progress.

Indeed, the activities of the East India Company were, after some initial stumbling, carried on with considerable enterprise and skill. Its agents tried so far as possible to fit themselves into existing patterns of trade by establishing factories, usually consisting of a very small number of agents, in any ports where the local rulers permitted, and did not, except in very few cases, try to intrude by force. On the other hand their ships were large and well armed and could resist Portuguese attempts to keep them away from coastal areas where they considered they had prior rights, or Dutch attempts to exclude them from particular ports (where they were not always so successful). Sometimes their ships could be used to blockade a port where the local authorities had turned hostile or were trying to screw too much in the way of bribes from the company, but only in the case of Ormuz (1622) was direct offensive action taken against a Portuguese possession, and this under pressure from the Persian ruler who made it a requirement for the continuation of their trading privileges. They were content from 1602 to use Bantam as their sole factory in Indonesia, though they sent individual ships farther east to the Spice Islands, but then Bantam was a clearing house in a complex trade system for many more commodities than the pepper which was the reason for choosing it initially. In 1611 they moved back to India and settled a factory at Masulipatam on the east coast, and then in 1612 to Surat. They got a licence from the Mogul emperor to trade there and, despite some local friction and a battle with the Portuguese in Swally Roads, near the entrance to the river leading to Surat, established that as their main station. From there they could send agents and establish small interior factories inside the empire, including Agra, then the capital, itself. They moved actively eastwards in 1612 and 1613 into Siam, where they established posts at Patani and Ayuthia, to Macassar in Celebes, and to Japan, where their factory at Hirado was to have a life of ten years.

Up to 1613 each voyage had been financed separately, and the proceeds had taken a long time to sort out while leaving no working capital to maintain factories or develop them. In 1613 joint-stock working was begun, and a presidency established at Bantam, the head of which was to oversee factories in the Far East and expand or contract commitments as the situation changed. This was essential as Dutch hostility was growing. There was friction at Bantam and open fighting at the Banda Islands when the company attempted in 1615–16 to extend regular operations into the Spice Islands proper, from which cloves, mace and nutmegs came. The factory at Hirado was intended to provide markets for English broadcloths in Japan, but failed to do so, as they were too expensive. The 1619 treaty with the Dutch involved the East India Company in paying for part of Dutch naval force in return for participation in trade of the Spice Islands. Though the presidency was removed to Batavia (the new Dutch centre), Dutch officials there soon made it clear they did not desire to have any association with the English. By 1622, too, the English had come to the conclusion that the factories in the Spice Islands, Siam and Japan were not paying and should be closed: The Dutch 'massacre' of company servants at Amboina in 1623 meant that withdrawal was hastened. But the company kept its presidency in the Far East, though now at Bantam again, traded extensively in Java, and especially in Sumatra, and through its factory at Macassar in Celebes continued to get the 'forbidden' products of the Spice Islands. The Far Eastern trade continued to play a considerable part in the company's activities. More and more it paid for its spices by cotton textiles exported from India, but the market for pepper at home was inelastic and re-export was only slowly developing for such products.

The company showed remarkable resilience, however, in developing its Indian trade. Here, on the east coast, the factory at Masulipatam from 1611 provided the basis for an expanding trade in cotton textiles, its expansion having much to do with the demand for such articles (notably calicoes) farther east, in exchange for spices. In the west, the

Surat factory was established in 1612. There was fighting with the Portuguese before they would accept its continuance, and intermittent friction with local officials in spite of imperial patronage, but, in general, it grew into a small, almost collegiate, society of factors, under a president. From Surat access to interior market places such as Ahmedabad, Broach, Burhanpur and Lahore was easy and the transport of goods to Surat offered no difficulty. The trade with Persia proved very attractive, and from 1613 onwards Persian silks were bought freely and sent back to Surat for transport homewards. The 'Treaty of Defence' with the Dutch in 1619 involved the company for a time in war with Portugal on a small scale, notably in the blockades of Goa and Mozambique (1621–3), but most notably in the capture of Ormuz in 1622, where the continuance of the trade in silk, as has been shown, was made contingent by the Persian authorities on a successful attack. From that time on the company enjoyed much profit from its Persian silk trade, even though it shared it with the Dutch, though here it was they who were the junior partners.

The thirteen distinct voyage stocks put together between 1601 and 1613 and worked out by 1617 meant the employment altogether of something over £500,000. The profit overall has been put at 155 per cent, but this is now regarded somewhat sceptically. The first joint stock, covering the ten years 1613–23, accounted for over £400,000 with an established profit of 87 per cent. The overlapping second joint stock was to run for fifteen years and to produce, for varying reasons, both a larger capital commitment and a much smaller profit, the costs of joint naval action with the Dutch being high and the exclusion from the Spice Islands temporarily expensive. But it was clear that the Mogul empire and the Hindu kingdom of Golconda alike were willing that the company's agents should trade freely, though Sir Thomas Roe failed to get any firm continuing treaty from the Mogul emperor. Sir Thomas Smith guided the company through most of this period, retiring finally from the governorship only in 1621, and with him were associated many of the richest merchants in the city. Admission was not at this time very difficult or expensive, but merchants with substantial capital of their own were able to make the most effective investments. The company, however, alarmed many theorists – including the government financiers – through its continued need to export bullion: something like £750,000 in money was used during the period as compared with the export of under £350,000 in goods. The company's continued expansion thus remained a matter of controversy, but if the balance of trade was favourable (as it was), little effective opposition could be mounted against it.

Trade with West Africa was not very active during the first quarter of the century. To begin with, it was largely a matter of individual enterprise. It centred not on the Gold Coast or the Bight of Benin, but on Sierra Leone (where, for example, John Davis was active from 1609), the Sherboro, Gambia and Senegal Rivers. Cargoes of ivory, together with some malagueta pepper and gold, were brought back. In 1618 John Davis was largely responsible for getting a charter for a new regulated company to monopolise the 'whole trade of Guinea and Binney', but which was in fact directed to the more limited areas already specified. Davis himself seems to have kept the whole of the logwood trade with Sierra Leone in his own hands until his death in 1626. The company, in its corporate capacity, made a considerable effort to penetrate the Gambia basin in the years 1618–21 in hopes of locating the sources of the gold which reached the coast. It failed in this and lost money in its efforts, but substantial quantities of other African products were brought back. After 1621 most of the trade was carried out by individual merchants or small merchant syndicates under the company's umbrella, and not much is known in detail of their achievement.

A certain limited amount of piracy continued in the Caribbean after peace had been signed with Spain, but English privateers before 1604 had partly given place to trading vessels. Some captains were only too willing to combine the two. But from 1605 onwards the Spaniards made a concerted drive to root out trading from the islands, and so far as the English were concerned they appear to have been largely successful, so that the trade in hides and sugar, hopefully begun, virtually came to an end. The northern coast of South America was more difficult to command. Until 1607 it appears that English as well as other European ships successfully traded tobacco with the Spaniards along the New Granada coast, but by 1607 this also had been checked and the Spanish inhabitants forbidden to grow tobacco. Trinidad and the Spanish settlements on the Orinoco were still more difficult to control. A very large trade in Trinidad tobacco, now selling for high prices in England, was done, but by 1612 it too had been virtually stopped by vigorous Spanish action. Guyana and the Amazon alone were left. Captain Charles Leigh's small colony on the Wiapoco (Oyapok) survived his own death in 1605 but came to an end shortly after 1606 owing to a mischance to a supply ship. Robert Harcourt left colonists there in 1609, who were still there in 1612. Sir Thomas Roe surveyed the coast in 1610 and reported that it was still partly open to commerce, and also explored the Amazon. In 1612 he established a settlement some 300 miles up the Amazon which he reinforced with a group of settlers from Ireland a little later. This had a long life, lasting for eight years as a cohesive group and for a further three as a series of small parties. Roger North's settlers on the Amazon in 1618 held on for some time also. The Portuguese in 1621 and 1623 put an end to English, Irish and Dutch settlements alike, though a few isolated groups survived for a time longer. So far as their contribution to English commerce was concerned, only the brief tobacco trade with Trinidad was large enough to count for much. The other factor of some significance is that some settlers managed to survive in Guyana and on the Amazon for a number of years, thus proving that tropical colonisation was not entirely out of the question for Englishmen. But the gains in tobacco and gold they made by trading were not large and it is unlikely that sugar, hemp, cotton and tobacco produced by their own efforts amounted to anything much. The incursion of Sir Walter Ralegh into the Orinoco basin in 1618, though dramatic (and for him fateful), was little more than an aberration, though had it succeeded and produced gold, even James I might have proved willing to challenge Spanish monopoly claims in that area.

The fortunes of the branches of trade which had traditionally made up the bulk of English exports were very different from those of the Levant and East India Company. They were highly erratic. They had some phases of prosperity and some of almost total ruin. Broadly the picture of the Russia and Eastland trades and the traditional cloth trade of the Merchant Adventurers begins on the whole favourably, takes a down-turn after 1610, enters a period of crisis (largely caused by state interference), and recovers so gradually and incompletely that a general economic decline of internal and external commerce, qualified only by the successes already recorded, appears to dominate the years 1620–24. The saga of the cloth trade fills most of the space in the economic histories. The 'new draperies', coloured cloths of lighter weight, formed the brightest element in the textile situation since they were mostly developing and at times booming in international markets. The Suffolk dyed heavy cloths were doing well, but the undyed 'short-cloths' of the traditional market were in some difficulty. The Dutch were developing their own basic cloth industry and bought fewer unfinished shortcloths and were able to compete in the Baltic and German markets with dyed cloths (to the detriment of the Eastland Company). On the other hand, the final closing of the Steelyard in 1597 and the expulsion of the Hansards did not lead to exclusion of the Merchant Adventurers from what was now the key German market. Stade and Hamburg (from 1611), as well as Middelburg in the United Provinces, were staples for English shortcloth disposals. There was a rise of some 20 per cent in exports in this area during 1604–14, and over all other exports (mainly finished cloths of one sort or another) an increase of perhaps 280 per cent in the London figures alone. The outports furnished a figure of about one quarter of the total cloth exports only. The attempt of Alderman Cockayne in 1614 to get James I to enforce the dyeing of all the heavier cloths before export was only too successful in the short run, and too disastrous in the longer.

The Merchant Adventurers were replaced by a King's Merchants' Adventurers Company, which was to take over all exports of this character. This was first met by a Flemish embargo (the Spanish Netherlands having revived as a market for short cloths), then one by Holland, and finally by the United Provinces as a whole. The Eastland Company may have benefited marginally, but the markets for most of the heavy cloths virtually disappeared. From 1615 to 1617 the ripples of the effects of this experiment affected much of the economy as a whole, even the growing new drapery sector. In 1617 the whole project was abandoned (though the proportion of dyed heavy cloth did permanently increase) and the Merchant Adventurers slowly clawed back about three-quarters but not more of their old market, though trade by 1622 fell back again for shortcloths to two-thirds of its estimated figure in 1610, and only slowly rose to some 80 per cent of its old figure by 1630. It can be argued that it was the elasticity of the East India, Levant and Spanish trades which kept the English economy from collapse.

A general 'decay of trade' struck much of Western Europe in 1620, and there were few signs of improvement for four or five years, so that the last years of James I were ones of appreciable economic difficulty. During that period the Russia Company, which began the period of peace well and profitably, fell victim to Dutch competition, a falling off in the Russian market, and to initial successful intervention in whaling at Cherry Island and Spitzbergen being followed by catastrophic losses at Dutch hands (with even a certain amount of bloodshed before the Dutch established a complete monopoly). The Eastland Company, too, did not wholly recover from dislocation of its cloth market and increased Dutch competition. These, combined with the failure of the Merchant Adventurers to win back the whole of their old market and the bad effects of continued raising of royal taxes on imports and exports, and the rake-off exacted by the Crown and courtiers through monopolies, accelerated a substantial decline in the traditional overseas trades and affected adversely the domestic market also. So the last years of peace were marked by much controversy in Parliament (unmanageable in 1621) and only partly appeased in 1624 by royal retraction of policies of state interference which were poorly conceived and almost catastrophic in their effects.

There is an element of paradox about the commercial history of this period. On the one hand there is the new development which has been sketched in a preliminary way, and on the other the older conventional picture of an England which had a short period of relative prosperity in the first half of the twenty-year period and which yet suffered in the second half of the period major commercial crises which had considerable effects on the direction and scope of colonisation and commerce. Yet the statistics, which are very imperfect, are often contradictory. There is no doubt that the years 1614–17 saw an economic crisis for the traditional cloth industry and that a partial recovery was soon followed by a further decline. It is less clear that these crises, stressed so much by contemporaries in the second decade, were so much real ones rather than the result of a shift of resources and the effect of growing-pains. There is undoubtedly a class of evidence which must be considered. Population was growing rather faster than agricultural production. Wages were also being depressed as a result of the hold of a limited body of powerful merchants on over-large sections of the economy, along with dislocation in older trades owing to changes in domestic and external demand and the depradations of monopoly-holding courtiers on established trades and the consumer alike. These factors created an atmosphere favourable to emigration.

But there were also less tangible factors, one being the growing unease inside the Established Church of those who felt that the day when the Church of England would become truly Protestant was receding rather than advancing and who were increasingly pessimistic about social trends as a whole. Open dissent during this period was not extensive, but as pressures on small property owners (and some not so small) increased, so, at the same time, did their dissatisfaction at the corruption and apparent decline in government and in the Church. If this was so, then the way was being paved for mass emigration. The first phase of this took place in the direction of Ireland, and it was also a factor in Englishmen leaving the country for the Netherlands, where economic opportunities and religious freedom went hand in hand. It was only at the end of the period, and then, unfortunately, in an atmosphere of boom followed by disaster in Virginia during the years 1618–24 that the transatlantic exodus began to take shape in carrying English families overseas in appreciable numbers. It is therefore peculiarly difficult in this period to equate new enterprise, basic changes in internal industry and external commerce, and the social and psychological effects of dissatisfaction with either overall progress or decline. Carl Bridenbaugh's picture of *Vexed and Troubled Englishmen* was considered by some when it first appeared in 1972 to stress too many disparate factors in leading Englishmen to seek change (his focus was ultimately on change by emigration), but it is easier for us now to appreciate that the spectrum of dislocation in the Jacobean period was greater than was formerly realised, even if it is not yet clear how far destabilising influences were operative before the end of James I's reign, and how many became effective only in the reign of his successor.

The peace years, however, were decisive for the creation of an English colonial presence in the western Atlantic even though achievement lagged well behind effort. For most of the reign of Philip III (to 1620),

Spain pursued an officially ruthless policy towards any English ships entering Spanish or Spanish-claimed areas. There are grim stories of ship after ship, some engaged in piracy, some purely in trade, others (the majority) in a mixture of both, being captured, their ships confiscated, their crews killed down to the last man, or, in exceptional cases, condemned to long periods in the galleys. Yet at the same time trade in the Caribbean continued and grew, and piracy declined, since Spanish settlers were more and more heavily taxed to provide the naval and fixed defences which were to keep the foreigners out. The Dutch now joined the French and English, and the harrying of Spanish official commerce went hand in hand with reprisals and the growth of peaceful trade. It is a confused picture which is only now beginning to clear. There is no doubt that Spain's islands and littoral settlements suffered severely, though her somewhat declining silver tribute continued. The outgoing fleets, however, were carrying more and more non-Spanish materials in the way of manufactures, to the special benefit of France but also appreciably of England. The relative cheapness of European goods bought direct from interlopers led to their taking a growing share of the colonial market in spite of all official Spanish precautions and reprisals. That such reprisals were extended well beyond the Caribbean is shown in the capture in 1605 of the *Castor and Pollux*, an English ship representing an Anglo-French syndicate, in what is now St Helena Sound, South Carolina. The trade goods designed for commerce with the Indians were confiscated and every one of the crew, it seems, was handed over to Indian tribes to use as ceremonial victims as they wished. Great attempts were made by Spain to hush this up, but it became known and caused deep resentment in England just at the time the Virginia Company was in preparation.

The Virginia Company was England's first systematic attempt to exploit North America and so is of great importance in English imperial history. But it was not an easy or complete success. In 1606 a joint venture, with western merchants and gentlemen taking responsibility for what was to be known as New England (partly explored by George Waymouth in 1605 and thought to provide a fur-trading as well as an agricultural base), and the much wealthier London venture, which was to plant the Chesapeake Bay area (where everything from naval stores to Mediterranean and sub-tropical produce was hoped for), were covered by a joint charter of 10 April 1606. James I even created a royal council for Virginia to oversee these and all other colonies and prescribe for their government and economic policies. The first expedition, in three ships, led by the *Susan Constant*, and under the command of the veteran privateering captain Christopher Newport, left in December 1606. Jamestown was founded well up the River James in May 1607, and then Chesapeake Bay had its first permanent English colony, though it was nearly five years before it could be considered even likely to last.

Why eventually should English people have begun to colonise overseas? The East India Company avoided anything like it. Ireland did attract many people and was a testing place for English settlement – after all, settlers there could easily return. But America? There are two sides to this. On the one side there was under-employment. Rising population and inadequate improvements in agriculture, together with the depression of wages by the power of the clothiers and the London merchant monopolists, produced it. To get out, even as a servant, was to have some chance to get a living. Then there were religious strivings, ranging from obstinate separatism to vague fears that the Church of England would never become Protestant but increasingly Popish. There was also another side. The land question was a difficult one. Gentry and merchant sons could not easily get lands in England: either it was tied up or it was too expensive. In England, land meant power, and in America, where there was plenty, it might provide power in the end. There was on both sides some hope of wealth. For the poor there was the hope that eventually they might find a product rich enough or land of their own to be able to be independent and so achieve a degree of upward mobility impossible in England; for the sons of the gentry and merchants there was adventure as well as land, hunting and venturing into new lands with always the hope of gold or some comparable riches to be won on their large new estates. In the beginning the Virginia Company encouraged all these hopes, but proposed to satisfy them only in the long run. For seven years all the men and women, when they came, were to be servants or officials of the company, serving for their keep and some of them for wages. This was chartered-company colonisation and it did not work. The arrangements forced on the company by the royal council for the years 1607–9 produced chaos in Virginia, more time being spent in feuds than in agriculture. Captain John Smith pulled the colonists together in 1608–9 and saved the company's honour though even he could produce no profits. Contingents of colonists were kept small in 1607 and 1608, but they, and the larger contingents sent in 1609, died off at an alarming rate, even though supplies were sent out in good time. Growing maize was an art few learnt quickly: it was easier to buy it or take it from the Indians when they had it. Experiments in viticulture, glass and ironmaking, the growing of woad, madder and such commodities, did little more than provide samples which were not worth persevering with. Indians offered some skins but no valuable furs, but they bought only relatively small amounts of iron, copper and beads, since they were not organised for large-scale commerce and had nothing to provide in return except corn and skins. The company saw its capital deteriorate fast. The native population offered more problems than had been anticipated. It was more numerous and better organised than the initial settlers had expected, and though it supplied essential foodstuffs which kept the colony alive in its early days, and continued to be a valuable source of maize, its ruling chief, Powhatan (to 1618), resented attempts to expand the settlement beyond Jamestown, and his associated tribal groups often harassed the colonists when they moved out of their limited settlement area.

In 1609 the company got a new charter. The unsatisfactory royal council was abolished, and the company was, with the aid of propaganda from pamphlet and pulpit, able to get subscribers from court, city and country. A great new venture went astray when all the officials were shipwrecked in Bermuda. Those who arrived proved to be 500 ignorant men who rapidly died off or were soon on the verge of starvation since they could not even trade peacefully with the Indians for corn. Too many gentlemen had been soldiers, not farmers, and had no idea of how to work on company farms: discipline gave way entirely. The shipwrecked crew from Bermuda built boats and eventually arrived in 1610, but the governor, Sir Thomas Dale, could think of no course of action but evacuation. He was about to take off when a relieving force appeared in the summer of 1610. A great effort kept the colony alive, under Sir Thomas Dale, and, for a time, Lord De La Warr, in 1610–11. Strict military discipline on company farms was established. A colony of a few hundred men learned to provide itself with basic necessities but continued to send only minor commodities to England (the most valuable export apart from some hardwoods was sturgeon). But King James had been under great pressure from Spain to give up all activity in North America. By 1609 he had reacted by broadening the company's base. In 1612 he gave it a broader backing still by admitting shareholders to some real measure of control. In all, some £36,000 was somehow raised between 1606 and 1613 to keep it afloat, largely on promises which were never fulfilled. But permission to run a lottery gave it an independent income from 1613 to 1621, and so it survived.

It was only the experiments begun in 1612 in growing an acceptable brand of tobacco, Trinidad tobacco, to which English taste ran, which slowly gave the colony commercial substance. By 1617 this had developed so far that it appeared that the colony had a staple (even if it was one the king detested) at last. In 1618 a cautious policy of holding on and slowly building up resources – which had assuaged Indian fears of conquest – changed. Sir Edwin Sandys in five years transformed the whole face of colonising enterprise. Land was to be distributed to investors; this immediately brought in new contributors. Groups of men under merchant or gentry leadership were to have allotments of large estates ('particular plantations') with some autonomy. A charter of liberties offered relief from harsh disciplinary laws, but also an assembly to give colonists some voice in their own affairs. Company servants were to have farms if they had survived seven (or in some cases five) years. All sorts of indentured servants, craftsmen and boy and girl apprentices were enticed or drafted to Virginia. Though there were now fortunes to be made in tobacco and everyone began growing it, corn was neglected. Too many people came out with too small a proportion of women and children; the death rate remained extremely high. But new glass and potash works were set up, a great ironworks was planned and begun, attempts to develop silk and vines renewed on a large scale. Plantations higher up the James River and not dependent on brackish water, like Jamestown, did well. The assembly of 1619 and its successors offered hope for a future for the colony. But Sandys was using the company's credit too fast. The lottery was stopped in 1621; news of the death toll made the company's propaganda seem false. The wholesale appropriation of tribal lands and the installation of white settlers brought about a long-deferred Indian revolt, and some 350 white persons died in the rising of 1622. The company made a last despairing attempt to supply reinforcements and relief, but it was at the end of its tether. James I dissolved it, replaced it by royal commissioners, and before his death had begun the organisation of the 1,500 or so survivors as a royal colony. At the very end of the period of peace, indeed, just after it had turned into one of war, the English government first took over responsibility for a colony in America and was forced, painfully, to develop a colonial policy.

Much was written and a good deal published about the Virginia colony, which was lavishly described and which continued to eat up men and money. Some illustrations from that literature reinforce what has already been said.

After the initial disasters it was possible to hope that relations with the Indians, which had been more often bad than good, could be stabilised. Ralph Hamor, in *A true discourse of the present state of Virginia, 1614* (1615) could say:

> now after five years intestine war with the revengeful, implacable Indians, a firm peace . . . hath been latterly concluded . . . by which means we shall not only be furnished with what commodities their country yieldeth, and have all the helps they may afford us in our endeavours, and may by lenity and fair usage . . . be brought, being naturally though ingenious yet idly given, to be no less industrious, nay to exceed our English, especially those which we hitherto and as yet are furnished with, who for the most part no more sensible than beasts, would rather starve in idleness (witness their former

proceedings) than feast in labour, did not the law compel them thereunto, but also, which will be most for our benefit, our own may without hazard, I might say with security . . . follow their several labours, whereby twenty shall now be able to perform more than heretofore hath been forty.

There were sceptics, too, who did not think the Americas, so far, offered much in the way of trade unless there were major changes. The 'free-trader' Robert Keale, in *The trades increase* (1615), after his attack on the East India and Levant Company monopolies, said:

I cannot find any other worthy places of foreign anchorage. For the Bermudas we know not yet what they will do; and for Virginia we know not well what to do with it, the present profit of those not employing any store of shipping. And for this other [tobacco?] it is yet but 'embrion', no question a worthy enterprise and of great consequence, much above the merchants' level and reach. And sure in regard of the great expenses they have been at, and the poor return that is made, they are much to be regarded and commended for holding out so long. I would wish that as many of the nobility and gentry of the land have willingly embarked themselves in the labour, so [that] the rest of the subjects might be urged to help to form and bring forth this birth, not of an infant, but of a man, nay, of a people, of a kingdom, wherein are many kingdoms . . . The Virginia Company pretend almost all that main [land] betwixt it and New-foundland to be their fee simple, whereby many honest and able minds, disposed to adventure, are hindered and stopped from repairing to those places that either [they] knew or would recover unfound even for fishing.

The picture four years forward, in 1619, from the Virginia side, was more lively, since Englishmen – mostly indentured servants – were being sent in large numbers into the colony (though many were still dying off there), and John Pory, after a few months, could report:

All our riches for the present do consist in tobacco, wherein one man by his owne labour hath in one year raised to himself to the value of £200 sterling, and another by the means of six servants hath cleared at one crop a thousand pound English. These be true, yet indeed rare examples, possible to be done by others. Our principal wealth (I should have said) consisteth in servants. But they may be chargeable to be furnished with arms, apparel and bedding and for their transportation and 'casual' both at sea and for their first year commonly at land also. But if they escape [i.e. survive], they prove very hardy and sound able men.

In 1622 Edward Waterhouse in his *A declaration of the state of the colony and affaires in Virginia* reported:

> In the last three years of 1619, 1620 and 1621 there hath been provided and sent for Virginia forty-two sail of ships, three thousand five hundred and seventy men and women for plantation, with requisite provisions besides a store of cattle . . . In which space have been granted fifty patents to particular persons for plantation in Virginia, who with their associates have undertaken therein to transport great multitudes of people and cattle thither, which for the most part is since performed . . .

The very extent of the plantation and its intrusion into Indian lands at length produced their reaction, as Waterhouse noted:

> on the Friday morning (the fatal Friday) the 22 of March, as also in the evening as in other days before, they came unarmed into our houses, without bows or arrows or other weapons, with deer, turkeys, fish, furs, and other provisions to sell and truck with us for glass, beads and other trifles . . . whom, immediately with their own tools and weapons, either laid down or standing in their houses, they basely and barbarously murdered, not sparing either age or sex, man, woman or child, so sudden in their cruel execution that few or none discerned the weapon or blow that brought them to destruction. In which manner they also slew many of our people then at their several works and husbandries in the fields . . . And by this means that fatal Friday morning there fell under the bloody and barbarous hands of that perfidious and inhumane people . . . three hundred [and] forty seven men, women and children . . .

The uprising could be turned to advantage, however, since the Indians could be enslaved and their lands taken from them:

> To conclude then, seeing that Virginia is most abundantly fruitful and that this massacre must rather be beneficial to the plantation than impair it, let all men take courage and put to their helping hands, since now the time is most seasonable and advantageous for the reaping of those benefits which the plantation hath long promised . . . Wherein no doubt but all the favour that may be shall be showed to adventurers and planters.

The Virginia Company indeed tried to capitalise on these events, but it was already nearly bankrupt and soon became wholly so. There was no alternative but for the Crown to step in and replace the company with an alternative regime.

Farther south, however, Bermuda was successfully colonised. In 1612, under the auspices of the Virginia Company, settlers went out and in 1614 a separate charter was granted. Proprietors divided up the land and brought out indentured servants and some women and children, to settle. Resources of the island were found to be attractive but limited; there was little disease and no famine. When tobacco came in in Virginia the Bermuda Company soon turned its attention to it, and the colony prospered. This was the first settlement to have been able to proceed to profitable status, at least for its proprietors, without a period of grim experiment and failure.

Colonisation and commercial exploration elsewhere in North America had had very mixed results. The northern colony of the Virginia Company proved a failure. Fort St George on the Kennebec River started in 1607 with great expectations of being a fur-trading and fishing base and also of developing an agricultural hinterland. But too much was spent on making it a military post in expectation of French resistance, the land proving totally unsuited for agriculture. The fur trade in 1607 was almost nil, the settlers having arrived too late, while the dreadful winter killed some and disheartened the rest. Though furs did come in in 1608, some masts were shipped to England and a serviceable pinnace built, the colonists evacuated the settlement in the autumn of 1608 rather than face another winter, and came home. The Plymouth merchants behind it had to be satisfied with summer fishing and fur-trading voyages, which did lead on from 1614 onward to some tiny fishing settlements on the mainland. In 1614–15 it seemed that Captain John Smith might do something more. What he did do was to put the region on the map and to give it the name New England. His own colony in 1615 never even crossed the Atlantic, but his booklet and map of New England in 1616 paved the way for permanent settlement which indeed began on Cape Cod Bay a few years later.

The first vital if very tentative steps were taken in the exploitation of New England on the initiative of a separatist group. Late in 1620 a party of some one hundred people landed at Cape Cod and moved across Massachusetts Bay to New Plymouth. The core of this party was formed by the members of one of the congregations of separatists (still occasionally known derogatorily as Brownists), the Scrooby congregation of 1607, who had followed the first pilgrims to the Netherlands. They got some merchant backing in London, since by this time furs and fish, obtained in the summer from the coast north of the Virginia Company colony, were coming in in some quantity. The original intention had been to settle on the fringes of the Virginia settlement, in the region of the Delaware or Hudson which were not yet firmly in Dutch hands, but they ended in Massachusetts. The Pilgrim leaders wanted to create not wealth but a self-supporting, self-perpetuating colony, a church congregation which was also a social and political unit. Even though they were a minority among the first settlers, the strong-minded separatists who lived through the first winter (nearly half of them died) brought into being a colony of some 300 people under the capable leadership of William Bradford. They had created by 1624 a self-supporting village community which revolved round the congregation. It is true it was hampered by obligations, ultimately amounting to £7,000, to London merchant backers which forced them to devote much energy to fur trading and fishing to pay off the debt (which took almost a generation), but, cultivating land cleared by Indians who had been killed off by plague, they provided an example of a colony in America which was a replica of English village life, however unorthodox its religious practices. This was to be of immense importance in focusing the attention of those Englishmen who had some reason to leave their homeland on New England and was to lead to rapid developments within a few years.

John Pory, after serving as secretary of the Virginia colony for three years, visited Plymouth in 1622. He may be taken as an unbiased observer, and he spoke well of both the location and the colonists, describing to Lord Southampton 'the excellency of the place':

First, the harbour is not only pleasant for air and prospect, but most sure for shipping, both small and great, being land-locked on all sides. The town is seated on the ascent of a hill . . . such is the wholesomeness of the place (as the Governor [William Bradford] told me) that for the space of one whole year of the two wherein they had been there, died not one man, woman or child.

The healthfulness is accompanied with much plenty both of fish and fowl every day in the year, as I know no place in the world that can match it . . . From the beginning of September until the end of March, their bay in a manner is covered with all sorts of water fowl . . . Touching their fruit, I will not speak of their meaner sort, as of rasps, cherries, gooseberries, strawberries, delicate plums and others, but they have commonly through the country five several sorts of grapes, some whereof I tasted, being fairer and larger than any I ever saw in the South Colony . . . So much of the wholesomeness and plenty of the country. Now as concerning the quality of the people, how happy were it for our people in the Southern Colony, if they were as free from wickedness and vice as these are in this place. And their industry as well appeareth by their building, as by a substantial palisade about their [town] of 2700 foot in compass, stronger than any I have seen in Virginia, and lastly by a blockhouse which they have erected in the highest place of the town to mount their ordnance upon, from whence they command all the harbour.

As touching their correspondence with the Indians, they are friends with all their neighbours . . .

The Plymouth colony, after its first misfortune, had done much to plan an effective pioneering settlement in New England which was soon to attract many others.

Sir Ferdinando Gorges, an enthusiast for New England ever since 1605, kept alive the interest of west of England gentry and merchants in the area. In 1621 he got the co-operation of a number of courtiers in creating the Council of New England, to which the crown granted a monopoly of licensing colonies in the area from 40° to 45°N., and from whom the Pilgrims eventually got a licence for their settlement. A few small additional fishing settlements on Massachusetts Bay were also authorised and set up. Eventually, there was to be a great share-out of lands among the members themselves, but they had not yet attempted it by the end of James I's reign. James had also approved in 1621 a scheme, headed by Sir Williams Alexander, for a Scottish colony in Nova Scotia, to be financed by part of the proceeds of creating a new order of baronets. Though a reconnaisance had been made by John Mason, an old Newfoundland hand, nothing had been done by 1624 to disturb the few French settlers who were already there. But if the Pilgrims were a tiny beacon of what was to come, the twenty years of peace had, apart from the fishery, produced very little in the way of commerce or settlement in North America beyond Chesapeake Bay. The slowness to achieve effective colonies contrasts with the almost continuous propaganda and repeated voyages for exploration or commerce. In the absence of state assistance or a strong corporate drive, New England, in spite of advantages for replicating English patterns of settlement which were soon understood, remained a potential rather than actual outlet for English settlement and exploitation.

Farther north, the Newfoundland fishery was in its heyday. Almost every year saw more English vessels come over and bring fish to be sold to Europeans from England and to provide a triangular trade with Spain, southern France and Italy. The number of ships rose from over 100 to over 200 and their average size increased. The result was that one branch of American trade boomed even throughout the period of depression towards the end of the period. But colonisation in Newfoundland did not produce profits. John Guy did very well with his little colony at Cupids Cove between 1610 and 1613, where colonists learned to grow root vegetables and to build workrooms where boats could be constructed in the winter, but the profits from furs were meagre and the intrusion of colonists into the large east coast region granted to the Newfoundland Company in 1610 was resented by the summer fishermen who felt the colonists had unfair advantages in starting the fishing early and choosing the best grounds for drying the cod. The colony did not grow and indeed ran down. Bristol's Hope in 1616 was a fresh start, but it, too, lasted only a few years. From 1617 onwards the company sold off parts of its holding to aristocratic speculators in England. Sir George Calvert took over Ferryland and had substantial buildings erected there by his agents. He went on to obtain separate and wide-ranging powers from the king over a good part of the company's territories which he named Avalon. Other speculators – Sir William Vaughan was the most eccentric with his Cambriola, and Lord Falkland, attempting to inject an Irish element – were less successful in even getting a foothold. In 1624 there were probably only between 100 and 200 settlers in Newfoundland, and most of them were working for the summer fishermen in order to make a tolerable living: the five months of winter weather were too severe for many.

The discovery of Hudson Bay in 1611 by Henry Hudson and the return of a few members of his crew in 1612 with the news (and also of their desertion of the captain to die in northern waters) created much excitement as it seemed to establish the existence of a North-west Passage. A North-west Passage Company (1612) found many subscribers and William Button was sent out with high hopes, but his experiences (he wintered on the western shore of the bay) seemed to establish that there was no western exit. The money had been wasted: 1613 was therefore a key year in the dampening of hopes of a passage. The company persisted for a time and William Baffin's voyages in 1616–17 did establish that it was possible to go north along the west Greenland coast to above 80° (while other voyagers had already established that even slightly higher latitudes could be reached on east Greenland coastal voyages) but ice barriers were found to shut off access to Asia across the Pole – a recurrent English vision since 1527. By 1620 it appeared to all but the most optimistic speculators that northerly and north-westerly ventures were bound to be fruitless.

Over the twenty years of peace England had then made great strides in the range of her commerce and the distribution of her factories and colonies. The factories in the East were successful enough – at least the balance between those which paid their way and those which were abandoned was very much in favour of the former. Many attempts at colonisation in the west had failed, mostly because of the smallness of their backing or from climate and disease. The Virginia Company alone of the purely colonial ventures had attracted substantial capital investment – the total for 1606–24 is put at about £200,000. Other settlements were small and only Bermuda can be said to have established firm roots. The tobacco trade was by 1624 considerable in extent, but royal intervention (to rake off profits as revenue) had distorted the trade and prices were beginning to fluctuate widely so that the tobacco-producing areas could do very well one year and extremely badly the next. Yet it was the only crop, except cod from Newfoundland, which paid its way. The cod fishery was by far the biggest and most profitable commercial activity in the western Atlantic, though it remained to be seen what occupation of the tiny islands in the eastern Antilles could lead to: was it to be the base for a real thrust into the Spanish Indies or a purely peripheral development as the Guayana colonies and commercial ventures had been?

At home the traditional trade with Germany, the Low Countries and the Baltic still depended, in spite of all the setbacks, on the traditional exports of short cloths as the backbone of commerce. But there had been major changes in the cloth industry. The export of dyed broadcloths had certainly gone up, but more important, the production of the new draperies, a wide variety of light dyed and finished cloths, had taken over more of the internal and external trade in cloth. Some were coming to be based partly on the import of Spanish wool which was frowned on by English producers. Others producers looked at the growing production of heavy woollen textiles on the Continent as threatening, and a certain growth in what had been almost dormant wool exports as sinister, so that well before 1624 export of English wool was prohibited and complex arrangements were also in force to prevent the export of Irish and Scottish wool to the Continent. A major change in the commercial set-up inside the British Isles was under way. Ireland was at peace. Native cattle and sheep production had gone up. The settlers in Ulster, Munster and elsewhere were producing hides and wool for export, as well as provisions, some of which were going to victual the fishing industry and western Atlantic colonising and trading ventures. Anglo-Irish trade was increasing, but Ireland was thought of as a rival by English mercantile interests. Her raw materials should, it was felt, be sent exclusively to the English market: the same view was current about American colonial products so that the beginnings of the classical colonial trading concept − colonies for raw materials inward and manufactured articles outward − was becoming accepted as an axiom, even if it had not yet been developed very far in formal regulations.

Above all there was well established a firm belief that the expansion of trade into new areas and with new products was beneficial to industry at home and invaluable as a means by which the Crown would obtain more revenue and the state, in general, be strengthened. The reign of James I was an era of continuing inflation, though the rate was tending to fall towards the end of the king's life. Inflation exaggerated fiscal problems for a regime which derived an important part of its revenue from the taxation of industry and commerce. For James I to bring the official values, on which taxes were not normally more than 5 per cent, into line with current prices was reasonable enough, but it did not always seem so to merchants or consumers. His further attempts to tax new products, or products brought in newly enhanced quantities, by impositions on top of the customs duty were resented. They were sometimes also unrealistic: at one time tobacco was charged 7s. a pound. The regional monopolies of foreign trade enjoyed by the chartered companies were considered by independent traders to be checks on enterprise. Monopolies of licensing and manufacturing, granted to courtiers and favoured merchants who shared the proceeds with the king and drove out all who did not receive licences from them to trade or manufacture, interfered with the course of trade and caused confusion and restriction of mercantile and industrial activity. The king was blamed for economic difficulties (some, like the Cockayne project, were very much of his causing, others were not). Thus there was the anomaly that merchants received great corporate privileges from the Crown, and were indeed able to expand the rate of commercial and colonial activity by this means, and yet felt themselves, frequently, to be unfairly exploited by the Crown, the source from which they had acquired their privileges. The friction interfered with colonial activity. The attack on monopolies in the 1621 parliament led to the dropping of the Virginia Company lottery which had been its financial standby; it led to the growing attack on the Newfoundland colonies in the interests of the fishing industry; it played its part in the disbanding of the Virginia Company. Merchant and gentry interests in trade conflicted with royal policies and provided one element in the controversies between king and parliament. It can be argued that they played some part in retarding both commerce and colonisation. Yet the Monopolies Act of 1624 stopped short of cancelling the overseas companies' charters, abolishing monopoly grants to individuals only. Yet by 1624 an empire in embryo, both in overseas trade and colonisation, was in being. How it would grow, and where, it was not yet possible to discern.

CHAPTER 7

Economic and Colonial Problems of a Divided Society, 1624–1642

The last year of James I's reign ushers in a very complex period in the domestic history of the British Isles, culminating in political crisis and civil war in all three countries. Over it lies the shadow of economic uncertainty, and, on the whole, decline, but this was not universal or continuous. In the spheres of overseas commerce and colonisation it is a strange mixture of continuity and novelty. In many branches of overseas commerce the trends of the previous period continue, and most economic historians link them closely with what went before, even though there are changes of emphasis and scale. On the other hand, there are features of great novelty in colonisation, for this is a period of rapid movement and development, in which foundations from which an outline picture of an English empire of settlement in the west definitely emerged out of the tentative efforts of the first quarter of the century. Within the period between 1624 and 1642 the North American colonies became a significant and powerful force in Atlantic relationships, while the West Indian islands, inhabited by persons of English stock, also transformed their position. The precise reasons for these changes were complex and are difficult to comprehend fully, just as the civil divisions resulting in war in Scotland, Ireland and England have produced many differing and often contradictory explanations. They involve complex inter-relationships between economic change, emigration, royal policies and the reaction of different areas ruled by Charles I to these policies.

It is important to stress that the period begins with war. War with Spain and then with France as well dominated the years 1624–30 and had scarcely cleared away fully until 1633. This war destroyed for a time Anglo-French trade, a smallish but significant part of England's commerce. It also broke up the more important Spanish trade, so affecting severely English commerce in her new draperies with the Spanish Indies, if nothing else. It revived privateering and piracy after piracy had begun to die down, and made the seas unsafe once more.

It affected adversely the trade of the Eastland and Russia Companies and the Merchant Adventurers' still basic trade in unfinished shortcloths, which over the longer term was also affected by the internecine struggles in Germany, the Thirty Years War. Because Portugal was part of the Spanish empire, war seriously affected the East India Company's dealings in the Indian Ocean. It involved totally new aggressive enterprises against the French in Canada and Acadia. War was accompanied by division between king and Parliament and a breach in relationships in 1629 which ushered in a novel period of direct royal government. This, in turn, was accompanied by royal financial demands on the trading community which found itself involved in loans which were not repaid and in new customs impositions in 1634, while at the same time the stick was accompanied by the carrot of lavish grants of exclusive privileges to favoured merchants and courtiers. The new independent royal policies of the post-1629 period, begun before war had ended, slowly modified the attitudes of numerous social groups towards the Crown.

It may seem strange that during a period when, for example, the Levant Company and the East India Company were both flourishing and developing the scale of their enterprise, Barry Supple (*Commercial Crisis and Change in England, 1600–1642*, pp. 120–31) should head his chapter on the years 1632 (when the wars were over) to 1642 (when civil war began) as 'The Declining Years'. The index which the number of shortcloths exported from London provides does indeed appear to show a low level of trade, the figure shrinking to something over 80,000 in 1633 as against a figure of around 100,000, but too much can of course be made of this indicator since the figures of exports of other textiles, new draperies and finished cloths of the older types, were rising. Whether the exodus of English families to New England and of English men, in the main, to Virginia and the West Indies can be put wholly in the negative side of the balance of trade is arguable: they were exporting bodies and capital, but they were also engendering a new flow of exports and imports, if still a marginal one. It is probably to this period rather than to the previous one that we can apply F. J. Fisher's dictum that 'goods were increasingly being shipped not to some cross-channel entrepot but to more distant regions whither they had previously been taken by continental middlemen, and imports were more frequently being obtained in or near the country of origin' ('Tawney's century', in F. J. Fisher (ed.), *Essays in the Economic and Social History of Tudor England*, 1961, p. 8). This is a complex topic but, in effect, the Levant, the West and East Indies and the regions to the north and west of Germany and the Low Countries were taking a higher proportion of English exports. Fisher goes on to stress the growth of 'a re-export trade in Asiatic and colonial produce', while Englishmen were also carrying goods between foreign ports without ever bringing them to England itself. 'This commercial expansion', he continues, 'took the form not only of a slowly increasing export of commercial commodities, but also of a rapidly increasing export of commercial and shipping services.' Re-export of goods brought to England was also stimulated by the development in the years before 1640 of a system of reimbursements of customs duties on such goods, which was in part at least an attempt to stem the supply of them direct to non-English markets from overseas sources.

The growth of direct trade to foreign ports and the development of a service industry in the hands of English shippers show that English competition with the Dutch in the carrying trade was not wholly unsuccessful, but the invisible exports which these elements created make it less possible to accept at their official value statistics of exports and imports, even leaving aside the question of smuggling. Why then can Supple classify the period as one of semi-depression culminating in depression in 1641–2? His explanation is that the period is one of decline in home production and marketing and a comparable fall in domestic consumption. This, apart from religion and politics, can provide part of the explanation for the mass emigration of these years – reaction against domestic depression, and the search for profits or even a measure of economic stability by moving overseas. Supple sees the Bishops' Wars of 1638–40 and even the political struggle of 1640–42 as, from the economic aspect, simple additional factors (involved, of course, with the increased financial demands of the Crown on the business community) in the drying up internal production and trade, so that he can say that 'The depression which settled on the economy in 1641–2 owed little to purely economic factors' but was primarily a crisis of confidence. This view may not be wholly acceptable, but there is certainly a significant element of truth in it. We might, perhaps, say that the Stuarts (Charles I in particular) when faced with an expanding world market, even though there was increasing competition to be found there, failed totally to carry out policies which would have kept the merchants as whole behind them and given home producers and consumers adequate incentives to expand both production and consumption. The English Civil War came about because of bad leadership in the commercial and colonial spheres as well as from disputes about the balance of political power or religious authority. It also came through economic dislocation and some decline in town and country, which produced protests from the poor and 'the middling sort' as well as the rich.

The crucial role in the foreign trade of England during these years continued to be played by a relatively small group of London merchants who held the majority of the strings in their hands and limited or prevented intervention by outsiders either inside London or in the outports. These comprised the directors of the Merchant Adventurers (strong and wary after their crisis under James I), the Levant Company and the East India Company, and the farmers of the royal customs, who overlapped appreciably in their directorships and comprised a merchant oligarchy which embodied the commercial imperialism of England in this period. Apart from the Merchant Adventurers, whose role was a holding rather than an expansionist one, much of the initiative in expanding English trade outside its traditional boundaries lay with them, and both the East India Company and the Levant Company showed considerable shrewdness and initiative in adjusting to local conditions and making profits out of them, while extending the range of their activities. At the same time, because they were a closely associated and identifiable group, unpopular in Parliament as oligarchs between 1624 and 1629, the Crown in its search for power and revenue untrammelled by Parliament was prepared to exploit their successes as far as possible. Customs duties were raised against their imports, loans in advance of the customs receipts were required from the farmers, and when it came to a crunch between Charles I and his Scottish and, later, his English subjects, they were selected to bear the brunt of his extra expenses and the working capital of the East India Company was sequestered when willing loans were not forthcoming. At the same time, in order to prevent their monopoly position becoming too unassailable or too profitable, Charles I and his advisers were willing to hand out to courtiers and to maverick merchants privileges which infringed the very monopolies which the companies held and make them fight to maintain their privileged position in the expectation that competition of one semi-monopoly against another would bring in a double return to the Crown. The merchants, in their turn, could manipulate the customs farm, to a certain extent at least, to serve their commercial ends, could connive at large-scale evasion of tax, and could charge high rates of interest for accommodating the Crown with loans, until they were forced to pay out capital in the crisis of 1639–41 which they had little hope of regaining. This domestic intermixture of commerce, finance and high policy gave the commercial scene, in the field of overseas trade, much of its character. The merchant oligarchy was caught between the nether and upper millstones. They had to support the king in order to remain solvent: they desired to attack the king in order to prevent the loss of their power and wealth. In the crises of 1640–42 they split, with the majority turning against the Crown and the minority holding on to their link with it until the last, so that they became embroiled on the royalist side in the Civil War.

As depression receded after 1625, the Merchant Adventurers regained and held much of their old grip on the cloth trade in Northern and

Central Europe. The shrinkage of the 'Old Draperies' was real. The heavier cloths, unfinished when exported, declined through competition with the new finishing industry of the Leiden area, the wars in Germany, a change in demand in various parts of Northern Europe and in Venice. Yet the emphasis on the decline by most economic historians is an exaggerated one. That they retained some two-thirds to three-quarters of their cloth exports throughout this period showed them as still the most important single item in the export trade as F. J. Fisher's figures demonstrate, and his 1640 analysis exemplifies (pp. 204-5 below). From the aspect of internal production, however, the shrinkage brought hardship and unemployment to the midlands and the north, accelerated by the weakening of the internal market in the late 1630s. However, the heavy scarlet-dyed cloths, Suffolks, remained in demand in Turkey and Persia as well as in Northern Europe. The growth of the 'new draperies' brought a measure of compensation, keeping in balance more or less the total textile exports, but without expanding their total. Colchester started the lighter, dyed cloths in East Anglia and they spread gradually through the area, each district often specialising in a particular named cloth. In Devonshire the tougher new cloths were serges, made of mixed wools, but lighter than the old, though not the lightest. The latter were made from imported long-staple Spanish wool. Some class the Wiltshire cloths 'Spanish' (and they spread well to the west from there) as 'new draperies', some as a third branch of the textile industry. They were poorly regarded by the wool-producing areas as relying largely on imported wool, but were highly sought after in warmer climates, especially in Spain and the Spanish empire. Finally, there were the cottons, mixed woollen-linen and cotton-linen weaves giving place to the beginnings of firm strong cotton cloth, the raw material imported from India and the Levant and to some extent the Caribbean, still confined to a small but growing home market but a sign of different things to come.

The tactical history of textile exports is one of sectional booms and declines, more of the latter than the former in the shortcloth trade, but also affecting some branches of the newer products as well. Much depended on the relations in any one year between the Merchant Adventurers with the Germans at Hamburg, with the Dutch at Middelburg, or the Hansa at Danzig, or whether they retained their staple at one place or moved to another. Over the whole northern picture the result is an uneasy tendency towards decline but no catastrophic changes. It was elsewhere, as has been shown, that textiles advanced in attractiveness. Yet no picture of English overseas commerce can decry the importance of the textile trades. They remained the mainstay of English commerce.

The trade with the Baltic carried on by the Eastland Company was untypical in that it was centred not in London but in Hull and Ipswich. It had suffered from Dutch competition in the earlier period, though from 1622 the Dutch were prohibited from trading to England in Baltic commodities, and also by the falling off of demand for English cloths, especially shortcloths, in this area. During the period 1624 to 1642 the average number of cloths which the company handled was some 32,000 a year, of which less than a third was shortcloths. The official value of goods sent out from England remained stable, being £144,000 in 1625 and £145,000 in 1635. It increased somewhat by 1640 and was augmented by company ships bringing salt direct from France and an occasional ship-load direct from Spain to the Baltic. Imports, on the other hand, were markedly variable. Corn (rye and wheat) might be high one year and low the next: after 1635, a 'high' year, corn declined as English production went up. What did increase, and became the staple of the import trade, was materials for the maritime economy – hemp, flax, linen and canvas. Pitch and tar were staples, too, and fairly significant in value; timber was important but values were not high even though quantities increased between 1635 and 1640; iron was becoming significant, while potash was a new and rising commodity derived from wood, indeed, but for soap not ships. A significant appearance of re-exports and of foreign commodities brought direct from foreign countries is evident in the latter years of the period. R. W. K. Hinton (*The Eastland Trade and the Common Weal*, 1957, pp. 33–52, 228, esp. p. 49) sees Charles I's policy of expansion of shipping and import control as benefitting trade in this area and creating something of a boom in imports towards 1640, though with a gap between import and export values which had apparently to be made up in silver exports. The significance of imports from the Baltic in providing material for ships and ships' equipment, as well as stores for extra-European activities, scarcely needs to be emphasised.

The Muscovy Company, under a new charter, received in 1623 fresh privileges from the first Romanov tsar, Michael I, freedom from custom being qualified by the royal right of preemption of goods imported. The company operated effectively as a joint-stock company between 1623 and 1635 in spite of Dutch competition. Some cloth was sold, though not any considerable quantity, and the trade in re-exports grew in return for Russian furs, skins, wax and flax. Exact figures of the scale of the trade do not appear to be available: it appears to have been comparable with that of Elizabethan times but no larger. To begin with, close contacts were maintained with the tsar, and the English ambassador, Fabian Smith, was well received. The Russians considered the company to be making good profits, but in the 1630s the joint stock was not being well-administered; Dutch competition was becoming stronger, so that the shareholders sold out to newcomers in 1639. They, in turn, proved to be so inefficient that debts led to bankruptcy in 1642, the governor Sir Henry Garaway being later imprisoned for financial misdealings. On the death of Michael I his successor expelled the company from Russia and its century-long existence was terminated.

The Greenland whale fishery operating at Spitzbergen did better after its detachment from the Muscovy Company and its reorganisation in 1620, having about fifty members and a fleet of between 2,000 and 3,000 tons, hired or owned, which brought sufficient whale oil home to make a profit and render England independent of the Basques if not entirely of the Dutch. Interlopers from Hull persisted in the trade and the company did not succeed in defending its monopoly successfully. Shipping was down to 400 tons by 1627–8, but increased thereafter. Its finances, too, were poorly managed and took some time to untangle after 1642.

The three companies, the Eastland Company, the Muscovy Company and the Greenland Company, thus showed only a modest degree of expansion over the period. The relative success of the first was balanced by the gradual decline of the second and the halting fortunes of the third. Little new in the way of increased foreign trade was to be hoped for in these directions.

If, over all, the East India Company made considerable progress during the period, the first few years were clouded by the Spanish war. In spite of Amboina and the Dutch attempt to exclude the company from the Spice Islands, company fleets combined with Dutch ones to repel Portuguese attacks and to carry on the offensive against them. From 1624 to as late as 1634, armed vessels had to be sent to India to protect ships passing Madagascar and the Comoro Islands from Portuguese attacks, while combined fleets took action against the Portuguese in the Persian Gulf in 1625, 1626, 1628 and 1629. Together, English and Dutch raided Bombay in 1626, while the Portuguese raided Swally in 1630. Hostilities between English and Portuguese died down slowly after peace had been made in 1630, while the Dutch-Portuguese struggle continued. These activities diverted the company from its avowed policy of avoiding military or naval actions and were very expensive so that an overall profit of only 12 per cent resulted from the second joint stock of £1,629,040, though a limited stock of £375,000 restricted to the Persian trade for 1628–30 produced a return of 60 per cent. The reaction of the directors was to reinforce the policy of non-intervention in Asiatic affairs, which was to prove much more profitable during the next decade.

It is now clear that the tradition that the company was excluded from the spice trade after 1623 is mistaken. Moving the presidency to Bantam, and developing the pepper trade in Sumatra, provided a steady profit for the company. They could get as much pepper as they could sell profitably in England and did not try to expand their operations beyond that. Cloves, nutmegs and mace they were no longer able to obtain directly from the Moluccas and the adjacent islands, but they obtained throughout this period most of what they could handle through the intermediary of their factory at Macassar in Celebes at only slightly enhanced prices. The Far Eastern trade thus remained a steady if not spectacular profit-maker for the company in spite of continued Dutch attempts at monopoly. It was based very largely on the exports from India of textiles to pay for pepper and the rest. Little in the way of English goods was sold in this sector. In India the position was very different. The spread of factories in eastern India was rapid – Armagon (1626), Viravaseram, Motipolli, Golconda and Petapoli (1630), followed a little later by the factories in Orissa at Hanparkur and Balasore. A crucial step was taken in 1639. Peter Day, factor at Masulipatam, acquired land to establish a textile manufactory at Madras (itself a novel development by a commercial company). The local feudatory who made the concession was to build a castle to protect it, so Day had Fort St George constructed to do so, the company remaining tributary to an Indian overlord. This led to the significant growth of Madras as a defended site in the 1640s, though K. G. Bassett has made it clear (in Bromley and Kossmann (eds.) *British and the Netherlands in Europe and Asia,* p. 97) that this did not involve a new positive policy of territorial acquisition by the company or a change in the company's subordinate standing in the Indian states system.

On the western side of India, Surat spawned factories in Sinde (1635) and Rajapur (1637). The company further developed the Persian trade and extended it in a new area by a factory at Basra (1640–41) and, having established itself in the pilgrim trade between Indonesia and India and Mecca, was shortly to establish commercial outposts at Mocha and Suakin on the Red Sea. These developments were costly but productive. Some £750,000 in bullion as against £350,000-worth of English goods were involved in the trade under the joint stock of 1631–42, but an investment of £420,700 returned an average of 35 per cent. Though Charles I had arranged with Spain in 1630 that one-third of the silver from the New World should be minted in London and not the Spanish Low Countries, he was reluctant to issue permits for the company to export silver from England to India. The company continued to acquire most of its Spanish rials in the Spanish Netherlands and claimed that, by doing so by bills of exchange and by exports of English goods, they opened the way to the expansion of other traditional branches of commerce with the Continent. The company however continued to be attacked by the bullionist economic writers of the time who remained alarmed at what they regarded as a dangerous net decline in the country's bullion resources. They were only partly mollified by the development of re-exports and by the institution of a draw-back system in 1635 which enabled the company to develop its re-exports rapidly without having to bear double customs duties (mitigating the effect of the new increase of impositions imposed in 1634). But N. C. Williams has shown (*Contraband Cargoes*, p. 68) that enormous frauds went on. From the company's minutes we know that their largest ship, the *Royal James*, had £58,000-worth of silk on board, quite apart from other goods, when it came up the Thames in 1633, yet the total value of the cargo was declared on oath before the London collectors to be no more than £796 − derived entirely from pepper, cloves and mace, calico and cotton yarn. Not a square inch of the vast quantity of costly silks was declared. If this happened once, it must have happened time after time. At this time the position of the company in India itself greatly improved. It managed to steer clear of involvement in political affairs and so remained solely a commercial venture so far as the Mogul empire and the surviving Hindu states were concerned. It paid bribes when pressed to do so rather than resist pressure and found that, on the average, this paid better than resistance which was much more expensive. This non-aggressive phase was not to last, but it was one of the principal foundations of the company's prosperity and later influence.

In the 1630s Portugal was under very heavy pressure from the Dutch in the East and at last began to consider opening some doors to the English. Dom Miguel de Noronha, Conde de Linares, at Goa made an agreement for a truce with the company's president at Surat which opened in a limited way the Malabar pepper trade to the company. This was done so that he might use the company's ships to keep open the sea lines between Goa and Macao which had been broken by the Dutch. Consequently the *London* was sent from Goa to Macao in 1635, but though the Portuguese at Macao accepted the goods she bought from Goa, both they and the Chinese at Canton impeded her attempt to obtain a full cargo in return. The return of the ship to Goa in 1636 with little profit (which was impounded by the new viceroy, Dom Pedro de Silva), did not lead to the continuation of the experiment. But it did give the company its first clear picture of the nature and possibilities of the China trade which it was to exploit more fully later, when more durably amicable relations with Portugal had been established.

Meantime a new threat to the company had arisen, this time from Charles I. Sir William Courten (or Courteen), who had burned his fingers in a Barbados venture in 1625–30, was outside the ring of the London monopolists but had friends at court, notably Endymion Porter, who had much influence with the king, and who was persuaded that much more profit could be gained from the Eastern trade than the company had achieved. Without formally modifying the existing

East India Company charter, Charles licensed Courten, Porter and a number of other courtiers and merchants to 'undertake a voyage to Goa, the parts of Mallabar, the Coast of China and Japan', himself making an investment (Samuel Morse, *East India Company and China*, Vol.I, pp. 14–30). Captain John Weddell sailed in April 1636 with four vessels headed by the *Dragon* and the *Catherine*, which arrived at Goa in October. They were strong enough to oblige the viceroy unwillingly to allow some trade and, unlike the company, they penetrated the Portuguese pepper zone and established factories at Bhathal and Cochin, leaving in January 1637 and arriving at Macao in June. The Portuguese this time were somewhat intimidated and did some trade with Weddell, but rightly feared that the Chinese would react unfavourably to their admission of other foreigners. Weddell took his ships up the Canton River and, in a complex series of episodes, which were to be paralleled at various times in the next two centuries, found the Chinese wavering between hostility and co-operation, the one when force was threatened or used against them (and Weddell did open fire on the Bogue Forts) and the other when they felt they had the whip hand. In the end Weddell did get something both from Canton and Macao, and his cargo of sugar, ginger, gold, silks, China root, porcelain, cloves as well as some American logwood from the Manila galleon, which came into Macao while he was there and to which he sold a pinnace. He got away unscathed and the *Sunne* reached England in December 1638 with a good cargo. The East India Company had sent out instructions that their factors were not to trade with what was known as 'the Courteen Association' (though Sir William Courten had died at the end of 1636 and his son William took his place in the syndicate). Before they set off for China, Weddell and Nathaniel Mountney took their two ships up the east coast of India, robbing where they could. They seized the cargoes of two Indian ships for which the Indian authorities, not unnaturally, blamed the company. In the end their factors had to pay compensation for the depredations of their rivals. In a sense they had their revenge when Weddell was lost at sea on his way home. It was not until 1641 that two further vessels belonging to the association, the *Bona Esperanza* and *Henry Bonaventura*, appeared in oriental waters, this time in an attempt to challenge the Dutch. They acquired some pepper, before they were attacked by a superior Dutch naval force and were captured. The result was that late in 1642 the association went bankrupt, but was not disbanded. It continued to issue licences to non-company ships to trade in pepper from the Malabar coast, and these had more success, though a limited one, between 1636 and 1643 than has usually been thought, before the effort finally faded out. Competition might have been good for the company, but a more principled and efficiently conducted operation could have had more success. As it was, the association was a thorn in the company's side, and an expensive one, but no more.

The prosperity of the Levant Company went hand in hand with that of the East India Company except that the latter cut off part of the supply of spices (or made them too dear to trade extensively) that reached the eastern Mediterranean. This came about in spite of the fact that English and French pirates in the service of the Bey of Algiers had trained a generation of Moorish captains who made piracy one of the major sources of revenue of the state. But most of the Levanters, stout, fast, well-armed merchantmen, were usually a match for them, especially when sailing in company, though they often had to fight their way through the central Mediterranean going or coming. Charles I made no attempt in the later 1630s to use his augmented navy to root them out, though he did clear the Irish coasts of pirates who were a danger to Levanters as to other English shipping. The company engaged in a good deal of inter-Mediterranean trade, comparable with the 'country' trade of the East India Company, carrying corn from Greece to Italy and from the Levant to Leghorn, Genoa and Marseille so that their commerce was not confined to trade between England and the eastern Mediterranean alone, but made them a major factor in the trade of much of the western Mediterranean as well, though in western Italy and southern France they had to compete with other English shipping since the monopoly did not extend so far. Newfoundland fish was brought direct to western Mediterranean ports and much wine and other Mediterranean produce carried to England in return. The main export of the company, however, was cloth, and it was specially prized, as it had been earlier, for its ability to sell heavy woollen cloth both dyed and undyed to Turkey and, overland, to Persia. There was also some considerable expansion in the selling of lighter woollen cloths of the 'new draperies' with many 'long westerns' and 'long Gloucesters' taking over in part from the dyed Suffolks.

The company too was prized because it could bring in major quantities of raw silk (to some extent in competition with the East India Company) from the Levant, whither it came mainly from Persia, and also carried growing quantities of raw cotton from Cyprus and Smyrna for the wool-cotton mixtures which were now being woven in England. Currants from Chios and other parts of the archipelago formed an important import also, so much so that, from time to time, a glut developed, though a certain amount could be re-exported. Though it is not possible to quantify the trade, it is clear that it expanded steadily and was in balance for most of the period, though there was an excess of imports over exports towards the end. The company was a regulated one, recruiting itself through apprentices, usually sons of merchant members, who, if they survived in their assignment to company factories and became rich enough thereby, were received into the company when they could pay its high premiums. The Levant Company, with its heavy import of raw materials and its considerable export of English goods, especially cloth, was highly regarded at the time. It seemed to offer many advantages over the East India Company, with its need for bullion exports. Together they were the mainstay of the oligarchy of London merchants whose concern with both companies overlapped. The link also with customs farming of some of their leading members, and the granting by them of loans to the Crown, left them at the centre of the London trading community as they had already become in the previous period.

The value placed on the Levant Company by contemporaries is illustrated by Lewis Roberts's *The treasure of traffike* (1st pagination, pp. 34–5), addressed to the Long Parliament in 1641:

> Besides the native commodity may be rich, and in itself, a necessary commodity, but the foreign a meaner, and tending peradventure more to excess and superfluity, than to need and necessity, as the great quantity of native cloths, that are yearly shipped into Turkey, by the Levant or Turkey Company, having their full workmanship, and perfection in England, brings in return thereof, a great quantity of cotton, and cotton-yarn, grogram-yarn, and raw silk into England (which shews the benefit acruewing to this kingdom by that Company) for here the said cloth is first shipped out, and exported in its full perfection, dyed and drest; and thereby the prime native commodity of this Kingdom, is increased, improved, and vented, and the cotton yarn and raw silk, that is yearly imported and brought in, is more (as experience tells us) than this kingdom can spend, vent, or any way utter, either raw, in the same returned as it is brought in, or wrought in this Kingdom into manufactories [= manufactured goods]: here the first as the most useful, native, and excellent, is to be first preferred and cared for, and the other yet so much cherished, that it may as much as possible it can, be wrought here, and perfected into stuffs, partly to give a consumption to the material it self, partly to set the poor artist [artizan] here on work, but principally to further the general commerce of the kingdome and country, and to help a valuable return, for the English cloth exported.

But what Roberts is saying also is that internal manufacturing capacity and marketing were not keeping pace with these valuable imports, and we are thrown back on the conclusion that inertia was overcoming enterprise in the field of domestic industry and even affecting external commerce.

The Spanish trade which had been coming on well before 1624 was hit by the war, though not entirely stopped, since some goods were carried each way by neutral vessels. From 1630 to 1642, however, it developed rapidly. The long staple Spanish wool fitted in so well with the still developing 'new draperies' that it formed a steady part of English imports, while both shortcloths and lighter cloths were exported, mainly for the Spanish American trade, and the customary iron, wine, hides and exotics were imported. How large a share of the American export trade the English merchants became heir to is not clear, but it seems to have been appreciable, though the French seem in the short run to have been the main beneficiaries of the declining Spanish contribution to the needs of their transatlantic empire. There were continued complaints about the height, rigour and uncertainties of the Spanish customs so that profits were said to be low, while the exchange was in Spain's favour. The East India Company would gladly have bought its silver rials there but had to go to the Spanish Netherlands for most of them. Lewis Roberts (*merchants mappe of commerce*, 1636, 2nd pagination, p. 23) says of the trade with both Portugal and Spain,

England brings them great stores of Newlandish fish, Irish salmon, pilchards, herrings, lead, tin, calves' skins [from Ireland?], bays, serges [new draperies] and other manufactures, and in return have only thence wines, fruit, oils, some indigo and sugars, ginger, and the like Indian commodities. East country [the Baltic via the Eastland Company] furnisheth them with corn, cordage, tar, resin, fir-boords, and other timber, and only returned thence the commodities above named; only it is ever lawful to him that brings corn to carry out rials of plate [silver] in return thereof.

The outports retained a substantial part of the Iberian trade and resisted further attempts to revive a monopoly Spanish company. Trade with France was cut off for the first six years by war, and though the Mediterranean end revived rapidly (especially with the aid of Newfoundland fish), the Gascony trade did not, and in the mid-1630s prunes and wines were the only imports from there.

West Africa saw a certain limited amount of English commercial development in these years, though it never became a major sphere of English enterprise. Increasingly in the 1620s partnerships like that of the Slaney family took over the more northern sectors. Humphrey Slaney was active on the Sherboro River down to 1637, and Nicholas Slaney at Sierra Leone, where he took over from Davis. Other trading voyages were also sent out, like that of the *Benediction* in which £8,000 was invested in 1628. The overriding impetus for new voyages was to locate the source of the gold up one or other of the navigable rivers, but all failed to do so. In 1631 Crisp, the Slaneys, William Clobery & Co. and John Wood, London merchant firms engaged in widely scattered trading ventures overseas, combined to get a grandiose trading charter from the crown. This aimed at nothing less than a monopoly of trade, comparable with that of the East India Company, for the whole of West Africa from Morocco to the Cape of Good Hope (20°N. lat. to 34°S.). The main practical objective was, like that of the Dutch at this time, to get a territorial foothold on the Gold Coast. The Digby family, influential at court, helped to get the charter through in hopes of profiting from the enterprise. Lewis Roberts (*merchants mappe of commerce*, 1636, 1st pagination, pp. 83–7) discussed the attempts to trade in Guinea and Benin, but described conditions specifically on the Gold Coast. The attempt to get a shore base was unsuccessful and trade was carried on by African boats which came out with gold to the ships anchored well off shore and exchanged small quantities of it for woollen cloths, linens and the like. The Dutch had, he said 'spoiled the golden trade' by their competition, the Africans playing off French, Dutch and English against one another, even though the English were known for 'the fairest and squarest trade'. But he had to admit that 'I hear not that these days the English frequenting that coast . . . make any great benefit thereby.' The company did not even maintain its English monopoly. Interloping English vessels, arrived to buy slaves, largely for Providence, the first of the English Caribbean colonies to use this type of labour. They were not in direct competition with the traders in pepper, ivory and gold, but rather the forerunners of what was to be in the future the greatest English trade in Africa, the slave trade.

The Newfoundland colonies and fishery both went through a very chequered period after 1620. Gillian T. Cell describes the years (beginning as early as 1613 and ending in 1631) as 'The years of disillusionment' (*English Enterprise in Newfoundland*, 1969, p. 70). This was so in the first place for the prospects of colonisation, but it was to apply also to the fishery from 1624 onwards. The Cupids Cove colony faded out slowly when its settlers dispersed or went home: it was harassed by fishermen who resented its pre-emption of fishing places. Sir William Vaughan settled a colony at Aquafort in 1617, moved it to Renews in 1618, and it was abandoned in 1619. He was still writing in 1630 as if 'Cambriola' still existed, but it had long since ceased to do so. Bristol's Hope was a small colony at Harbour Grace which survived from 1616 to 1631 at least, but whose ultimate fate is obscure. Sir George Calvert began a settlement at Ferryland in 1621 and his agents there built and carried it forward during the following years. Lord Falkland, with whom Calvert was associated, launched a colony from Ireland, where he was Lord Deputy, in 1623, and Irish and English colonists settled for some years on Trinity Bay. This was still active in 1626. Calvert was the only projector to persevere for some years, since he planned a long-term colony where Catholics might settle. His own visit in 1627 led him to bring out his household to Ferryland in 1628 but the winter was too much for him and he set out, unsuccessfully, to transfer most of his colonists to Virginia in 1629. In 1622 his patent for Avalon had given him wide powers, superseding other grants already made, and his settlers held on at Ferryland for some time, at least until 1638. Sir William Alexander received in 1625 a paper grant of a large province called Alexandria, with the idea of settling Scots there, but did nothing about it.

The fortunes of the fishery during the latter part of this period were drastically affected by the war. The French and English fishermen fought and damaged and captured each other's ships. The French sent out the Marquis de Rade to harass English fishermen in 1628: Calvert mobilised fishermen and settlers against the French and succeeded in taking a number of prizes. It took some time after peace was made to re-establish good relations. Moreover, the wars cut off the supply of fish both to France and Spain and so destroyed part of the value of the trade, the marginal profitability of which was largely based by this time on foreign exports. This trade gradually revived after 1630 (though there was controversy over whether foreign ships should be allowed to carry fish direct to Europe or even be used in the trade with England). A fresh danger arose in the 1630s from Barbary pirates, who intercepted Newfoundlanders making for Spanish or Mediterranean ports. The overall effect was to cut down the extent of the trade, but not by a great deal. By 1640 it had regained much of its former scale and importance, only to be hit, once again, and more drastically, by the civil wars from 1642 onwards.

The Kirke family took their chance of intervening in the general area when they got up an expedition to capture Canada in 1628, which they did and took over the St Lawrence fur trade from the French. They had to give it up in 1633 when Sir David Kirke, as he now was, turned again to Newfoundland. His object was to monopolise the carrying trade in fish to Europe and be empowered to exact a levy from all foreign vessels engaged in the inshore fishery. In spite of opposition from the west-country fishermen, who had in 1634 got the Privy Council to impose restrictions on the settlers in the interests of the fishermen, and so helped to accelerate the decline in colonisation, Kirke did get a charter, again superseding all others, for the whole of Newfoundland, in 1637, though he was to respect the rights of inshore fishermen and did not obtain his monopoly of trading with Europe. What he did do was to take over Lord Baltimore's house and the remaining settlement at Ferryland, bring out settlers to take on a tax-collecting role, and, with his patrol boats, scour the coast taking levies from French, Dutch and Basque ships, not without some resistance. How successful he was over all is still obscure. The fishermen were hostile to him and became more so when he declared for the king in 1642 and tried to divert Newfoundland shipping into royalist hands. However, he did not get outside support and the fishermen continued to operate on traditional lines, though much hampered in both their domestic and their European trade. Newfoundland had proved itself unsatisfactory for colonists, not least because most fishermen resented their having any control of the shore places or of the timber which they employed for stages, flakes and cookhouses. But the industry itself was very much at the mercy of events in Europe and at home for its prosperity, and though it remained a substantial element in the English economy, it ceased to occupy the leading position it had held in the early part of the century.

In 1624 the whole question of Virginia was in suspense. The company was being dissolved and decisions to erect a royal administration were slowly taken and put into effect, though for several years the governors under the Crown were drawn from earlier Virginia settlers and officials like Sir Francis Yardley. The count taken of the settlers in 1624 and the muster roll of 1625, which included some new settlers, showed that of some 7,000 sent out there were, except for a few hundred who had come home, only some 1,200 left. But many of them were either in possession of land on which they could grow tobacco or were the indentured servants of such people. Tobacco had found and would keep a market in England even if it was heavily taxed and if the price fluctuated wildly from year to year, but it was a protected commodity, Englishmen being forbidden to grow it at home and Spanish imports being either forbidden or limited by quotas. Virginia in 1624 had a virtual monopoly of the English tobacco market, though it had soon after, from 1630 at least, to compete with Caribbean islands as well as with Bermuda, and later still with Maryland.

What emerged fairly soon after the liquidation of the company was that the established London merchants firms would not touch the Virginia trade with the longest of poles. The settlers thereupon built up connections with a new group of merchants outside the monopolistic ring, some of whom had been planters themselves, or who acquired plantations for themselves, as absentees, in Virginia. Chief among them was Maurice Thompson and, inside the colony, the secretary, William Claiborne. To begin with, the great tobacco estates continued to be dominated by the old land-accumulators like Yardley, Francis West and Wyatt who had created and profited by the first Virginia boom, but they gradually gave way to new men such as Claiborne, planters who were as much merchants as landowners and whose contacts with the ring of London merchants with whom they had their connections kept the tobacco trade sewn up into a tight little package. Ships sent out from London by one of the specialist merchants or a firm composed of several of them simply collected the tobacco crop from the landings at the plantations of the contacts of their charterers or owners and sailed back to England. It is true that there were small-holdings on which tobacco was grown by free settlers or by indentured servants who had survived their bondage and had acquired their fifty-acre head rent, but these grew only slowly. So too did diversification. Corn growing and cattle rearing were gradually to take a place in the colony's economy, while trade with the Indians on the frontiers, now more for skins and furs rather than subsistence corn, was developed, especially by such able entrepreneurs as Claiborne.

Before 1630 emigration picked up and continued to increase throughout the decade. The greatest number of those who came were indentured servants. A few of them were black and, if there was no observed discrimination at first, they were gradually singled out for special treatment before the law, so that the slow transition to chattel slavery took place by 1640. But free settlers came too in some numbers. They were attracted by cheap land and by the instant, if unstable, profits which tobacco offered. It is hard to trace the gradually increasing flow of men and a few women, but they accumulated to something between 8,000 and 10,000 by 1642, making up a sizeable population. The war against the Indians of 1622-9 enabled the Virginia settlers to seize as much land as they could and to clear the Indians – native Americans, as they now insist on being called – altogether from the peninsula between the James and York Rivers in the 1630s.

The large plantation-owners continued to dominate the council, and when the first independent royal governor, Sir William Harvey, came out in 1630 he found that giving way to his council composed of the major planters was the only easy road to a measure of peace and quiet. But even that was not enough. Harvey showed some independence in Indian policy, in an attempt to control the production of tobacco so as to prevent gluts and shortages, and also, under orders from home, in facilitating the establishment of Maryland, farther up Chesapeake Bay, well beyond all but one of the Virginia settlements. A crisis in 1635 saw Harvey shipped home by the settler élite and a long wrangle in England brought to the support of the settlers the devoted group of London merchants to whom they were attached. On the other side, the royal supervisory body, a committee of the privy council, was dominated by friends of Harvey. In the end Harvey was rehabilitated and a concord worked out, but it did not last long and finally Harvey was recalled, with the government left in the hands of one or other of the councillors, until the arrival of Sir William Berkeley as governor in 1640.

Berkeley immediately began building up an estate for himself and aligning himself with the planter oligarchy. Charles I had already given official recognition to the assembly, which had met fairly regularly most years since 1624 without recognition, and while this gave the smaller proprietor in the newly formed counties some representation, it was usually dominated by the governor and council. As relations between king and parliament worsened in England, the Anglican community in Virginia was gradually mobilised by Berkeley behind the king. But the merchants with whom Virginia dealt were mostly parliamentarians. Thus the war, when it came in 1642, slowed down though did not stop the tobacco trade, and led to more cargoes being sent direct to the Continent and to the appearance of Dutch vessels to take tobacco and substitute Dutch imports for English. This was a gradual process and was never completed since some tobacco continued to go to England and some vessels with imports still came from there even though war was on.

Maryland was a thorn in the side of Virginia. In 1629 Lord Calvert, having spent a cold winter in Newfoundland, came to Jamestown to seek out a warmer territory on which he could plant his colony of mainly Catholic retainers and supporters. He was rejected by the Virginia governor and council because he would not, as a Catholic, take the oaths of uniformity and supremacy. But he kept up a barrage of requests to Charles I for a grant and got one shortly before his death in 1632. The Crown had neglected to assure Virginia of its old boundaries under the Virginia charter and assumed the power to redistribute lands not occupied by the Virginia settlers. Thus the 1632 grant allocated to Calvert all the land north of the Potomac River to the Delaware River and cutting across the Eastern Shore of Virginia. This grant also included Kent Island where William Claiborne had begun an effective plantation in 1631 as an extension of Virginia, based on his contacts with the Indians, with whom he had built up a considerable trade, and also on the agricultural prospects of the island. The second Lord Baltimore went on with his father's plans, and in 1634 sent out his brother Leonard Calvert to act as his representative at the head of a small body of settlers who established themselves at St Mary's, on a branch of the Potomac, and began to create an equivalent to Jamestown there in the summer of 1634. The Maryland grant, when put into operation, was quite different from anything the mainland of North America had yet seen. It conveyed absolute authority to the proprietor subject only to the king and with a rather vague provision that he should consult with his subjects. Administration and justice, not to mention the distribution of lands, were solely in his hands. Provision for an assembly was made, and in the end it came to exert more influence than had been anticipated. The principal objective was to set up a Catholic colony where English Catholics might find security and freedom to worship without the intermittently enforced restraints and penalties imposed on them in England. But there were not enough Catholics who wished to go, and any plan to exclude Protestants would have brought resistance from Charles I's ministers, so that toleration was insisted on as a matter of policy, and an appreciable number of those who sailed on the *Ark* and the *Dove*, many of them indentured servants, were Anglicans. The Jesuit mission, led by Father Andrew White, largely financed the colony through the society. It aimed at missionary work among the Indians as well as the provision of religious services to a Catholic community and the conversion of Protestant settlers. But Protestants were eventually allowed to set up places of worship as well. Leonard Calvert, the proprietor's brother and first governor, established manors and let out farms, creating an elaborate organisation for very few people. He also took on Claiborne, who resisted the infringement of his rights, until finally the Calverts had to capture Kent Island by force in 1638. In spite of the objective of living by a mixed agriculture, the colonists were soon thriving by growing tobacco. But not very many survived to do so. The death rate was and remained high. What used to be thought of as a population of 1,000 by 1640 has been reduced by modern research to less than half that number.

The two Chesapeake colonies shared a little world of their own. There were few women, a high proportion of indentured servants, but no towns to speak of, since both Jamestown and St Mary's remained administrative centres only. The colonists lived, when they survived, on the proceeds of extensive tobacco and fur trading with the native inhabitants. They traded from riverside plantations with small coastal vessels which in turn supplied cargoes for ships to take to London, or later on, and especially after 1642, to Amsterdam, and they imported all they needed in return for tobacco from England, and later Holland, producing little for themselves. They were in a real sense colonies, providing raw materials for the colonising country and accepting in return its manufactured goods. But they could turn, in emergency, to carry on their commerce with a comparable trading power, the United Provinces.

Much of the Caribbean enterprise of the period 1604–24 had centred, as has been shown, in 'the Wild Coast' from the Orinoco round to and up the Amazon, but a considerable amount had been learned about the limitations of the Spanish hold on the Caribbean islands. The Windward and Leeward Islands were either uninhabited or left to the Caribs, while many small islands adjacent to the large occupied islands were also vacant. Consequently, as the mainland experiments petered out and the war with Spain began, a more positive policy of penetrating and occupying the islands developed. English promoters began to send settlers to the Leeward Islands (and so, at the same time, did the French and Dutch), confident at least that if they resisted Spanish attacks they would not be repudiated by the Stuart monarch, as Ralegh had been, and might even rely on royal patronage, a somewhat mixed blessing as this was to prove. The success of the island colony of Bermuda was also a considerable encouragement. If tobacco and subsistence farming together could produce prosperity there, why could not also the healthy (as compared with Guyana and the Amazon) unoccupied islands. Sir Thomas Warner's first tentative settlements at St Christopher's (St Kitts) from 1624 onwards were complicated by both Carib raids and French competition which led to the division of the island, but he was able to show it was healthy and that profits could be made from tobacco culture, while it proved possible to co-operate with the French against the Caribs.

Sir William Courten settled on Barbados for a tobacco experiment, sending out a considerable number of indentured servants and tenants between 1625 and 1628, and in 1628 got apparent royal co-operation through a grant to the Earl of Pembroke 'in trust for Sir William Courten'. The chaotic state of royal grants to courtiers by Charles I meant in fact that in 1627 and 1628 the Earl of Carlisle also received grants in proprietorship of 'the Caribee Islands', which he took to be all the Windward and Leeward Islands. His connections in the City and at court were good, while Courten was something of a maverick, and so Carlisle was able to send an expedition to the West Indies, invade Barbados and remove Courten's representatives, and proceed to take control also of St Kitts – where Warner submitted and stayed on as governor – and Nevis, later adding Montserrat and Antigua (1627), and the almost useless Anguilla, Barbuda and Tortola, not without resistance from both French and Caribs. Some of the tiny islands never became of any significance, while Carlisle was only interested in getting revenue as a non-resident from his grant, so that most of the initiative in settlement came from London merchants and a few courtiers.

The pressure of unemployment at home and the more deep-seated social and religious discontents brought to the islands a flow of adventurers and indentured servants. It was found that even a tiny patch of land could provide subsistence from tobacco culture. Richard Dunn (*Sugar and Slaves*, 1974, p. 18), shows that Barbardos from the outset was the most populous and successful plantation in the Indies, though at first the inhabitants were far from rich. Until the 1640s the Barbadians formed a simple community of tenant farmers. Islands' tobacco proved to be of better quality than that of Virginia and commanded a better price in England so that it was less of a gamble than it remained in the Chesapeake region. Moreover it could be easily disposed of to Dutch and French shippers without going through the burdensome English customs network.

The attractions of the Leeward Islands proved to be remarkable and, apart from one devastating Spanish raid on St Kitts and Nevis in 1629, external interference was lacking. The population of Barbados grew very rapidly, but it is now clear that earlier estimates of the rate of growth were greatly exaggerated. Poll-tax payers, Richard Dunn has found, increased from some 1,200 in 1635 to nearly 9,000 in 1639, and he would therefore put the total population in 1640 at about 10,000 while he does not think the other islands contained as many (p. 55), so that 20,000, the figure for 1639 accepted by Carl Bridenbaugh (*Vexed and Troubled Englishmen*, 1974, pp. 427–8), may be too high, though earlier writers placed it at twice that number. But even so it was a very substantial migration, if still too much in the end for so small an acreage of arable land and a commodity with such a fluctuating price record. After 1640 there was in Barbados a rapid switch to sugar production and a complete alteration in the economic and demographic picture of the island. The Dutch trained the English in sugar production and took most of the product back to Europe.

Before the Spanish war was over another very different venture was begun. A group of powerful members of the dissolved parliament of 1629, the Earl of Warwick and John Pym among them, began the occupation of Santa Catalina, which they renamed Providence Island, and another island, Henrietta, off the coast of what is now Nicaragua, adding to it in 1631, Tortuga, not far away from the Hispaniola coast. Colonists were sent to plant there and produce tropical commodities, but the primary objective was to carry on raids in the Elizabethan style against the Spanish-held mainland and islands, Charles I giving them a charter in 1630, the year he made peace with Spain. Tobacco, corn and cotton flourished, but the main energies were directed to attacks on Spanish settlements. In this case the Spaniards were not willing to tolerate English intervention: Tortuga was taken from them in 1635. It was only in 1641, however, that a major Spanish force was sent against Providence and Henrietta and drove the English out with some difficulty. This colony was a Puritan one, and its organisation in England had some political importance, as A. P. Newton showed (*Colonising Activities of the English Puritans*, 1914), but it was in a sense anachronistic. The newer tactics of Europeans were usually to trade illicitly and profitably with the Spanish colonists. If, however, they lost some £33,000 and a number of lives in the colony, one of their privateers in 1642 took a Spanish prize worth £50,000 and probably recouped their losses, though their colony had gone.

The major overseas achievement of these years was the creation of New England. The literature of the Plymouth colony, the so-called Mourt's *Relation* of 1622 and the detail in John Smith's *Generall historie of Virginia* (1624), excited curiosity and inspired action, which even so remained somewhat uncoordinated until 1628. The keynote to a critical and constructive attitude, and also an emphasis on the religious character (even if in this case the author was an orthodox Anglican) of the intended settlers is given in William Morrill's verses, *New England* (1625), in the preface to which he warned his readers: 'What can we expect from false relations, but unhappy proceedings, to the best intended, and most hopeful colonies. So that want of provisions, and right information, begets in the distracted planter nothing but mutinies, fearful execration, and sometimes interitures [decays].' New England should not have to go through the pains of early Jamestown. But more than that:

> I only now and ever desire that my best intent may for ever wait upon all truly zealous and religious planters and adventurers, who seriously endeavour the dilating of Christ's kingdom, in the propagating of the gospel, and so advisedly undertake so weighty and so worthy a worke, as that they and theirs may parallel these worthies of the world in all external, internal, and external abundances.

The parallel attempts of the aristocrat-dominated Council for New England from 1621 onwards floundered, only one of its members, Sir Ferdinando Gorges, being prepared to risk, and lose, his fortune in New England. Various religious groups at odds with the Anglican establishment – reformers rather than separatists as the Pilgrims had been – gave subsequent attempts to occupy further parts of New England down to 1629 a purely tentative character, but in total they prepared the way well for the effective occupation of Massachusetts Bay and indicated that settlement in Maine would prove a tougher proposition. The Council for New England could and did grant licences to plant. Scattered and transient settlements, mostly for fishing, brought only one stable settlement, Naumkeag (the later Salem), into existence. In 1628 the New England Company gave effective backing to John Endecott for it to become the second New England town. In 1629 this group was transformed into the Massachusetts Bay Company, chartered by the Crown, which was intended, in the words of C. M. Andrews (*Colonial Period of American History*, Vol.I, 1934, p. 371), to 'be both a religious refuge and a profit-making plantation'. The dismissal of parliament and the establishment of an authoritarian and High Anglican regime by Charles I determined large numbers of non-separating Puritans to join the venture, so that, gaining its main impetus from East Anglia, the *Arbella* was able to lead a founding fleet to Massachusetts in 1630. At Yarmouth, on board the *Arbella* on 7 April 1630, John Winthrop, governor, Richard Saltenstall and other men of substance addressed their *Humble request . . . to the rest of their brethren, in and of the Church of England*, stressing their debt to the

Church of England 'our deare Mother' and 'blessing God for the parentage and education': they were not leaving 'as loathing that milk wherewith we were nourished' but to 'endeavour the continuance of her welfare, with the enlargement of her bounds in the kingdom of Jesus Christ', and asking for their prayers 'in our poore cottages in the wilderness'. It is necessary to stress this aspect of the emigration since in fact they became, in spite of their intentions, effectively separatist from the Church of England. They did, moreover, take the revolutionary step of transferring the charter and its headquarters to New England, so that in effect they aimed to set up an independent 'Commonwealth', which was how they were always to describe Massachusetts. Winthrop's idea envisaged a 'City upon a hill' as a spiritual entity but also, to begin with, as a veritable unified urban settlement. The safe arrival of the fleet at Salem from 28 June onward and its dispersal outwards to the Charles River was followed by the founding not of one but of half a dozen settlements which became the nuclei for a series of villages, though Boston, partly by chance, partly by design, became the capital and centre of government.

The settlement was not without its initial suffering and hardships, even though most of the emigrants were households of men of some substance and their families and servants. But from 1631 onwards they were able to evolve a technique of establishing townships not only on the coast but in the interior, where the nucleated village, enjoying much local autonomy but firmly under the governance of the General Court at Boston, could settle and cultivate, fish and hunt – and above all, of course, build – so that within some eighteen months of its founding each settlement, with few exceptions, was able to regard itself as viable. This triumph in settlement was achieved and maintained only by the flow of capital goods and of settlers from England which every year poured into the bay and led to the earlier townships spawning new ones further inland or along the coast. The villages were centred round the church – a condition of recognition of a township, an area with a village nucleus at the centre, was that it must have a minister, while a local executive, 'selectmen' as they came to be called, ran the affairs of the township within a framework of general laws. To begin with, church membership was assumed to be the right of all, but it soon became a privilege to be granted by the founders of each township and later to be acquired only by an individual declaration of conversion which was acceptable to the congregation.

The government of the Commonwealth, too, was confined to the freemen named in the charter, or co-opted by them, so that it had a somewhat oligarchical character. At the same time, there was close liaison between the ministers, the founding groups in the townships and the General Court with its annually elected governor, the executive head, who was almost invariably John Winthrop while he lived. The ministers exercised individually much influence in their own townships, and collectively, in close co-operation with the General Court, established a considerable degree of uniformity in which the non-use of the Prayer Book and the suspicion and repression of antinomianism were the negative aspects, while the positive ones soon approximated to 'Independency' or, in more modern terms, congregationalism, so that the new branch of the Church of England rapidly moved far away from it. On the other hand the continued flow of emigrants each year involved considerable problems of dispersion and assimilation, but also brought a continued inflow of capital and capital goods, many having left resources in England which could be called on to subsidise or capitalise them for some considerable period. The leaders were men of education and substance and were rewarded by the grant of substantial farms of their own. They were also experienced businessmen, so that Boston rapidly became a town where the traders and craftsmen stayed and where business enterprises flourished. Townships were manned by, on the whole, experienced peasant farmers, with a few men of substance and education in most of them, and their objective of an early subsistence and capacity for self-sufficiency in essentials was soon achieved. Where it was not, help might be forthcoming from the General Court or the township might move to more promising land; the inflow of new immigrants might force the division of a township or its splitting, one group moving off to found a new settlement. The early advantages of cleared land (the Indians who had cleared it had died off before 1620) were soon replaced by the struggle to clear enough additional ground for subsistence agriculture and pasturage so that townships became absorbed in their own immediate problems. Boston, Charles Town, Cambridge and Salem became the active political centres quite rapidly, but the rise of Boston (carefully chronicled in Darret B. Rutman's *Winthrop's Boston*, 1965) to a sizeable town of 2,000 inhabitants in a decade emphasised the urban element in the new society. It provided a vehicle for internal exchange, for distribution of immigrants and their belongings, and a base for fishing, fur-trading and other enterprises which were conducted on businesslike and usually successful lines. Apart from furs and fish, a little sassafras and some fine timber there was little that could be sold in England or Europe, so self-sufficiency was enforced on the colonists. The tide of immigrants, which perhaps reached 20,000 before the end of the decade, kept the colony solvent since capital was available to purchase supplies in England beyond the returns from exports.

The Plymouth colony in the 1630s took on a more expansive character in supplying livestock and agricultural produce to the new colony, and became less self-centred as it, too, expanded slowly, even if it regarded Massachusetts as too embued with secular ideals and not rigid enough about admission to the gathered church. But Massachusetts was rigid enough. Natural expansion went on to distribute the inflow of immigrants, but what we might term unnatural expansion also took place. Orthodoxy became such that even a minor difference on church government led John Hooker to lead his congregation inland to found the Connecticut River towns between 1636 and 1639, whose union under the Fundamental Orders of the latter year created Connecticut (later to expand southwards and eastwards). Between 1636 and 1638 also a heterogeneous group of exiles left Massachusetts: the highly individualist Roger Williams founded Providence Plantation and a number of antimonian incompatibles settled on Rhode Island and laid the foundations of Newport. In 1638, too, a new colony from England created New Haven to the south-west of the Connecticut River towns and formed a closely integrated settlement. This formed a barrier against the Dutch pushing out from New Amsterdam, settled in 1624–6. To the north of Massachusetts, New Hampshire, under John Mason, attracted a few settlers and a number of tiny fishing settlements and small groups of farmers sent out by Sir Ferdinando Gorges laid foundations for Maine, thus bounding Massachusetts by the Merrimac River. To these northern outposts, too, dissidents from Massachusetts came and formed an appreciable part of the small communities.

The core of Massachusetts throve, however, as no other European colony in North America did and confidence in its permanence and continuity was well expressed in the foundation of Harvard College at Cambridge in 1636 to continue the production of godly ministers, educated on mainly English lines. But New England lay under threat. Grantees like Gorges revived the Council of New England and attempted unsuccessfully to establish some superior frame of government over the colonies. The Laudian administration of Charles I woke up in 1635 to the drain of population and the rival church or churches emerging across the seas and attempted, with only very limited success, to stem the tide of emigration. Massachusetts was told to send over its charter for scrutiny and refused. It ignored the condemnation of the charter in 1638, but it lay under threat of armed intervention from England if Charles I had not been preoccupied first with the Scots and later with Parliament as well. It is significant that Massachusetts took the opportunity, when dissension had turned to civil war in England, to declare herself a commonwealth to herself. This, then, was no ordinary group of colonies. Its roots within a decade were deeply sunk; its ideologies were formed on lines dead contrary to those laid down by Charles and his ministers between 1620 and 1640. Above all the New England colonies, unlike those on the Chesapeake, Bermuda and the Caribbean islands, were not complementary in their economies to those of England. The settlers there were a new breed, a new kind of Englishmen in a New England indeed.

At the end of the period of direct rule by the Crown there were strong views that the Chesapeake was the really effective area for English colonisation from the point of view of the state's interest, while the rush of colonists to Virginia in the years before 1640 might support this view. George Donne, a propagandist for the Chesapeake in 1639, denounced New England as in no way suitable to be recognised as a dependency of the Crown; and no suitable partner for Virginia:

> In that country it is a question undecided, though your Majesty hath a firm interest, whether the inhabitants acknowledge you their king or whether they, by your Majesty, are worthy to be acknowledged subjects. Much [might be] available for comfort for assistance [that is to Virginia from New England] (if occasion should be) might such a complantation prove, were not the people themselves in their manners and lives both infectious and pestilent. They in religion, their country in its barrenness are not unequally fruitful . . . These fanatics choose rather, without policy or religion, to be misled by their elders than be guided by the true pastors of their selves or governed by their natural sovereign. Almost it exceeds a wonder how many of fair quality alien[ate] and sell their whole estate in their old [age] to shuffle themselves, wives and children into their New England . . . What a commonwealth amongst such precisions is likely to flourish where zeal is preposterous, cruelty a justice, confusion a law not difficult to be resolved? As colony there can be none, it were dishonour to the name so to entitle it.

Recent historians have disagreed about the relative significance at the time of the Chesapeake and New England colonies, and the debate continues. There has been much discussion of the status of English overseas commerce as a whole, centring round the year 1640, for which F. J. Fisher has analysed the London customs returns which are full for that year ('London's export trade', *Economic History Review*, Second Series, vol. III, 1950, pp. 151–61), while these figures and also the share of the outports have been discussed by J. D. Gould and W. B. Stephens in the same journal (vol. XII (1969), pp. 28–48; vol. XXIV (1971), pp. 249–57), so that a synthetic picture emerges. The export from London of shortcloths was still as high as 87,427. Fisher and Lewis Roberts give values of between £6 13s 4d to £10 a cloth, giving a range of money values (affected of course by inflation over the whole period from 1600) between some £533,000 and £874,000. Other cloths and hosiery, mainly the new draperies, were officially valued at some £455,000, making an overall cloth total of between £1,000,000 and

£1,300,000. Against that we must remember the 1564 estimate of over one million pounds, so that it does not look good after nearly eighty years of inflation. In addition, in 1640, other English manufactures were valued at £26,873, minerals at £34,555, agricultural products a mere £11,878 and re-exports £76,402, making only some £150,000 in all, though official values and real values are not necessarily the same. But it remains true that the apparent predominance of the cloth industry continued, and may still have comprised 75 per cent of total exports. To these must be added the exports of the outports which are thought to have declined from about 25 per cent to some 17 per cent. The trade picture cannot be said to have been favourable. The new factors keeping English exports going were first, of course, the new draperies and then, the newest element, re-exports, stimulated no doubt by the drawback of customs from 1635 onwards. So far as the cloth trade is concerned, diversified exports to a much wider range of markets was the principal achievement. This is not so evident in Fisher's picture, in which the really new element is re-exports only. This springs wholly from the trade of the East Indies, Levant and tobacco concerns in markets only newly developed. It must be stressed that a major element in overseas trade was goods which did not appear in the English customs accounts. Fish imports from Newfoundland do not appear in the accounts, while the principal trade in Newfoundland fish was direct to Italy, southern France and Spain; Virginia tobacco was going direct to Hamburg, Caribbean to Amsterdam by 1640; Baltic stores were going directly to Spain. No values can be placed on these new overseas trades. We must also consider that some of the new trade was 'coloured' by false customs declarations as has been suggested, as well as by straight smuggling. We still lack any breakdown of English goods sent to the colonies in the west, the Caribbean, Bermuda, the Chesapeake and New England by 1640: the total was considerable and almost wholly manufactured goods, including cloth. We must, however, bear in mind that the estimates of economic historians to the value of the western settlements are on the low side, and their attitudes cool. Charles Wilson's (in *England's Apprenticeship*, 1965, pp. 56–7) is that

> The rush of newly promoted companies to settle the Americas and West Indies did not at once bring profits or employment. These are in every sense 'adventures' and as yet their importance was largely potential. Most were divided by discussions over policy, often as much a source of loss as of gain to their promotors . . . Here and there some individual might reap a personal profit from these new ventures beyond Europe. A few made large fortunes. But for some time they were not to bring much comfort to an economy in the throes of reorganisation.

There is much in this, of course, but it is truer of the early part of the first period, 1604–24, than of the second, 1624–42. It will be clear, however, that the export of people and the capital they brought with them created in the 1630s an important contribution to the shipping industry, and the human cargoes and the goods carried along with them were a wholly new and a major feature of English overseas commerce, even if they perhaps involved more loss than gain at this time to the English economy as a whole.

Lewis Roberts, in the tract *The treasure of traffike* which he addressed to the Long Parliament in 1641, took a very different view and spoke like another Hakluyt:

How had ever the name of the English been known in India, Persia, Moscovia, or in Turkey, and in many places elsewhere, had not the traffic of our nation discovered and spread abroad the fame of their sovereign potency, and the renown of that people's valour and worth? Many parts of the world had, peradventure even to this day, lived in ignorance thereof, and never dreamt of the inhabitants of so small an island, had not the traffic of the merchants by navigation made it famous over all those remote regions . . .

It is not our conquests, but our commerce, it is not our swords, but our sails, that first spread the English name in Barbary, and thence came into Turkey, Armenia, Moscovia, Arabia, Persia, India, China, and indeed over and about the world; it is the traffic of their merchants, and the boundless desires of that nation to eternise the English honour and name, that hath induced them to sail, and seek out all the corners of the earth. What part is there unsearched, what place undiscovered, or what place lies unattempted by their endeavours and couragious undertakings? Most of which hath been accompanied with such fortunate success, that they have contracted leagues and amity with the Mogul, Persia, Turk, Moscovite, and other mighty foreign princes in their sovereign's name, and to his honour; which ever in our father's days was not known to us.

This outburst of Welsh rhetoric had some substratum of truth: much had indeed been done to spread the map of English commerce, already coloured in outline, as Hakluyt had demonstrated, in Elizabethan times, but now reinforced by solid trade. But the actual results of all this enterprise in the Old World (and Roberts ignores the New) were not yet sufficient to make a major impact on the overseas trade of the country as a whole, so as to transform, as he suggests, the impact of England on the non-European world. But several important steps forward had been taken. Nevertheless, bleakness for the common people, rising discontent among the growing 'middle sort', and frustration by the leading merchant groups presaged the necessity for change and laid a train for the unexpected explosion in 1642.

So many things changed so rapidly once war had begun that only a brief epilogue is possible. The short-term effects of the civil wars of 1642–9 on commerce and expansion have not been calculated in detail. Since the Parliament held London and the major ports and the main cloth-producing areas throughout (except Bristol for a time), trade was able to go on. How far it could reach productive sources depended on a multitude of factors: accessibility to the ports, the availability of labour, the dislocation or otherwise of communications (though sea communications were scarcely interrupted). The south-east was cut off from most of its coal for four years and this affected many industries. Cloth exports continued in some quantity; minerals also for much of the time. Imports in demand were iron, timber and all the Baltic specialities. The Eastland Company therefore had some revival of prosperity. On the other hand the Muscovy Company was stopped in its tracks when it lost its privileges in 1645 and was finally excluded in 1649. The élite group which administered the Merchant Adventurers, the Levant Company and the East India Company had a very mixed experience. The farmers of the customs lost their monopoly and paid £150,000 in fines for extortion; the East India Company lost their £60,000 loan to Charles I. East India Company merchants held on to their links with the king too long for comfort. But apart from a certain purging of royalists, the companies were not deprived of their monopolies (this was reserved for the monopolists in branches of internal commerce), even though there were intermittent demands for the freeing of trade. But, of course, ships might be hired or commandeered for war purposes and in general the pattern of trade was interfered with. None the less even the Merchant Adventurers managed to keep their traditional cloth trade going (though the German market after over twenty years of war was sadly impaired); the East India Company did not lose any of its factories, though it kept more of them going by the country trade from port to port than before. The Levant Company, like the East India Company, found that the demand for luxury articles decreased rapidly. Saltpetre and alum were more important than silks and spices. Some re-exports also helped the balance of trade. Parliament could not do without foreign trade and tried its best to keep it going from Newfoundland to China. But even after fighting had ceased to be general in 1646, it was slow to pick up towards its pre-war level.

The position of the American colonies was very different. The West Indian islands, Bermuda, Virginia and Maryland all found themselves progressively cut off from commerce with England as the English demand for tobacco tailed off and their royalism made the parliamentarians less willing to trade with them. Trade did not cease but it dwindled almost to nothing. On the other hand, the Dutch soon taught the Barbadians and other islanders the art of making sugar and their ships took most of the tobacco, and later sugar, to Europe in return for Dutch goods. In the Chesapeake, too, Dutch and, later, New England shipping largely took the place of English and there was a change of markets from London to Amsterdam for imports as well as tobacco. New England provisions were exchanged for tobacco and sugar where appropriate also. Inter-colonial trade for the first time became appreciable. But all these colonies had to try to become more self-supporting. Immigrants ceased to come during the first Civil War, but in the West Indies, especially when Lord Willoughby took over as resident royal governor in 1646, royalist immigrants took shelter, some bringing property with them, some not. The same sort of thing happened on a lesser scale in the Chesapeake. In Virginia, a parliamentary party developed with the result that Puritans were expelled or left. They found refuge in Maryland, hungry for settlers and willing to allow a variety of faiths. They were to prove there a Fifth Column which undermined for a time the Catholic ascendancy. By contrast, royalist emigrants strengthened both Virginia's colonial strength and its Anglican commitment.

The effects on New England were more fundamental. Settlers ceased to come and so the inflow of capital ended. On the other hand, an appreciable outflow of Puritan recruits to the parliamentary forces began. A wide spectrum of New Englanders helped to defeat the king, Sir Harry Vane and the Reverend Hugh Peter being the two names which achieved most prominence. Very few ever returned. Massachusetts declared its independence of each side, but it was wholly parliamentarian in sympathy. But Massachusetts was also forced to attempt to develop its own resources. Its ironworks on the Saugus, the first major industrial enterprise in English North America, could still attract some English capital as late as 1643, and was invaluable during the remaining years of war, even if it outlived its usefulness and died in 1650. New Englanders were driven to build more ships to replace those which came from England. They traded tobacco from the Chesapeake and the West Indies and what was not sold to the local Indians was exported, along with their fish, direct to the Atlantic islands, Spain and Portugal. The basis for the transformation of Massachusetts into a great trading centre was being laid. Elsewhere, the long visit of Roger Williams to England to give comfort to the cause of Parliament and, not so popularly at the time, of toleration in religion, led him to acquire in 1644 a parliamentary charter to unite the Providence Plantations, so that Rhode Island came into existence as a more or less united colony. Connecticut had to strengthen its links with Saybrock and New London to the east and New Haven in the west, and though they did not formally unite, they were strong enough collectively to deal with the Dutch without being taken over by them. The New England colonies united for military purposes against the Indians and the Dutch and achieved a wholly new sense of unity. Indeed, the opportunities which the lack of supervision from England provided enabled the colonies on the Chesapeake and in New England to gain a sense of identity and a capacity for co-operation which they were not to lose once imperial supervision and attempted control were revived and strengthened.

The tone of religious dedication to a colonising task pervades one of the early New England classics, Edward Johnson's *Wonder-working providence*, completed in 1651 (J. F. Jameson (ed.), 1910, pp. 153–4). His fourth chapter is headed 'Of the abundant mercies of Christ in providing liberal supply for his New England people'. He says that, while God was more concerned for their spiritual than for their temporal welfare, none the less:

> you shall see He who commanded the fruits to spring out of the earth, when none were, can much more cause this corner of the earth to be fruitful to you, and this you shall attain by means; although he have caused the fowls of the air, the grass of the field to depend upon Him in a more immediate manner, yet you hath he taught to sow, reap, carry into barns, and spin, and indeed herein the Lord hath answered His people abundantly to the wonder of all that see or hear of it. And that whereas at their first coming it was a rare matter for a man to have four or five acres of corn, now many have four or five score, and to prevent men from sacrificing to their nets, the Lord hath taught them to labour with more ease: to great admiration also enlarged it, for it was with sore labour that one man could plant and tend four acres of Indians' grain, and now with two oxen he can plant and tend thirty. Besides the Lord hath of late altered the very course of the heavens in the season of the weather, that all kind of grain grows much better than heretofore.

In Newfoundland the English share in the fishery declined somewhat and with it the colonies of settlement there, but the fishery still continued at a substantial level. That Providence and Henrietta Islands were overrun by the Spaniards robbed the parliamentarians of any foothold in the West Indies, but made them even more anti-Spanish than they were to begin with; on the other hand, they gave every support short of military aid to emergent Portugal after the 1640 Revolution. This opened up the Portuguese empire to English penetration and turned the precarious links of the East India Company with Goa into a firm treaty, to their great mutual advantage. Thereafter the English hung together with the Portuguese against the Dutch on the one hand and the Spaniards on the other.

The civil wars then broke some patterns and retained others. They cleared the decks for new imperial enterprises, commercial and colonial, after the establishment of the Republic. The intervention of the Dutch and the necessity to recover the royalist colonies reinforced the strong mercantilist tendencies of the English trading classes as a whole, and no sooner had the decade ended than the Navigation Acts began the formalisation of the control of shipping and trade as an essential tool of state policy.

CHAPTER 8

Ships and Money, 1604–1642

Elizabeth I outlived most of her contemporaries and near contemporaries who had been the dominant people in maritime affairs during the 1580s and 1590s. A notable survivor at the queen's death in March 1603 was Charles Howard. Created Earl of Nottingham in 1597, Howard reigned as lord admiral from 1585 until his enforced retirement in 1619, five years before his death. His continuity of service through the change of dynasty in this high office is a warning against any facile assumption that the difficulties encountered under James I were caused by the advent of lesser men and lower standards with the passing of the Tudor age.

Nottingham was very much the great office-holder when office was at once a responsibility to be discharged and a property to be exploited. His place in England's hall of fame as a fighting seaman is secure on account of his leadership in the Armada campaign and, to a lesser degree, the Cádiz expedition of 1596. But sea-going episodes, which were no more than brief interludes in a career largely spent ashore, tell us little about his influence upon the development of the sea forces of the realm. In this context Nottingham is an enigmatic figure. We have already seen him as a frequent promotional participant in privateering ventures. We must also, if we are to understand his public role, recognise that as lord admiral he derived an income from the costs of cases, including prize cases, heard in the Court of Admiralty. He thus had a legitimate interest in the privateering movement which went far beyond his personal involvement in particular enterprises.

If Monson is to be believed, this interest was not conducive to the good of the regular element of the sea forces in the closing years of the war when there were signs of emerging differentiation between squadrons of royal ships and squadrons of private ships and increasing competition between them for seamen. The Elizabethan state was already confronted by the chronic manning problem of the sailing-ship era, the insufficiency of seamen to meet both civil and military demands and the reluctance of seamen to serve on board royal warships when opportunities existed for service on board private ships which paid higher wages. The problem was of interest to Monson because he underrated the contribution to the war effort of the privateers, believed that they possessed unfair advantages over the queen's ships in the competition for seamen and was convinced that he and Richard Leveson would have snatched the treasure fleet during the Atlantic campaign of 1602 had it not been for the disruptive effect of the manning problem upon the co-ordination of their movements.

Monson called for reforms in a paper entitled 'The Abuses of Our Seamen and the Corruptions that are Tolerated' (M. Oppenheim (ed.), *The Naval Tracts of Sir William Monson*, Vol. II, Navy Records Society, Vol. 23, pp. 237 ff.) which was prepared for the principal secretary, Sir Robert Cecil, in 1603 and embellished by the author at some later date. The chief obstacle, as Monson saw it, to remedying the situation was the interest of the lord admiral 'in all such prizes as these unprofitable ships take'. He continued by arguing that 'if it be true, as it is held to be, an easier thing to cure than to discover a disease, then may there be hopes of amendment of these enormities and abuses. But the first thing that must be obtained is the consent and countenance of the lord admiral; for I have showed that these abuses are crept in by his permission, or at least his officers'. These passages should not be construed as a personal attack upon Nottingham, to whom Monson owed his advancement to command at the beginning of the century and his continuous employment at sea for many years thereafter, but rather as a *critique* of the office which he held. This office was fast becoming an anachronism. Nottingham was the last medieval admiral of England with an income largely derived from legal jurisdiction and first titular head with no administrative functions of an immature modern navy. Not surprisingly, therefore, he was by and large the willing prisoner of a profitable system, little aware in the sense that later generations understood the term of the good of the service.

Although administratively powerless, Nottingham was a grand personage whose influence in matters relating to the sea was by the early years of the reign of James I unrivalled. He had built up through the accumulation of prestige, through the judicious exercise of patronage and through the careful cultivation of James, both before and after his accession to the throne, a personal ascendancy which functioned through a network of social and familial relationships. People who owed their rise to him occupied high positions afloat and ashore. Richard Leveson, who was to die comparatively young in 1605, was vice-admiral of England. Sir Robert Mansell, a distant relative, relinquished the command in the English Channel in 1604 to become treasurer of the navy. Mansell thus joined forces on the Navy Board with Sir Henry Palmer, the comptroller, and Sir John Trevor, the surveyor of the ships, to form a powerful triumvirate backed by Nottingham and virtually irremovable. He was succeeded in the channel command by Monson, himself a follower of Lord Thomas Howard, who held this post until 1616. The Howard monopoly of influence was further reinforced, though difficulties arose later on, through the appointment of Henry Howard, first Earl of Northampton, as lord privy seal and lord warden of the cinque ports.

We can see this influence at work at a fairly humble, day-to-day level in the early career of the future master shipwright, Phineas Pett, a son of Peter Pett the Elizabethan master shipwright of Deptford. Phineas Pett recalls in his autobiography (W. G. Perrin (ed.), *The Autobiography of Phineas Pett*, Navy Records Society, Vol. 51, p. 9) how, having nearly made a false start by trying to attach himself to the Earl of Essex, he became a follower of the lord admiral:

> In the latter end of March succeeding, or beginning of April 1597, by the means of one Mr. Gilbert Wood, one of the Lord Admiral's Chamber, a especial good friend of mine, I was presented to the Lord High Admiral of England, at his Manor at Chelsea, where his lordship was pleased not only to accept me as his servant, but also openly showed such extraordinary respect of me as I had much cause to give God thanks, who no doubt had stirred his honourable heart to regard me, but a simple and mean fellow, even far beyond my expectation or desert, and this was the very first beginning of my rising.

Phineas completed in 1599 a purveyance of timber and plank in Norfolk and Suffolk to the lord admiral's satisfaction, if not entirely to that of Sir Fulke Greville, then treasurer of the navy, who was an enemy of Phineas's friend and patron Sir John Trevor the surveyor. He thereupon received in 1600 a relatively minor post at Chatham and, more importantly, assurances from the lord admiral 'of better preferment to the utmost of his power'. In 1601 he was appointed an assistant to the master shipwrights at Chatham.

The rise of Phineas Pett owed much to his considerable professional skill, but the backing of Nottingham remained indispensable. In 1605 his elder brother Joseph, a mastershipwright, died, thus creating a vacant mastership. By a grant of letters patent obtained in 1603, Edward Stevens of Limehouse, builder of the queen's galleon *Warspite*, held a right of general reversion to the next vacancy. On grounds which are legally obscure, Nottingham succeeded in having Stevens's reversion set aside in favour of Phineas.

> Presently after my brother's decease, it pleased my very good lord, the Lord High Admiral, to grant his warrant for my entrance into my brother's place, to the effect of my letters patent, notwithstanding

the claim made unto it by one Edward Stevens of Limehouse, who had formerly procured a general reversion of all the Master Shipwright's places, but by reason the fee was mistaken, wherein his Majesty was abused and charged with an innovation, he could not prevail in his claim, albeit he often petitioned the Lords of the Council and made great friends against me; yet it pleased God by the noble favour of the Prince my master, and the Lord Admiral's countenance, I enjoyed my place with a general approbation both of the State and Officers; and so finished the year 1605. (Perrin, (ed.), *Autobiography*, p. 27).

We shall see from another perspective the strength of the links between Pett, Nottingham, Trevor and Mansell when we come to the commission of inquiry into the navy of 1608–9.

This commission was appointed to investigate the 'very great and intolerable abuses, deceits, frauds, corruptions, negligences, misdemeanours and offences . . . committed and done against the continual admonitions and directions of you our High Admiral by other officers of and concerning our Navy royal, and by the Clerks of the Prick and the Cheque and divers other inferior officers, ministers, soldiers, mariners and others serving, working or labouring in or about our said navy . . .' (A. P. McGowan (ed.), *The Jacobean Commissions of Enquiry, 1608 and 1618*, Navy Records Society, Vol. 116, p. 2). The charges themselves were hardly novel. We have seen that similar accusations and counter-accusations were current during the lifetime of the late queen and that they were endemic to a system which permitted badly paid servants of the Crown to augment their incomes out of favours, fees and perquisites of office. No man of ability would have accepted office at the contemporary rates of remuneration had not opportunities for its legitimate exploitation been publicly recognised as the reward of services rendered.

Responsibility for preserving the fine distinction between legitimate and illegitimate exploitation of office and for seeing that the state was not cheated belonged to the principal officers of the Navy Board who might themselves be the principal profiteers. The most effective restraint upon unbridled acquisitiveness was the existence of faction within the board itself as during the relatively successful period of the Hawkins–Winter rivalry. Monopolisation removed a practical curb upon the tendency of office-holders and administrators to regard the institutions which gave them employment as existing primarily to advance their own interests. It also aroused the resentment of those excluded from office and jobs and furnished them with accusatory material in the event of their finding a powerful personage willing to act as the focus of discontent.

In 1608 the monopoly was shaken by a bitter quarrel within the Howard family which led to the emergence of Northampton as the leading critic of the naval administration and to the first Jacobean commission of inquiry. While it would be wrong to dismiss Northampton and his followers out of hand as being motivated solely by personal animosity and self-interest, their chief objects seem to have been to discredit and topple the administration. They certainly do not seem to have been equipped with a programme of structural administrative reform calculated to eliminate the conditions which gave rise to the abuses of which they complained. This may help to explain why, in addition to James I's reluctance to get rid of Nottingham, the commission ended with things very much the same as when it began, despite damaging evidence of misappropriation and waste.

Naturally enough much of this evidence emanated from hostile deponents, but Phineas Pett hardly cut a convincing figure before the commission in trying to explain the affair of the ship *Resistance* which accompanied Nottingham on an embassy to Spain in 1605: an affair reminiscent of the use made by Marian and Elizabethan naval officials of royal equipment and property in private ventures to Africa.

He [Phineas Pett] deposeth that in *anno* 1605, Sir John Trevor, Sir Robert Mansell and this deponent were aboard of a ship called the *Resistance* of the burden of eightscore tons or thereabouts in ordinary merchandise, which ship was employed in the Admiral's last voyage of embassage into Spain as a transporter. And being asked whether this was a transporter for the King's service or not he answereth that he was commanded by Sir John Trevor and Sir Robert Mansell to make ready the said ship for the King's service, and that she carried in her for that voyage biscuit, the quantity whereof he knoweth not, but sayeth that it was as much as she could well carry besides her other lading; which other lading was lead of Mr. Alablaster's for the kintailling [ballast] of the said ship, of what quantity he likewise knoweth not. And he sayeth that the said lead was appointed to be delivered at Seville in Spain, and that he this deponent fell into the Groyne with the said ship the next day after My Lord Admiral, *viz.* on the Tuesday and departed thence on the Saturday then next following. But whilst he remained at the Groyne, Sir John Trevor and Sir Robert Mansell told him that by reason of the short passage My Lord Admiral had into Spain, there was no use for the navy of that biscuit which was in the *Resistance*, and that he this deponent might therefore go to Lisbon or St Lucar and there sell the same. And that they reported as from My Lord Admiral, that because this deponent was a shipwright, he might in the harbours where he should put in take view of the Spanish ships and galleys, and of the manner of their building. And concerning the said lead he sayeth that the contract made betwixt this deponent, Sir John Trevor, Sir Robert Mansell and Mr. Alablaster the owner of the lead, was to this effect *viz.* that if the *Resistance* should go no further than the Groyne then Sir John Trevor and Sir Robert Mansell should at their charge provide shipping to deliver the said lead at St Lucar, which was done in the said ship by this deponent accordingly, and delivered at St Lucar by the appointment of Mr Alablaster's factor. But for the quantity of the said lead he referreth himself to the accounts thereof. Howbeit, the said factor paid to this deponent for the freight threescore pounds or thereabouts, which sum was afterwards divided betwixt Sir John Trevor and Sir Robert Mansell and this deponent as the owners of the said ship. And touching the biscuit he sayeth that the most part thereof was sold at Lisbon and the rest at St Lucar, saving some small quantity which was reserved for the provision of the ship to bring her home again to England. And for so much of the said biscuit that was sold at Lisbon he sayeth that it was sold for 32 *reals* a *kintar* which is an hundred and eight and twenty pounds English weight a *kintar*. And that which was sold at St Lucar was sold much about the same rate, the money proceeding whereof this deponent received and sent £300 thereof by bill of exchange to Valladolid where the court of Spain was, to Sir John Trevor and Sir Robert Mansell according to their former appointment; and for the rest he was accountable unto them at his return into England . . . (McGowan (ed.), *The Jacobean Commissions of Enquiry*, pp. 11 ff.)

Pett's deposition and those of deponents hostile to him, including the shipwright Thomas Norris who was to be a member of the second commission of inquiry in 1618, points to the conclusions that the *Resistance*, though owned by Mansell, Trevor and Pett, was fitted out at public expense for service as a transport in the fleet attending Nottingham on his diplomatic mission to Spain and was employed during this service as a merchantman, having been laden with a consignment of lead on behalf of the London merchant Alablaster. There are grounds also for believing that a quantity of public stores, though here the details are shadowy, was treated by the owners as disposable cargo and that the crew was pressed at the expense of and paid by the Crown. This affair and other malpractices which came to light during the depositions of April 1608 to June 1609 have earned for the early Jacobean naval administration a reputation among historians of having been one of the most 'corrupt' in the history of the English navy. Constant repetition of this theme, however, has led to some fossilisation of thought, one consequence of which is a blurring of the difference between corruption and misappropriation. Another consequence is a tendency to assume that when we have established the existence of nefarious practices we have said all that needs to be said about Mansell, Trevor and Pett. But this is hardly so, for underlying their conduct as owners of the *Resistance* are a set of assumptions about the navy which illuminate its problems. We can detect in their behaviour the survival of the medieval concept of the navy as the multitude of shipping of the realm and of its corollary, the interchangeability of the warship and the merchantman. Seen in this light the ideas of the principal officers were at variance with the facts of technical progress in that they had not come to terms with the growing differentiation between the two. In many ways they typified the Nottingham era with all its anachronisms.

Yet, by way of contradiction, the same decade witnessed an ambitious attempt to transcend the limitations of warship design which continued to provide grounds for equating the armed ship with the man-of-war. In October 1608 there was laid down at Woolwich under the direction of Phineas Pett the *Prince* or *Prince Royal*, envisaged by its creator as the first fighting ship with three gun-decks. The *Prince* was not in fact the prototype of the later three-decker, having two gun-decks with full batteries and a half upper gun-deck. Nevertheless, besides being the heaviest warship yet built in England, she met a demand for superiority in armament over any other vessel afloat: an aspiration akin to that which inspired the *Dreadnought* battleship of the Fisher era.

The *Prince* was caught up in the conflicts of 1608–9 for Northampton and his allies among the shipwrights sought to outflank the defences of the Nottingham faction by bringing about the downfall of Pett. Prominent among the technical critics of the *Prince* were the 79-year-old Elizabethan master shipwright Matthew Baker, a veteran opponent of the Petts, and Edward Stevens, who had good reason to believe that his career prospects had been damaged by Pett's advancement. The attack took the form of criticism of the materials used by Pett and his ideas of ship design. So hard fought was the controversy that the king himself became involved. In May 1609 he went down to Woolwich in company with Henry, Prince of Wales, in whose honour the ship was to be named, to inspect the works, listen to the conflicting evidence of the experts and pronounce judgement thereon. The day ended in victory for Pett, which meant victory for Nottingham, Mansell and Trevor.

By that time all these things were thus performed and his Majesty wonderfully satisfied, and it growing somewhat late, his Majesty returned again into the hall where he formerly sat; and being placed, and the room filled as full as it could be packed, his Majesty began a most worthy and learned speech for conclusion of the business, the scope of his words tending first to a full declaration of the satisfaction he had received touching this great business, wherein he expressed with many effectual speeches what content he received in bestowing his pains that day to so good a purpose; next his Majesty addressed himself to give thanks to the Lord Northampton for his great care and diligence to search out such errors in the Office of the Admiralty, wherein his Majesty and the State were abused, with encouragement for him to go forward with prosecuting his commission, notwithstanding his Lordship had been misinformed by being drawn to question this present business; next his Majesty directed his speech to Mr Baker, Bright, Stevens and the rest of the informers, very bitterly reprehending their malicious practices, more to bring to effect their own private ends than out of any consciable care of the good of his Majesty's Service or benefit of the State, repining at the preferment I had and the countenance of the Prince, his son, and therefore combining together to disgrace and ruin me, though otherwise they envied one another and were at controversy who should be preferred to my business; with many good exhortations to will them to beware how they did abuse the Majesty of God and himself, his substitute, with malicious informations in which he could do no less than think them perjured, as in the prosecuting of this whole business was too apparent to himself and all the world, whereby they deserved to be severely punished, if he should censure them as they worthily merited.

His Majesty then began to shew me a very pleasing countenance and turned his speech to me, willing me not to be discountenanced with these proceedings against me, since he was now sufficiently persuaded of my honesty, integrity and abilities to perform what I had undertaken, advising me not to refuse counsel of my fellow servants since it was his service, wherein we ought to join together for his good and the honour of the State; . . .

Then the noble Admiral [Nottingham], as his Majesty was rising, humbly besought his Majesty to license him to speak a few words, as well to declare his own innocency concerning these unjust accusations, as to clear me in the point both of my sufficiency and my care and honesty to perform the service entrusted to me, to which his honourable request (though it grew now to be late) his Majesty most willingly condescended. (Perrin (ed.), *Autobiography*, pp. 62 ff.)

Pett's victory in the battle over the *Prince* was to be tarnished in the 1620s by renewed doubts concerning the quality of her timbers. But for the moment it was an indication, though by no means a guarantee, that the outcome of the commission of inquiry would be favourable to the Nottingham group in the administration.

It was, however, significant that the king in his concluding speech at Woolwich, as reported by Pett, should have made a point of encouraging Northampton to prosecute the work of the commission with all diligence. James I had a shrewd appreciation of the usefulness in the search for efficiency and economy in the management of the navy of publicly exposing its administrative incumbents to the rancorous criticisms of personal enemies and professional rivals. This was perhaps his chief interest in it, for he disregarded the commissioners' recommendation that 'the offenders be condignly punished'. According to Sir Robert Cotton, Northampton's principal agent in the affair, it pleased the king to remit their offences 'upon hope and promise that ever after they would each one of them in their places respectively perform their duties justly and carefully. And for better direction of them in their present function and charge it pleased His Highness to command the Earl of Northampton to draw up a book of ordnances for the Navy Royal which with great pains he performed and presented to His Majesty. And this is the sum of the whole year's service' (McGowan, (ed.), *The Jacobean Commissions of Enquiry*, pp. 5 ff.). Apart from James's personal reluctance to humiliate Nottingham by dismissing his associates and followers, king and council may well have considered that, given the inbuilt defects of the machine, the interests of efficiency and economy might be better served by retaining the current team, appropriately chastened, than by surrendering control to its victorious enemies, many of whom were clearly motivated by personal ambition and resentment.

There was a good deal to be said for this solution. Northampton and Robert Cotton, though thwarted of their chief objectives, had had the better of the argument in 1608–9 and were on the look-out for grounds on which to base a new attack. In theory this threat should have encouraged a drive for administrative reform from within. In practice the lack of improvement was evident enough to prompt an attempt by Northampton and Cotton to institute a new commission of inquiry in 1612. Though blocked by legal obstacles and royal prejudice, they seem to have at least stimulated a burst of rebuilding and repair, at costs, however, which could hardly be considered economical.

Perhaps the worst feature of these years was not so much the continued exploitation of the navy by its servants as the apparent lack of direction and purpose in its management. It had already been accepted, as is evident from the building of the *Prince*, that, whatever her defects, the future lay with warships of increasing might and power: ships that were bound to render obsolescent both the interchangeability of warship and merchantman and the age-old assumption that armed merchantmen had a place in the front line of the national sea forces. Yet, with the sea forces on the brink of a break with their past history and traditions, there is no sign of any serious consideration having been given by the administration to the character and size of a naval establishment commensurate with contemporary needs, much less to the problem of how such establishment might be most effectively financed. This is why it had only collapsible defences when under attack from the second commission of inquiry in 1618.

The commission of 1618 was a much more formidable body than that of 1608–9. At its head was Sir Lionel Cranfield, future Earl of Middlesex, a man of exceptional financial and business skills, who had recently achieved overdue economies in the administration of the royal household and wardrobe. His aim with regard to the navy was to 'effect that work which hath been so often attempted in vain, both in his Majesty's times and the late Queen's'. Sir Thomas Smythe was a governor of both the Muscovy and East India Companies; Sir Richard Weston, future Earl of Portland and lord treasurer of England, a collector of customs at London; Sir John Wolstenholme, a farmer of customs and a member of the company of Merchant Adventurers; Nicholas Fortescue, a commissioner of the royal household; John Osborne and Francis Gofton, both remembrancers of the lord treasurer; Richard Sutton, an auditor of the navy accounts; William Pitt, a member of the Muscovy Company and a former official in the Exchequer of Receipt. The naval experts, the only commissioners not to have been members of the commission of inquiry into the royal household in 1617, were John Coke a future secretary of state who had served as deputy treasurer of the navy (1598–1604) under Fulke Greville, now chancellor of the exchequer, the master shipwright Thomas Norris, a deponent in 1608–9 and William Burrell, master shipwright to the East India Company and yet another rival of Phineas Pett. Its membership reflected the pressure of interests, particularly City interests, which favoured domestic economy, administrative efficiency and the existence of a strong navy.

Although England was not faced in 1618 with a threat of invasion, the probability of a major war in the near future between the great powers of continental Europe was a warning in the face of its unpredictable consequences against complacency in the matter of naval defence. Another factor which persuaded members of both the privy council and commission that the time was ripe for a searching review of naval costs and efficiency was the evident growth of Dutch maritime power and influence. These were years when the Dutch were fast making themselves masters of the North Sea herring fishery, sending their fishing fleets into English waters with a complete disregard of English protests unsupported by naval power. In *Mare Liberum*, a work dedicated primarily to demonstrating the alleged illegality of Iberian monopolistic claims in colonial waters, the Dutch jurist Grotius asserted that fishing rights 'ought everywhere to be exempt from tolls, lest a servitude be imposed upon the sea, which is not susceptible to a servitude'. Another disturbing development, which in view of the interdependency of different branches of Dutch trade could not be isolated from the problem of the fishing industry, was the growing capacity of the Dutch mercantile marine to outpace the Eastland Company in the Baltic trade. This created fears that the Dutch might secure a grip on the carriage of timber and other essential ship-building materials to the ports of Western Europe, including those of England, and impede the traffic of English cloth to the Baltic region.

The anti-Dutch sentiments of the commissioners are unmistakable. Cranfield himself made hostile comments on 'merchant strangers'. John Coke wrote to George Villiers, first Marquis of Buckingham, that 'whereas formerly no stranger was permitted to pass up the Medway to come amongst the ships, now the Low Country men daily haunting that way both know the river and the state of the Navy and carry thence fuller's earth for the dressing of our cloths, and store of gold and silver'. As if anticipating the Medway disaster of 1667, he also noted that 'from Flushing in Zeeland to the ships at Chatham with a good wind and tide one may pass to do mischief in less than ten hours'. There was considerable support for the view that the king was helpless without the ultimate sanction of naval force in dealing with the Dutch.

A third factor was the danger of piracy. This had been a problem since the first decade of the century, for the predatory restlessness in the seafaring community survived the Anglo-Spanish peace of 1604. It had proved easier to unleash the sea-dogs than to put them back into their kennels. The pest of piracy, much of it mounted from remote harbours on the Irish coast, had frequently prompted merchants to demand protection from the Crown. The decreased lawlessness among European seafarers after about 1615 did not provide much respite. If anything, insecurity at sea became more pronounced through an explosive upsurge of the piracy endemic in the Barbary states, particularly among the Algerines, whose name in the 1620s was to become hated and feared by Western Europeans.

The commission reported to the Privy Council in September 1618. Though critical of waste, inefficiency and overmanning both afloat and ashore, it was primarily concerned with recommendations for the future naval establishment, its cost and its management. As far as the naval establishment was concerned, its recommendations were a blend of tradition and change. They took for granted the role of the merchant marine as a component of the national sea forces, the regular element being regarded as 'sufficient with the ships of His Majesty's subjects without foreign aid to encounter the sea forces of any prince or state whatsoever'. At the same time, however, an unmistakable differentiation was underlined between royal warships and armed merchantmen.

> The number of small vessels built in former times were a means to draw on many needless employments and charges, and withal neither able to perform service nor give reputation to the state, whereas these greater ships will not so easily be sent out and when they are abroad will carry with them more power and honour, and keep the seas with more respect and command and when there is need of small ships they may be had from the merchants. (McGowan, (ed.), *The Jacobean Commissions of Enquiry*, p. 288)

The function of the royal warships was to provide a powerful squadron which should be the backbone of the massed fighting strength at sea. Having made a distinction between the function of the royal warships, or the greater bulk of them, and that of the private armed ships enrolled in the national sea forces, the commissioners recommended a permanent establishment of thirty efficient ships, the classification of which anticipates the rating system of later days. It was to be headed by four 'royal ships', the *Prince Royal*, the *White Bear*, the *Merhonour* and the *Anne Royal*, all of 800 tons or more and all currently serviceable. The proposed second class numbered fourteen ships of 650 to 800 tons, which were described as more useful than those of greater burden and less expensive to build and maintain. Eight such ships already existed, and six would have to be built to replace five worn-out vessels and four galleys. The third class was described as 'middling ships' of 450 tons, of which three would have to be new built. There was to be a fourth class of two 'small ships' of 350 tons, of which one would have to be built. Lastly, there were to be four pinnaces of 250 tons and less. This recommended establishment, though numerically smaller than that of Elizabeth I, was heavier by over 3,000 tons. The commission admitted that the achievement of this establishment required the building of ten ships, but it claimed that the standard might be reached in five years by the construction of two a year and that the total cost to the Crown during this period of restoration would be £30,000 a year, which was considerably less than the recent annual charge 'in the time of decaying'.

The recommended establishment, though undoubtedly based upon a comprehensive grasp of the problems of naval defence in an age of chronic financial difficulty, was less innovatory than the constitutional proposals for the future management of the navy. They amounted to nothing less than a proposal that the existing system should be scrapped and that the commission itself should be the body responsible for executing the programme which it had recommended. This meant in effect dismantling the Navy Board and the vested interests clustered around it. The hand of the commissioners was undoubtedly strengthened by the fact that, having been appointed by the Privy Council to effect economies and to improve efficiency, they had produced a reasoned report showing how these aims could be achieved. The ranks of the opposition were already thinned by the removal from office in May of Sir Robert Mansell, who had been compensated by the receipt of £3,000 from his successor, Sir William Russell of the Muscovy Company, and an appointment as vice-admiral of England. Even so, it is doubtful whether a recommendation which threatened so many interests would have won acceptance had it not been for the impact upon the business of factional rivalry at court.

The key figure here was the youthful George Villiers, Marquis of Buckingham, who had since 1616 been climbing the hills of power and preferment through the affection and favour of the king. To reach the summit he needed to sweep away the influence of the Howards. There, perhaps the main target was the lord treasurer, the tough ex-seaman Thomas Howard, first Earl of Suffolk, who was suspended from office in 1618. The removal of the ageing Nottingham was also of advantage to Buckingham and his clients. By aligning Buckingham, who possessed what Northampton had lacked – the doting affection of the king – with the cause of naval reform, its advocates could hope to win the battle at court. They therefore mounted a campaign in favour of Buckingham's appointment as lord admiral.

There had already been talk of Buckingham as successor to Nottingham, and possibly some tentative negotiations, in the spring of the year when the privy council was considering the investigation of naval finance. Now John Coke emerged among the commissioners as the driving force of a pro-Buckingham bandwagon, one of his tasks being to persuade the favourite that acceptance of the appointment would increase the substance of his influence and power.

That the frame of our commission to execute what we have projected for the navy may not be mistaken as derogatory from the lord admiral's power – the true grounds there of are briefly these. That in bodies politic as well as natural the parts must have a symmetry and proportion to the head. That this proportion in kingdoms requireth a subordination of officers and magistrates rather than senates or synods, and that therefore the lord admiral as a chief officer of the state receiving his virtue and motion from the first mover the king must thereby move and guide all others contained in his orb. First, the principal officers that have their patents anciently from the king may notwithstanding depend upon the lord admiral for the recommendation of their ability and worth. Secondly, that all under officers that have lately procured patents during life may again be reduced to the ancient manner of grants from his lordship during pleasure only. Thirdly, that even this temporary commission may wholly depend upon his authority and protection. Be pleased, my good lord, to consider that the lord admiral's greatness is not to have a market under him of base and unworthy people that betray the king's honour and his by the sale of places, havoc of provisions, and ruins of the ships, but his true and real greatness is the power and greatness of the king, the confidence of his favour, the trust of his service, and the reputation and flourishing estate of the navy. (Historical Manuscripts Commission, Twelfth Report, Appendix, Part I: *The Manuscripts of the Earl Cowper, K.G., Preserved at Melbourne Hall, Derbyshire,* Vol. I, p. 99)

The intention therefore was to bring the lord admiral out of the administrative shadows in which he had lingered since the mid-1550s. When Buckingham accepted office with the title of lord high admiral it was as effective chief of the service at the head of a standing commission responsible for the government and administration of the navy. The commission itself was hardly distinguishable from a committee of the Privy Council, the lord high admiral being its representative within the councils of state. Buckingham therefore may be fairly said to have fulfilled many of the functions of the later office of first lord of the admiralty. Nottingham retired with generous financial compensation. And the principal officers, with the exception of the treasurer, Sir William Russell, were suspended.

It is also clear from Coke's correspondence with Buckingham in the autumn of 1618 that the commissioners recognised that changes in the form of naval government were of themselves insufficient to improve the cost-effectiveness of the navy. To achieve the aims set out in their report to the Privy Council they would have to establish control over holders of the expanding network of offices and jobs within the naval service. This could only be done through the abolition of practices which were sacred to early seventeenth-century official careerists: venality of office, grants of reversion and patents of tenure for life. Whichever way one looked at it, however, practices hallowed by centuries of tradition and fortified by legal concepts of office as property could hardly be abolished by frontal attack. The removal of officials with life tenure was extremely difficult by any method other than financial inducement: the method employed in the cases of Nottingham and Mansell. Radical reform therefore of the sort in which the commissioners professed an interest remained for the present an aspiration. This was largely for financial reasons since it would have been impossible to find the money for dispossessing officials by legal methods. They could only make recommendations concerning the granting of office during pleasure and the restriction of reversions to take effect with the passing of the existing generation of officials.

The commissioners entered upon what was to prove a ten-year period of naval management burdened with the legacy of the past and restricted by the financial problems of the Stuart monarchy. Nevertheless they tackled the building programme designed to bring the fleet up to the desired strength with commendable energy. Writing in 1626, Coke stated that, in the first five years of the commission, ten new ships were built and the rest repaired in accordance with its propositions and that the state of the navy at the end of those five years was much better 'than ever it was in my memory and exceeded the navies of former times, the greatest of which came short of this in burden above 4,000 tons. And since this lord admiral's time there have been built at Chatham two new docks and a great structure of storehouses, and many reparations done at Portsmouth' (*Manuscripts of the Earl Cowper*, Vol. I, p. 285). Coke has been described as a creature of Buckingham. He certainly campaigned zealously for his appointment in 1618 and had an interest in his reputation as lord admiral. We should not, therefore, accept these claims uncritically. There is, however, general agreement among historians, including the most severe critics of Jacobean naval administration, that the standing commission was at least an improvement on its predecessors and that, as far as the ordinary upkeep of the navy was concerned, it achieved its stated objectives.

The ordinary upkeep of the navy was one thing; operational efficiency was another. Coke's comments were made in response to demands for an inquiry into the state of the navy. These demands arose out of dissatisfaction with its operational performances. The first operation under the commission's management was the expedition, ostensibly in collaboration with Spain, led by Sir Robert Mansell into the Mediterranean in 1620 against the pirates of Algiers. In retrospect, the expedition is chiefly remarkable as having been the first passage beyond the Straits of Gibraltar of an English naval squadron. It can therefore be seen as the first step towards the gradual development during the seventeenth century of an English Mediterranean policy and the emergence of England as a Mediterranean naval power of the first rank within less than a century. While it would be fanciful to attribute to James I and his advisers a consciousness of England's future destiny within the inland sea, it is interesting that Spanish statesmen in these first years of the Thirty Years War were, despite agreement on the desirability of international action against piracy, uneasy about the consequences for the interests of Spain of this extension of English sea power.

'The dawn of England's career as a Mediterranean power,' wrote Sir Julian Corbett in *England in the Mediterranean* (Vol. I, p. 97), 'was as unpromising as her first attempts at colonisation.' It is difficult not to agree. The mobilisation of a fleet of six royal warships, ten well-armed merchantmen and two pinnaces was decided upon in 1619. Partly because of political hesitations and partly because of financial and organisational difficulties, it proceeded slowly. Not until the autumn of 1620 did the squadron get away. The appointment of officers was as haphazard as in the days of the late queen. The command was given to Mansell as vice-admiral of England. He had last seen service at sea in 1604. The post of second-in-command went to Sir Richard Hawkins, author of *The Observations òf Sir Richard Hawkins knight, in his voyage into the South Sea, anno domini 1593*, which was to be published posthumously in 1622. Sir Richard, who was about sixty years old, had last been at sea in 1594 when the voyage on which the *Observations* is based was terminated in the Pacific when he was made prisoner-of-war by the Spaniards. He seems to have owed his appointment to the demands of London merchants and shipowners who considered him a suitable representative of their interests. Third-in-command was Sir Thomas Button, the highlights of whose career had been resourceful conduct at Kinsale in 1601 and leadership of an exploration in Hudson's Bay in 1612. Ship commands went to professional seamen, including a sprinkling of adventurers and ex-pirates, and courtiers.

Mansell's expedition is largely remembered for its failure to destroy the pirates' nest. Many historians, accepting uncritically Monson's strictures upon its conduct, have written it off as yet another example of Jacobean inefficiency and Mansell's incompetence. Corbett, on the other hand (*England in the Mediterranean*, Vol. I, pp. 100 ff.) brings out the cautionary nature of Mansell's orders with their emphasis upon the desirability of obtaining satisfaction by forceful diplomacy rather than by a hazardous frontal assault upon Algiers. The risk to the ships played a part in this thinking. It would also seem, in the light of Corbett's investigations, that the English government, though irked by the activities of the Algerines, neither wished to push the quarrel to an irreparable breach nor to destroy Algerine maritime power. It must be remembered that, as a Northern Protestant power, England faced the risk of becoming involved through the dangerous international situation in war with Spain, in which event, collaboration with the Algerine corsairs could well become the order of the day. The affair seems to warrant more investigation as an aspect of the history of international relations. It cannot be written off as a piece of 'gunboat diplomacy' that went hopelessly wrong.

James I, despite recent events in Bohemia and the Palatinate which touched his honour as father-in-law of the 'winter king', Frederick the Elector Palatine, never abandoned his efforts to rescue Frederick from the consequences of his own follies through diplomatic efforts, including negotiations for a marriage between his son Charles and a Spanish princess.

The breakdown of the marriage negotiations and the death of the king opened the way, largely at the instigation of Buckingham, to war with Spain. A Spanish war was, from Buckingham's point of view, an attractive proposition. Spain was in popular opinion the national enemy. Men could still be stirred by the call to arms against the power and wealth of the Spanish monarchy. The words of Sir Benjamin Rudyard, M.P. for Portsmouth, in 1624 vividly capture the depth of anti-Spanish sentiment.

> Now, let us a little consider the enemy we are to encounter, the king of Spain. They are not his great territories which make him so powerful and so troublesome to all christendom. For it is very well known, that Spain itself is but weak in men and barren of natural commodities. As for his other territories, they lie divided and asunder, which is a weakness in itself; besides, they are held by force and maintained at an extraordinary charge. Insomuch, as although to be a great king, yet is he like that great tyrant who was said to have 100 hands, but he had 50 bellies to feed, so that rateably, he had no more hands than another man.
>
> No sir, they are his mines in the West Indies, which minister fuel to feed his vast ambitious desire of universal monarchy: it is the money he hath from thence, which makes him able to levy and pay soldiers in all places; and to keep an army continually on foot, ready to invade and endanger his neighbours.
>
> So that we have no other way, but to endeavour to cut him up at root, and seek to impeach, or to supplant him in the West Indies. By part of which course, that famous queen of most glorious memory, had heretofore almost brought him to his knees. And this our undertaking (if it please God to bless it) must needs effect it sooner and quicker: the whole body of the kingdom being united and concurring in a perpetual supply to this action, so that he will have no free time given him to rest. (L. F. Stock (ed.), *Proceedings and Debates of the British Parliaments respecting North America,* Vol. I: *1542–1688,* p. 62)

The Spanish war was Buckingham's one serious attempt to rally the House of Commons, including its Puritan members, to his support. Although the attempt was to fail because men both distrusted his motives and doubted his competence, he provided his opponents with their naval war with Spain.

It began inauspiciously since the yield of parliamentary subsidies fell short of what was required to meet the cost of war. Nevertheless there was much talk, as in the 1590s, of expeditions to the Caribbean, the Azores, the Canaries, the Spanish coast and, more innovatory, the Mediterranean. The fleet assembled to revive illusory glories was in appearance imposing. It consisted of nine royal warships, thirty armed merchantmen, a number of Newcastle colliers and transports having on board an army of 10,000 troops. It was under orders to weaken and disable the King of Spain by taking and destroying his ships, galleys and vessels of all sorts, by spoiling his provisions in the coastal towns, by intercepting his outward- and homeward-bound fleets and 'by taking in, and possessing some such place or places, in the many of his dominions, as may support and countenance our successive fleets'. We would not be far wrong if we detect here unmistakable echoes of the strategic plans of the second Earl of Essex in 1596-7.

When we turn to the leadership, however, we are bound to be struck by the lack of experience of war, especially of war at sea. Of the men who had led the fleet into the Mediterranean in 1620, Mansell had excluded himself from selection as commander by coming out into the open as an opponent of Buckingham. Button was out of favour. Richard Hawkins was dead. The appointments of 1620 had at least taken into account experience, however remote, at sea. Those of 1625 were influenced by the lack of progress towards the professionalisation of the naval officer. Two seamen of some standing, John Pennington and Sir Henry Palmer, were given responsibility for the defence of trade in the Narrow Seas against the Spanish Dunkirk squadron, the direct descendant of that organised by the Spinolas around the turn of the century. The fleet for foreign service was officered on medieval lines, the leadership being entrusted to soldiers and courtiers.

At its head as admiral-of-the-fleet, lieutenant-general and marshal of his majesty's land forces was Sir Edward Cecil, Viscount Wimbledon, a nephew of the late principal secretary Robert Cecil, Earl of Salisbury. Wimbledon, born in 1572, was an experienced soldier who had reached the rank of colonel in the Netherlands campaigns. He was recalled from the Netherlands, where war between Spain and the Seven United Provinces had flared up again in 1621, to take command. The vice-admiral was Robert Devereux, third Earl of Essex, a future parliamentary general in the Civil War, who had also reached the rank of colonel in the Netherlands. The rear-admiral was William Fielding, first Earl of Denbigh, who was the husband of Buckingham's sister Susan. The paucity of maritime experience was further reflected in the membership of the largely courtly council appointed to serve Wimbledon. Its senior naval member was Sir Thomas Love whose only recorded service hitherto was command of a ship in Mansell's expedition. The other seamen on the council of war were Sir Samuel Argall and Sir John Chudleigh, commanders of merchantmen on the same expedition, and Sir John Watts who seems to have been a grandson of the Elizabethan London privateer, John Watts. William Monson, now very much on the beach, commented upon 'the want of expert men to advise what had been practised in fleets' and wrote scathingly of 'sailors put into the habit of gentlemen and made knights before they knew what belonged to gentility, nor were ever expert but in poor petty barks' (M. Oppenheim (ed.), *Naval Tracts of Sir William Monson,* Vol. III, Navy Records Society, Vol. 43, p. 166).

Though deplored by Monson then and by navalist historians since, the appointment of the colonels was not the last seventeenth-century experiment in military leadership of the navy. The republican council of state in a search for discipline and loyalty was to select the officers, known to history as the generals-at-sea, from the commissioned ranks of the New Model Army. As not even the most convinced navalists would attempt to deny that the leadership of the republican generals, among them Robert Blake, did much to advance the rise of English sea power, it must be presumed that the fault of Wimbledon and his colleagues was not that they were soldiers but that they were failures.

The failure was no doubt partly of their own making. In one striking respect Wimbledon anticipated the achievements of the generals-at-sea. His instructions for battle attempted to substitute a regular order for the chaotic tactical legacy of the Elizabethan seamen and seem, in the cautious words of Sir Julian Corbett (*Fighting Instructions, 1530–1816,* Navy Records Society, Vol. 29, p. 50), 'to contemplate the whole fleet going into action in succession after the leading ship, an order which has the appearance of another advance towards the perfected line'. For the rest, however, his concept of leadership was hardly inspiring. Departing from the style of Drake, he reverted to the idea of the commander as chairman of a committee and caused to be added to his official instructions from the king an authorisation to undertake an enterprise that might be dangerous as long as it was by the advice of the council of war. By recommending and consenting to this clause Wimbledon made himself dependent upon a disparate group of subordinate officers. He thus weakened his own authority without divesting himself of responsibility for the consequences of such decisions as might be made in council.

Wimbledon, however, is entitled to some consideration. It would be understandable if when he read the first draft of his instructions he did not much like what he saw. They were produced following a council at Plymouth, attended by both Charles I and Buckingham, at which Lisbon, Cádiz and Sanlúcar, the port for Seville, were mentioned as possible targets. No settled plan was decided, largely, it would seem, because the king and the lord high admiral wanted victory without risks.

If you be constrained to put on land to burn any of the shipping, magazines of provisions, or provisions, and shall find that that town or port where such provisions are, may be kept as a surety to us, and a thorn in the sides of the enemy, you may then upon good council and deliberation, put a convenient garrison into the place or give us advertisement, that by holding of such a place we may the rather bring the enemy to reason. And though that which we have least in contemplation is the taking or spoiling of a town, yet if you shall find any rich town, that without any great hazard you may take, you may do well to remember the great cost we have been at in this fleet, attempt the taking of the town, and being gotten, be very careful for the gathering together and preserving of the riches towards the defraying the cost of the fleet . . . (C. Dalton (ed.), *Life and Times of General Sir Edward Cecil, Viscount Wimbledon*, Vol. II, pp. 383 ff.)

The target therefore became the subject of debate in council after the fleet had put to sea. Several places, including Gibraltar, were put forward before the choice finally fell on Cádiz.

The chances of a successful attack on foreign territory were low. Buckingham and the commission had done a worthwhile job in restoring and maintaining the peacetime navy during their first five years of office. They were overwhelmed by financial disorder in their efforts to equip an expedition for overseas service in time of war. The strain upon the royal finances of the continuously rising cost of war, already apparent in the days of the queen, played havoc with the policy of Charles I. Even with parliamentary goodwill and understanding, which was not altogether lacking in 1624–5, it was impossible to raise a public revenue sufficient to satisfy the financial hunger of the war machine. The preparations were impeded by shortages of all kinds, including food, drink and clothing. There were difficulties in manning the ships, seamen who had been pressed into service deserting at every opportunity. The quality of the levies raised for land service was, if anything, even poorer. At the beginning of September, Wimbledon, having made a survey of the condition of the land and sea force, informed Buckingham that 'the wants are many' (Dalton (ed.), *Life and Times*, Vol. II, p. 129).

By all rational considerations the expedition should have now been called off. To send a fleet on foreign service so late in the season with unwholesome food, bad beer and inadequate clothing was asking for trouble. The expedition did not in fact get away until the beginning of October after frantic efforts to make good the deficiencies. Within four days of leaving Plymouth the ominous decision was taken to put five men on four men's allowance.

Whereas by the contrariety of the wind, we may be put to a further expense of victuals than we are provided for, and being at this time far from any place whereby our wants may be supplied, to prevent such inconveniences as may hereby ensue, these shall be to require you forthwith, upon the receipt hereof, to give present order, that to every mess there may be five, until we shall be better enabled to make further provisions (Dalton (ed.), *Life and Times*, Vol. II, p. 389)

By the time it arrived off Cádiz, twenty-one days after clearing from Plymouth, it was too enfeebled by sickness and damage to recapture the glories of 1596.

An ill-coordinated assault was none the less attempted. Led by the Earl of Essex, the fleet glided into Cádiz Bay with instructions to anchor off Port St Mary, which was situated on the opposite side of the bay to the town of Cádiz. The choice of anchorage was a sign of uncertainty within the collective leadership concerning the eventual target. An obvious reason, consistent with the idea of an attack upon Cádiz, was that Port St Mary lay outside the range of the fortifications of the town, thereby providing a secure anchorage. Another reason for the choice, however, was that Port St Mary lay within an easy march of Sanlúcar and was regarded as a suitable landing point for any army. There are good reasons for supposing that, had the leaders focused their minds upon Cádiz and launched an immediate attack thereon, its weakly manned defences might have been in trouble. As it was, the dilatory proceedings of the council and the cautious resolve to attack neither the town nor the shipping within the inner harbour until the fort of Puntal at the entrance to the harbour was taken allowed the Spaniards to reinforce the defences. Six days after their arrival, the leaders, conscious of the increasing enfeeblement of the army and of the poor showing of the auxiliary armed merchantmen, accepted defeat and withdrew.

The fleet struggled home in a state of collapse. Wimbledon's flagship, the *Anne Royal* (formerly the *Ark Royal* of 1588), staggered into Kinsale harbour in mid-December with 160 sick on board, having lost by death 130 men. According to John Glanville, recorder of Plymouth and secretary to the fleet, whose journal (A. B. Grosart (ed.), *The Voyage to Cadiz in 1625. Being a journal written by John Glanville*, Camden Society, New Series, Vol. 32) contains a vivid account of conditions, the ship was brought to anchor only with the help of volunteers from ashore. The Earl of Essex fetched up at Falmouth in the *Swiftsure* and several ships of his squadron in an equally distressed condition. Sir John Eliot, vice-admiral of Devon, reported from Plymouth on the state of the ships and crews which arrived there. He noted the high death-rate of both seamen and soldiers, which he attributed to the scarcity and corruption of the provisions and the want of clothing. The virtual collapse of the victualling and medical services in the wake of the expedition as well as of the machinery for paying the seamen left a scar on the Stuart navy which led to the festering within it of anti-royalist sentiments.

Although contemporary reaction to the Cádiz disaster was to search for scapegoats among the leaders, the truth seems to be that early Caroline England simply could not afford to be at war. Yet war was so much a continuous activity of the seventeenth-century state that neither Charles I nor Buckingham seriously contemplated disengagement, despite the fact that English security interests in the 1620s hardly demanded conflict with any of the great continental gladiators. Besides being unequal to the task of terminating the war with Spain, they compounded their problems by entering upon war with France with the ostensible object of giving support to the beleaguered Huguenots of La Rochelle, that symbol of a state within a state which the French Crown was determined to reduce to obedience. In the then state of international relations, especially of the growing tension between Spain and France, this was rather as if Britain had declared war on the Soviet Union during the Russo-Finnish conflict of 1939–40. The French war is chiefly memorable for the three unsuccessful efforts of 1627–8 to relieve the Rochellais. It was during the preparations for the third attempt in 1628 that Buckingham, who had intended to command in person, was assassinated at Portsmouth.

The first of the La Rochelle operations, launched in June 1627 with Buckingham in command, was directed against the off-shore Isle of Rhé. It was hoped that its occupation would be a first step towards the relief of La Rochelle and would also furnish a base for operations against French shipping, the idea being that the campaign would, in some degree, thereby pay for itself. Although a fleet and an army of 7,000 men were assembled with much difficulty, the 1627 expedition gave a better account of itself than did that of 1625. The army, which was inadequately trained, got ashore without opposition, but failed to reduce the castle of St Martin to which the garrison of the island had withdrawn. Buckingham laid siege to the castle, but a prolonged siege was out of the question owing to sickness and shortages. None the less the army hung on until the autumn, largely, it would seem, in the expectation of reinforcements from England, which, however, came too late to be of useful service. With the approach of winter and the arrival of troops from the French mainland, the attempt had to be given up. The chance, slender as it was, of relieving La Rochelle had now gone for ever. The expeditions of 1628 sailed for La Rochelle at the end of April and in September; the first under the Earl of Denbigh, the second under Robert Bertie, first Earl of Lindsey. Their object was to throw supplies directly into the city from the sea. During the winter of 1627–8, however, the French government had planted a formidable chain of obstacles in the inner and outer approaches to the port, with the result that neither commander was able to break through. The withdrawal of Lindsey after a comparatively brief campaign was followed by the surrender of La Rochelle.

The evidence in the correspondence of John Coke, now secretary of state (*The Manuscripts of the Earl Cowper*, Vol. I, pp. 346 ff.) indicates that the same, perhaps even worse, financial difficulties as had impeded the fitting out of the 1625 expedition were also at work in 1628. Coke spent some time at Portsmouth during this summer trying to hasten the equipment of the fleet that was to have been led by Buckingham. He was informed at the end of May by Sir Allen Apsley, who was responsible for victualling, that the creditors were so much disheartened they would not do anything more on trust. In response to a request from Buckingham for fireships to accompany the expedition, Coke replied that there could be no work on fireships where no money could be obtained, that, if the fleet waited for fireships and the fireships for money, the available victuals would be consumed before it got to sea. By the end of June he was writing to Buckingham in what seems to have been despair about the state of things at Portsmouth.

> By this large account your grace may perceive that there remaineth no more here wherein my service can be of use. For though the officers have sent a warrant to Mr Boate to make ready the *Triumph*, the *Warspite* and the *Esperance*, yet they have taken no order for materials or for monies or for repairing the graving place here. I have continued here almost 6 whole weeks and have spent already all the king's money in his service and my own, in an inn where I have lodged not only with a continual oppression of seamen, victuallers, and workmen, but as if in a hospital with a confluence of sick men. Give me now leave to say freely that not only my abode here will be of no use, but that every day while the fleet stayeth in this harbour it will be less ready and worse provided to set to sea. (*The Manuscripts of the Earl Cowper*, Vol. I, p. 355)

Apart from operations under letters of marque by the privateering Kirk family against French settlements in Canada, which are chiefly interesting as the first round of the Anglo-French conflict for dominion in North America, king and council now came to terms with their incapacity for offensive warfare. The proposed fleet for 1629, at an estimated cost of some £66,000, was geared to almost entirely defensive purposes, in particular the defence of commerce and fisheries.

This switch to defensive warfare was the prelude to the termination of hostilities with both France and Spain by treaties of peace. Peace, however, by no means solved the problems of naval finances. Charles I and his advisers, though not faced with external security threats such as had troubled the Tudor dynasty at different times in the sixteenth century, were highly conscious that the long-term independence of the island realm, the safety of its trade, the prosperity of its shipping industry and the survival of the transoceanic plantations as extensions of England demanded that she make herself sovereign of the seas. It was no coincidence that John Selden's *Mare Clausum seu Dominium Maris*, with its claim to an exclusive sovereignty over the waters 'which flow between England and the opposite coasts and ports', should have been published in 1635 after having been in preparation for some years. It was no coincidence that, when Phineas Petts's masterpiece, the first true three-decked English warship, was launched at Woolwich in 1637, it was given the name *Sovereign of the Seas*. The flow of royal proclamations for the regulation of colonial affairs designed to keep the North American plantations dependent upon, and useful to, the mother country was also significant of the consciousness of sea power. At this stage in their history the North American plantations were considered to be important not so much as reserved markets for the products of English industry but as suppliers of raw materials. In particular, it was hoped that the virgin lands and forests would enable England to substitute America for the Baltic region as the source of timber, hemp, pitch and tar, the raw materials of the shipbuilding industry and hence of sea power. Early Stuart statesmen were already dazzled by the vision of a self-sufficient maritime empire independent of the goodwill and interests of foreign producers and foreign dealers for the stocking of the royal dockyards.

These ambitions, however, could not be achieved unless a solution were found to the problems of naval finance. These were very complex problems. Their political aspect, the inability of the Crown in ordinary circumstances to command a revenue sufficient to meet the cost of the armed services without parliamentary consent, is well known. The same is true of the constitutional aspect of Charles I's attempt after the dissolution of Parliament in 1629 to raise a sufficient revenue by recourse to methods of taxation allegedly inherent in the royal prerogative and hence not subject to parliamentary control. The political and constitutional tensions which bedevilled naval finance under the early Stuarts, and for that matter under Elizabeth I as well, coincided with distinct, though subtle, changes in the relationship between the mercantile marine and the navy royal.

The mercantile marine was an element of maritime strength because it both furnished a reserve of armed ships for service as fleet auxiliaries and privateers and fostered the growth of a seafaring population whose technical skills were an essential ingredient of national power at sea. The navy royal and the mercantile marine were thus interlocked as complementary components of the navy of England and were to remain so throughout the era of the broadside sailing ship. But the limitations of the merchantman-of-war, to use the sixteenth-century nomenclature, had been exposed under Elizabeth I in the Armada fight and the various overseas expeditions in the years following 1588. The recommendations of the commission of 1618 for the naval establishment were in line with the lessons of experience, for they distinguished sharply between the respective roles of the king's ships and the merchants' ships, clearly equating the latter with an auxiliary service. The growing differentiation between the royal warship and the armed merchantmen was accompanied by an equally important differentiation between merchantmen which were sufficiently powerful to protect themselves against enemy raiders in wartime and pirates in peacetime and those which were not. The stoutly built ships of the Levant Company, for example, were well able, especially when sailing in company, to look after themselves against both Spanish and Algerine raiders. Indeed, they kept the Mediterranean open to the English flag throughout the Spanish war and afterwards without benefit of naval support. The Levantmen, however, were untypical of the majority of English trading ships. Their self-sufficient independence was in marked contrast to the appeals for protection at sea against enemy raiders and pirates with which the Crown was assailed from the days of the queen onwards.

Trade had of course sailed in company under convoy of larger ships in the Middle Ages. But this was a form of self-help since the protecting ships were furnished by the mercantile community. The situation which arose in the Spanish war was different. It constituted a call upon the Crown for the provision of armed protection for traders incapable of protecting themselves. Then calls became especially insistent after the formation of the Dunkirk squadron and the rise of a threat to trade in the Narrow Seas. The question naturally arose as to how such protection should be funded. Since it was indisputable that vested in the royal prerogative was a right in time of emergency to call upon ships and seamen to serve in the defence of the realm, it was at least arguable that vested in the same prerogative was the right to substitute money for ships since the Crown was required to provide the ships to protect its subjects at sea. This seems to have been the thinking behind a scheme proposed in February 1603 to assign a number of warships to protective duties, the cost thereof to be met by voluntary contributions from all parts of the kingdom. The novelty of the scheme lay in the idea that the whole of the kingdom, not, as traditionally, the coastal areas alone, might be called upon to support the navy. Opposed by some merchant shipowners, who claimed that they could sufficiently arm their ships, and abandoned on the death of the queen only a few weeks after it had been first mooted, the proposal was never put to the test.

Although nothing came of them at the time, the proposed voluntary subscriptions of 1603 contain at least a hint of the existence in the Privy Council of the idea of a national navy financed on a national, albeit voluntary, basis. Contributions were again invited in 1618 when it was proposed to raise a fleet for service against pirates in the Mediterranean. The invitation was extended on this occasion to the ports and maritime communities. In this sense it was a less ambitious scheme than that of 1603. None the less the fact that it was extended to the very people who were accustomed to provide ships in an emergency points to the development of the doctrine that the gap between the king's men-of-war and the armed merchantmen was now such that, instead of ships, their equivalent in money was needed.

There were precedents therefore for the proposals made by king and council in February 1628 to solve the financial crisis afflicting the navy by imposing a tax, in advance of approval being given by Parliament when it assembled, 'to be cast up and distributed among all the counties at a proportionable rate' (quoted by R. J. W. Swales, 'The ship money levy of 1628', *Bulletin of the Institute of Historical Research*, vol. 50, p. 175). Letters were sent to the sheriffs instructing them to summon the justices of the peace and explain the policy for financing the navy in defence of the realm. The levy was expected to raise £173,411, the heaviest demands among the counties being made on Devon, Somerset and Yorkshire, and the heaviest among the cities and boroughs on Westminster, Southwark, Exeter, Gloucester, Bristol and York. The majority of counties were assessed at less than £6,000; the majority of cities and boroughs at less than £200. Four days after the dispatch of the letters, however, the scheme was abandoned, probably because of the risk that, in a volatile political situation, the proposed levy would be assailed in Parliament as an arbitrary attempt to deprive people of their property.

The abortive efforts of 1603 and 1628 and the limited proposals of 1618 pointed the way to the levy of ship money by Charles I in the 1630s during the period of non-parliamentary government. Though certainly unpopular for much the same reasons as the levy of 1628 would, if attempted, have been unpopular, ship money must not be dismissed as a revenue-raising expedient designed to enable Charles I to impose arbitrary rule. The levying of ship money was a systematic attempt to break through the fiscal barriers which barred the way to the creation of a national navy. Charles had talked in 1628 of building twenty new ships a year. This would have meant an annual expenditure far greater in real terms than that envisaged by any of his predecessors over the last century and far greater than he could afford. It was one of his wilder dreams. Even so, though he failed to reach it, he was carrying to its logical conclusion the naval policy of Henry VIII. The three-decked, 100-gun *Sovereign of the Seas* completed the process which had begun with the warships of Henry. She also heralded the new age of the ship-of-the-line and of a disciplined professional navy which it called into being.

In the 1630s, however, the *Sovereign* symbolised the as yet unattainable. This is not the place to enter into the constitutional and legal arguments against the levying of ship money, beyond noting that they did exist and were employed by its opponents. It is important at the same time to recognise that not all the arguments surrounding ship money favoured the opposition and that, although resistance to payment increased, especially after the Crown became entangled in an unpopular war with the Scots in 1638, the initial response must have provided Charles and his advisers with grounds for satisfaction. Despite the lack of a professional bureaucracy for the administration of local affairs, the first levy of 1634 was successful. The receipts of Sir William Russell, treasurer of the navy, were £79,586 against an expected yield of £80,609 and an actual expenditure on the navy of £88,000. In 1634, however, the writs were issued only to the sheriffs of the maritime counties and allowed for a fairly free measure of self-assessment. The writs of 1634 could be fairly presented, and seem to have been accepted, as an extraordinary levy upon the coastal regions of money in lieu of ships to provide the means of protecting the fisheries and trade of the kingdom at a time of international turbulence at sea. It is interesting to note that London, source of the most powerful armed merchantmen, was permitted to provide ships instead of the equivalent in money. The favourable response of areas accustomed to providing in kind for the sea service may well have owed a good deal to chauvinistic aspirations to sovereignty of the seas when both the Dutch and the French were known to be developing their navies.

The reaction to the writs of 1635, which extended the assessments to the inland regions, was much less favourable. Apart from the breach with custom in the extension of the levy to the inland areas, there was widespread resentment at the imposition of what was clearly designed to be a new annual tax, especially as the writ of 1635 was accompanied by much stricter directions from the Privy Council governing the methods of assessment. One of the standards by which the emergence of discontent can be measured is the flow of complaints from all over the kingdom against the rate assessments. Although the Crown could be reasonably well satisfied by the annual yield, the gap between anticipated and real receipts widened steadily from 1635 onwards. In 1635, out of £199,700 which ought to have been paid in, £4,836 was uncollected. In 1637, when the sum required was £196,400, the amount uncollected rose to £17,738. In 1638, when the much smaller sum of

£69,750 was required, more than one-third was unpaid. And in 1639, when the last writs were issued, only £43,417 was raised towards a target of £214,400 which included money instead of ships from London.

The story of ship money is therefore a story of diminishing returns. The evidence is that the income was shown to be delivered to the treasurer of the navy and was delivered to the treasurer of the navy. A feature of these years were the annual summer cruises of the 'ship money' fleets, usually composed of about nineteen royal warships, probably less in 1639, plus auxiliary armed merchantmen. They seem to have done a real service in showing the flag and providing some kind of protective shield to both fisheries and trade. There was, however, no breakthrough of the sort that was to occur under the republican government towards establishing English sea power as a major factor in international affairs. Although the income, in the early years of the experiment at least, was large compared with that available to James I and larger again compared with that available to Elizabeth I, rising costs took care of the apparent advantages enjoyed by Charles I, as also did the problem of paying off the debts incurred during the financial disasters of the 1620s. By international standards the fleets of the 1630s were comparatively weak. The limitations were demonstrated in October 1639 when a Spanish armada sent to the relief of the army in the Netherlands was destroyed in English territorial waters off the Kentish coast by a Dutch fleet under Maarten Haarpertzoon Tromp, with Pennington's squadron unable to assert, within sight of its own coasts, the doctrine of sovereignty of the seas.

The divisive effects of political and social tensions within Caroline society spilled over into the navy. The navy of the 1630s may be seen as marking an advance towards a national state navy financed by a national tax. At the same time it displayed a marked lack of social and professional solidarity. The Crown remained heavily reliant on noblemen and courtiers to command both fleets and ships. And the practice, so much complained of later in the century by Samuel Pepys, of permitting well-connected young men to take ship with their friends and associates as supernumaries on summer cruises, was already a cause of discontent. For the Crown was also dependent upon what might be called 'professional-seamen' officers, usually able men of non-aristocratic origins who acquired their advancement as a result of proven ability and experience at sea. Some idea of the gulf between the world of aristocratic volunteers and that of professional seamen may be gathered from the letters written by the youthful Viscount Conway when serving in 1636 as a volunteer on board the *Triumph* during a summer cruise (H. M. C., Fourteenth Report, Appendix, Part II: *The Manuscripts of His Grace the Duke of Rutland preserved at Welbeck Abbey*, Vol. II, pp. 34 ff.).

Social divisions among the officers could have even more sinister symptoms, reflecting the existence within society of irreconcilable differences and foreshadowing the failure of the king to retain the loyalty of the navy when civil war began. In 1637, for example, a fleet was sent against the pirates' nest at Salé under the command of William Rainsborough, aged about 50, a resident of Wapping greatly experienced in the Levant trade and the ways of the North African pirates. The vice-admiral and second-in-command was the twenty-eight-year-old Sir George Carteret. Rainsborough appears to have been the senior of a group of captains from Wapping or adjoining parishes, all of whom were possibly part-owners of such ships in the force as were armed merchantmen. Although Carteret's appointment certainly had Rainsborough's agreement, or even his support, relations between the two men were not happy. And Carteret on his side expressed dissatisfaction with the conduct of two Wapping captains, the rear-admiral Brian Harrison, and Thomas White, captain of the *Expedition*. The uneasy relationship between Carteret and the other officers seems to have given rise within the fleet to a 'Court *versus* country' situation: a speculation supported by later events, for in 1642 the Wapping professionals went over almost to a man to the parliamentary side, while Sir George emerged as an ardent royalist.

It is one of the ironies of history that the Caroline fleet, in which he took such pride, should have deserted the king on the outbreak of civil war. The desertion was to a great extent the result of Charles I's fatal flaw: his inability to win the trust of men whom he needed. The time was perhaps not ripe for the creation of a reliable corps of professional officers. And Charles cannot be blamed for having failed to foresee the consequences of this lack. Despite his interest in the navy, however, he failed to win its loyalty. A factor of importance here was the royal insensitivity. As Archbishop David Mathew (*The Age of Charles I*, p. 281) reminds us, 'The fashion in which courtiers overflowed into the fleet was uncongenial, as was the privileged way of life reflected in the summer flagships.'

Beneath its frothy social glitter and its gilded ornamentation, the Caroline fleet was seething with discontent: the discontent of professional seamen officers with what they regarded as subordination to courtly privilege and the discontent of the pressed seamen of the lower deck with their intolerable conditions of service, including those chronic grievances of the English seaman, inadequate victualling and poor and irregular pay. This widespread discontent, given an emotional driving force in a strongly Protestant service by alleged Catholic sympathies of the king, tipped the balance decisively in 1642 in favour of Parliament and contributed to its ultimate victory. Charles I's failure to retain the loyalty of the fleet was in great part a failure of personality. But it also reflects the Crown's inability to overcome fiscal obstacles to the creation of a truly professional national navy and, in the end, its continued lack of full control over the service.

It is perhaps a measure of Charles's remoteness from the navy in which he had taken so practical an interest that he was unaware of the extent to which popular sympathy within the fleet was on the parliamentary side at the outbreak of civil war. When he took the queen to Dover as war approached for her passage to the Netherlands, he was politely received by Sir John Mennes, commander of the *Lion*, and his crew with the result that he believed himself to be assured of the loyalty of the fleet. The reality of the situation became clearer with the siege of Hull in the spring of 1642, when the lord admiral, Algernon Percy, fourth Earl of Northumberland, seeking to avoid involvement in the struggle (he was eventually to acknowledge the authority of Parliament), pleaded that he was unfit to serve because of ill-health. Control thus passed to his deputy, Robert Rich, Earl of Warwick. Warwick (1587–1658) had experience of military service in the Netherlands and of leadership at sea in raids under the auspices of the Providence Company against the Spaniards in the Caribbean. He was the key figure in securing control of the navy for Parliament. He acted quickly to exploit the widespread parliamentary sentiments, to which he himself was committed, to assert his authority. Royalist officers were rapidly deposed, and on the whole generously treated, with the result that the ship-money fleet provided Parliament with a ready-made weapon in the struggle ahead.

It is also an irony of history that many of Charles's aspirations were realised after his execution by his enemies. In its isolation and insecurity, and shaken also by the partial mutiny of the navy in 1648, the regicide republican regime put its trust in sea power. Exploiting financial resources which had been barred to Charles I, it asserted English sovereignty of the seas by putting to sea fleets which far surpassed those of either the Tudor or Stuart monarchy. In the words of an apprehensive Dutch commentator, these fleets were 'a mountain of iron'. During the wrangles over ship money the king's opponents had frequently challenged him to demonstrate the existence of a state of emergency as the only means of justifying the imposition by royal prerogative of an extraordinary tax. When in power after their victory in the Civil War they provided their own answer. The condition of English sea power was a permanent emergency.

A Note in Conclusion

The change in the circumstances of England between about 1550 and the start of the First Civil War was a dramatic one. In the mid-sixteenth century the population was still less than two and a half million; by 1600 it had reached three and a half million; after about 1620 it began gradually to slow down the rate of increase, but there were well over four and a half million by 1642. The increase in the number of people in England affected every aspect of her internal and external relations: moreover she was, after 1603, in control of Scotland and Ireland also, giving her between one and two million additional population. In 1550 the greater number of her towns and cities were very small. A county town might have a population of 1,000, a few of the larger provincial towns, like Bristol or Norwich might have over 5,000 people but not more than 10,000. If there were many more hands able to work, there were as many who had to be fed. London by 1640 had grown from 50,000 to well over 250,000: a dozen cities or towns had more than 20,000 people; the county towns were in the range, in the south and east at least, of 3,000 to 5,000. These figures are very imprecise but they give, better than any other single factor, a measure of the changes that had taken place.

The basic need was for more corn to be grown, though corn had also to be imported well before the end of the period, and the bad harvests of a decade like that of 1630–40 could cause hardship and even death on a considerable scale. London was now surrounded by farms which produced a wide variety of produce for the city market. Farming was changing rapidly in the corn-growing areas: yeoman farmers were using larger fields and less labour − except for casual labour in harvest time − while pastoral farming in the less fertile areas − much of Wales, for example − was directed towards the meat markets of London and the larger towns, while Ireland increasingly supplied more cattle. There was, however, a lack of permanent employment for agricultural labourers, and smallholders were being pushed out of business by more economical production on the large farms, though a good many landless families were able to push into thinly occupied areas and develop new holdings as squatters, so that internal colonisation absorbed a substantial number of people. New industries, tied to the towns where the suppliers of the raw materials and machines of an elementary type were centred, were spread over the countryside: coal, iron, metal-working of all sorts, glass-works, potteries and so on, were industries growing up alongside the domestic spinning and weaving and the works for fulling, and dyeing of the new draperies and the older finished cloth, while the traditional unfinished-cloth industry was being more highly organised on a domestic basis.

In 1550 many parts of the country were intensely local in their contacts; villages or groups of villages were almost self-sufficient: after a century communications had opened up. Though roads were still poor, many rivers were in use. The internal market had proliferated at the same time as industry developed and population rose. This meant that there was an entirely new range of demands arising as new products came into use, and many of these came from distant parts. Tobacco was only one of them, but by 1642 its use had spread throughout England. At the same time there was much variety in the goods which could be sent abroad. The cloth industry remained dominant in its new and old guises, but alongside it was a very great differentiation of products for the internal and the overseas market, with a corresponding demand for comparable products from abroad, especially from overseas.

The fourfold inflation of the century – at its most rapid in the later sixteenth century, slowly declining in the seventeenth – proved advantageous to almost all independent producers and to merchants. It tended, in an era when wages were being held down by the action of government and masters alike, to lower real wages for those employed in town or country, causing severe hardship and at times famine, though probably the artisans gained from the upturn in urban activity. Yeomen, some gentlemen, many entrepreneurs and very many merchants did well. The amount of capital available for investment in new industries – most of them very small, a few very large – was growing, and a substantial part of it was being applied to the development of trade with the overseas world. The merchant fleet grew under Elizabeth partly because of new opportunities in trade and also because its value as an auxiliary to the royal ships became greater as the century went on, while privateering also encouraged it. In the years of peace after 1604 down to the Civil War, the merchant fleet went on increasing and, faced with intense Dutch competition, managed to retain a substantial share of new trade in European waters and, especially, outside them. Alongside the growth of the man-of-war cum merchantman, the fluctuations in naval power have been traced. The restoration, in part, of the decayed Henrician navy after 1560 was followed, after a period of indecision, by the development of a new and effective breed of royal fighting ship, the qualities of which outreached those of all but the greatest of Spain's galleons. Though, after 1604, there was a period of decline and indecision, there was no absolute neglect of the navy and some new vessels were built to maintain a moderately effective fleet, though it did not show up well in the wars of 1625–30 and by 1642 it had been virtually replaced by a new and formidable fighting force of powerful vessels. The mercantile marine and the royal navy grew more distinct: the former having a much more specialised task in competing with the Dutch bulk carriers of the period than any previous competition had offered.

On the basis of expanding population and increasing capital resources – coexisting with periods of bad weather and harvests and probably increasingly hard times for much of the working population – it became possible for England to build up, round her chartered companies, a favoured position in overseas trade in markets such as the Levant and India. It enabled her to send several hundred thousand people to Ireland, the North American mainland and the Caribbean islands to settle, and, in the case of the Chesapeake and the West Indies, to provide new materials (if still mainly tobacco) for English consumption or re-export. Re-exports or direct colonial trade with continental Europe were indeed where the new overseas activity showed itself most graphically in the period from about 1612 onwards, but especially after 1630. The New England colonies removed people from England who did not contribute much towards England's trade, and even involved a net loss of capital goods, but Ireland flourished and, on the whole, the new settlers did well, and even the Irish labourers under new English and Scottish masters saw some improvement in their standard of living. Emigration was first of all encouraged, and much money was lost in the early Virginia experiments before that colony returned a profit, but well before 1640 it was coming to be seen as a drain of skills and capital and bodies which might debilitate the body politic. But the emigration of so many persons dissatisfied with the ecclesiastical establishment possibly held back the development of civil strife, which emerged by 1642 for social, political and constitutional, as well as for religious, reasons.

England in 1642 was a very much better-integrated country than she had been in 1550. Her gentry and nobility held the counties together and merchant oligarchies ruled the towns, but the attempt of the Crown to gain a great measure of independent strength by tightening its grip on local government, by inventing new-old taxes, by restoring the Church and introducing absolutist doctrines into it, was vitiated by failure to afford either an army or an effective paid local bureaucracy. When subjected to the strain of even a minor war with Scotland, the local ruling groups, with a good deal of pressure from beneath propelling them, took up an effective stand against the central government. War was by no means inevitable in 1640 or even for the greater part of 1641, and its outbreak in 1642 was the result of many convergent strains and accidents, but it broke down the longest period of internal peace England had ever had. At least from 1560 to 1638 there had been no serious fighting on English soil – though religious and social revolts had occurred from time to time – and this was the basic reason why England was able to emerge as a much more significant factor in Europe and overseas by mid-century. It was one of the major factors propelling her into overseas trade and colonisation. If many of the working people in country and town remained at a low level of subsistence, and though plague still struck at London and elsewhere from time to time, with dreadful effects, the country as a whole was stronger than it had ever been by 1640, even though many people at the time were worried by bad harvests and temporary trade depression as well as by other things. That it was also so badly governed that discontent eventually produced war is another matter. Civil wars did not, however, destroy the gains which had been made in the previous century's accumulation of strength and England's capacity to operate effectively over great areas of distant Asia and newer-found America. At the same time the oceanic and industrial revolutions which were to bring her to world power were still far out of sight.

Index